D0771547

THERE'S
SOMETHING
IN THE WATER

THERE'S SOMETHING IN THE WATER

Environmental Racism
in Indigenous and
Black Communities

Ingrid R.G. Waldron

Fernwood Publishing
Halifax & Winnipeg

Copyright © 2018 Ingrid R.G. Waldron

All rights reserved. No part of this book may be reproduced or transmitted in any form by any means without permission in writing from the publisher, except by a reviewer, who may quote brief passages in a review.

Editing: Fazeela Jiwa
Cover image and design: Dave Ron
Printed and bound in Canada

Published by Fernwood Publishing
32 Oceanvista Lane, Black Point, Nova Scotia, B0J 1B0
and 748 Broadway Avenue, Winnipeg, Manitoba, R3G 0X3
www.fernwoodpublishing.ca

Fernwood Publishing Company Limited gratefully acknowledges the financial support of the Government of Canada, the Manitoba Department of Culture, Heritage and Tourism under the Manitoba Publishers Marketing Assistance Program and the Province of Manitoba, through the Book Publishing Tax Credit, for our publishing program. We are pleased to work in partnership with the Province of Nova Scotia to develop and promote our creative industries for the benefit of all Nova Scotians. We acknowledge the support of the Canada Council for the Arts, which last year invested $153 million to bring the arts to Canadians throughout the country.

Canada Canada Council Conseil des arts NOVA SCOTIA Manitoba
for the Arts du Canada

Library and Archives Canada Cataloguing in Publication

Waldron, Ingrid, author
There's something in the water: environmental racism in indigenous
and black communities / Ingrid R.G. Waldron.

Includes bibliographical references and index.
Issued in print and electronic formats.
ISBN 978-1-77363-057-1 (softcover).—ISBN 978-1-77363-058-8 (EPUB).—
ISBN 978-1-77363-059-5 (Kindle)

1. Environmental policy—Canada. 2. Hazardous waste sites—Canada.
3. Blacks—Canada—Politics and government. 4. Native peoples—Canada—
Politics and government. 5. Racism—Canada. 6. Equality—Canada.
7. Canada—Ethnic relations. I. Title. II. Title: There is something in the water.

HC120.E5W35 2018   363.700971   C2017-907865-8   C2017-907866-6

CONTENTS

This book is dedicated to my family: my late father, Dr. George Waldron, my mother, Myrna Waldron, and my sisters, Marcia Waldron and Terri-Lynn Waldron.

ACKNOWLEDGEMENTS

The Environmental Noxiousness, Racial Inequities, and Community Health Project (the ENRICH Project), upon which much of this book is based, has been an amazing ride over the last six years. Although challenging, exhausting, and frustrating at times, the project has been an intellectually stimulating and exciting endeavour that has brought me into contact with politicians, artists, media, social and environmental activists, faculty and students in a wide range of disciplines, and diverse community leaders from across Nova Scotia.

I owe much of this to Dave Ron, a social and environmental activist who asked me to take on the ENRICH Project in the spring of 2012. As the ENRICH Project's first research coordinator and, later, a volunteer working with the project, Dave has shown unwavering commitment and support over the past six years by conducting literature reviews, helping to organize events, creating promotional material for events, updating the project's website, and providing general advice and feedback on the project's direction. He even designed the cover art for this book! Although Dave and I have had many heated debates over the years about the direction the project should take, they were rooted in our shared passion for community, equity, and justice.

I would also like to thank my good friend Doug Macfarlane for supporting me throughout the writing process for this book and in general. His insights and advice were invaluable and, most importantly, so was our promise to each other when we first met — that we would be "friends for life." We have both stayed true to that promise. Thanks for holding me down.

In completing this book, I also owe a unique debt to members of the Mi'kmaw and African Nova Scotian communities that invited me into their lives, and with whom I have been fortunate to have developed relationships over the past several years. I would particularly like to thank the following community leaders for granting interviews, organizing and participating in focus groups and other events, delivering presentations, and sharing their wisdom: Jonathan Beadle, Dorene Bernard, Louise Delisle, James Desmond, Mary Desmond, Cathy Hartling, and Alan Knockwood.

In addition, I would like to acknowledge the indispensable help of the members of the ENRICH Project's Lincolnville Water Monitoring Program Committee who volunteered their time to develop and successfully implement a project that built community members' skills to test their own water. Thank you, Wilber Menendez Sanchez, Fred Bonner, Courtney Bonner, Angele Clarke, and Robyn Beckett, for a great job done in Lincolnville.

Thanks also to the many volunteers, research staff, and faculty that have given generously of their time to support the ENRICH Project over the last six years. I owe much to the local organizations Ecology Action Centre (EAC), Nova Scotia Public Interest Research Group (NSPIRG), and East Coast Environmental Law Association (ECELAW). I also appreciate the support of the College of Sustainability, the Healthy Populations Institute, the School of Nursing, and Faculty of Health at Dalhousie University.

Last, but not least, special thanks go to Lenore Zann, who was the first Member of the Legislative Assembly (MLA) to return my call and meet with me to discuss the ENRICH Project and environmental racism in the province. Her commitment to and passion for social and environmental justice issues has been inspiring to me and to the community members with whom she has developed relationships over the years. Most importantly, our collaboration led to the development of the *Environmental Racism Prevention Act* — the first bill of its kind in Canada.

Preface

A RISING TIDE LIFTS ALL BOATS?

Strategic Inadvertence and Other Shortcomings of the Environmental Justice Lens in Nova Scotia

> If the problem of the twentieth century was, in W.E.B. Du Bois's famous words, "the problem of the color line," then the problem of the twenty-first century is the problem of colorblindness, the refusal to acknowledge the causes and consequences of enduring racial stratification. (Murakawa 2014: 7)

As I jumped out of a taxi outside Province House in Halifax on April 29, 2015, I noticed a journalist from a popular online news site approaching me with a smile on his face. He wanted to congratulate me and my team on our efforts to have the *Environmental Racism Prevention Act* (Bill 111) (Nova Scotia Legislature n.d.a) introduced by New Democratic Party (NDP) Member of the Legislative Assembly (MLA) Lenore Zann in the Nova Scotia Legislature. I had been collaborating with Zann to develop a private member's bill on environmental racism since earlier that year, and the day had finally come for her to introduce it. I smiled cautiously at the journalist, expressing both my satisfaction that the bill had reached this stage and my skepticism that it would eventually become legislation. After all, since a bill asking the government to address environmental racism had never been developed in Canada before, I was being careful about expecting too much, particularly given Nova Scotia's complex history of racism.

It is not lost on many Canadians that Nova Scotia has had a long and rather unique history of racism, being perceived as rather slow to address the structural and institutional impacts of that history on Mi'kmaw and African Nova Scotian communities. The government's failure to understand or acknowledge the complex and specific ways in which race is implicated in environmental policymaking is, perhaps, not surprising to many in this province. This failure was illustrated by former provincial environment minister Margaret Miller's response to journalist Jacob Boon's questions in the January 21 edition of *The Coast* (Boon 2016) about the legacy of environmental racism in Nova Scotia and how the province could better protect marginalized communities. In this article, her assertion that the province does not have to "look at any segment or any part of our community as different than another" is the kind of "colour-blind" ideology that is emblematic of broader attitudes in Nova Scotia and the rest of Canada. This enables Nova Scotia Environment to continue averting its eyes from the ways in which its environmental policies disproportionately harm Mi'kmaw and African Nova Scotian communities. It also legitimizes practices that maintain the racial order by failing to acknowledge the structural manifestations of racism in Nova Scotia historically and in the present day.

I liken this lack of acknowledgement to the kind of "strategic inadvertence" that Professor Michael Eric Dyson accused Barack Obama of displaying throughout his presidency. In his book, *The Black Presidency: Barack Obama and the Politics of Race in America* (2016), Dyson argues that Obama's public policy approach has reflected a kind of universalism that contends that if unemployment, income insecurity, and poverty experienced by *all* Americans are addressed, those who are most affected by those social ills will benefit. As I look back on Obama's presidency, it is clear to me that his public policy approach failed, as significant disparities between whites and African Americans in income, poverty, health, and other social ills persist. I agree with Dyson when he argues Obama's philosophy that "a rising tide lifts all boats" was ineffective because it failed to help those most affected and most in need. Rather, public policies work best when they are strategic and directly target social ills in communities that are most affected. For those who argue that environmental racism is an issue of class and not race, I maintain, as Dyson has done several times, that "race makes class hurt more" (*Democracy Now* 2005). In other words, for non-white or racialized peoples, the added burden of racism deepens existing inequalities and disadvantages they are already experiencing related to class, such as unemployment, low income, poverty, food insecurity, and residence in under-resourced neighbourhoods.

By and large, the environmental justice movement in Nova Scotia and Canada engages with a "race by proxy" approach (Dyson 2016) because it fails to make race explicit, obscuring it within discussions on class. This type of strategic inadvertence mutes the specificity of Mi'kmaw and African Nova Scotian experiences with racism and environmental hazards in Nova Scotia. If Nova Scotia Environment truly believes that all communities are deserving of equal protection from environmental hazards, it must begin to investigate and seriously question the ways in which environmental policies play a role in unequally burdening Mi'kmaw and African Nova Scotian communities with environmental and health risks. Avoiding the topic of race in environmental policymaking simply *does not work.*

This book addresses one of the many limitations of the environmental justice movement in Nova Scotia — the tendency to subsume race within class in discussions about where industry gets placed in the province. Therefore, in this book I centre race as a fundamental analytical entry point for understanding the spatial patterning of industry in Indigenous and Black communities, while acknowledging that a sustained focus on race must be accompanied by an engagement with the ways in which environmental racism manifests and is sustained within the context of the intersecting dynamics of class, gender, sexual orientation, ability, and other social identities. Perhaps the inability of many people to acknowledge race as a defining factor in social relations and policymaking can be attributed to narrow conceptualizations of racism that focus on individual malicious acts — the acknowledgement of which requires "evidence" and "proof" — rather than subtler or systemic forms of racism that are entrenched within institutions and decision making (Pulido 2000). For example, focusing on individual cases of facility siting and looking for malicious intent on the part of decision makers doesn't get us very far in understanding the subtle racist ideologies that underpin environmental policy and other social structures, inevitably harming Indigenous and Black communities. Furthermore, since Indigenous and Black women in Canada and Nova Scotia experience marginalization due to race, gender, and the feminization of poverty (Gazso and Waldron 2009; Gazso, MacDaniel, and Waldron 2016; Waldron and Gazso 2018), an unwavering focus on race must be accompanied by an analysis that acknowledges the intersectional identities of Indigenous and racialized peoples as well as how this informs the spatial location of individuals and communities, exposing them to varying levels of social and environmental risk.

As a professor whose scholarship has long focused on the marginalized intersectionality of Indigenous and Black bodies, it often frustrates me when I speak with individuals who are stubbornly unwilling to acknowledge the reality of racism in this province and country. While many of these individuals seem to have no problem acknowledging disproportionality with respect to class, income, poverty, gender (for example, the fact that women and children are among the poorest groups in Canada), and other social inequalities, they do not acknowledge how those social inequalities often create greater vulnerability in

Indigenous and racialized communities. Also problematic are those individuals whose limited understandings of the ways in which social inequalities intersect cause them to attribute Indigenous and racialized peoples' experiences solely to class and income.

Black feminists (Hill Collins 1990; King 1988) have long argued that race, gender, class, and other social identities cannot be separated because they function interdependently and accompany an individual into every interaction or experience. In other words, challenging monolithic conceptions of communities requires an understanding of how these multiple social identities operate *in* and *through* one another to produce diverse experiences. Such an analysis appreciates the complex relationality of these multiple identities that frame individuals' social, economic, and political lives. In addition, an intersectional analysis requires attendance to the historical, material, and structural contexts and conditions within which social inequalities are produced; the meanings assigned to them; and the interrogation of white privilege and power and their accompanying ideological rationales for dominance.

While I argue that race must be a fundamental analytical entry point in the struggle for environmental justice in Nova Scotia and Canada, I also assert that one cannot fully understand how environmental racism manifests within the structures, policies, and practices of Nova Scotian society without an appreciation for how race intersects with and interprets other social identities. As Sherene Razack (1998: 13) argues, the multiple identities individuals hold simultaneously produce hierarchies of privilege and disadvantage that impact social relations:

> These complex operations of hierarchies of gender and race point to contradictions and cracks in hegemonic systems and illustrate the central importance of understanding how various systems interlock to produce specific effects.

It is also important to emphasize that our failure to consider our own complicity in the subordination of others is to perform what Razack (Fellows and Razack 1998: 336) refers to as "the race to innocence." In other words, understanding where all people, and in particular Indigenous and racialized peoples, stand in relation to one another requires a consideration of the role that complicity plays in relations of power. Such an analysis makes visible how our lives are scripted by multiple narratives and "shifting hierarchical relations" in which we experience varying levels of privilege and disadvantage in our relationship to patriarchy, capitalism, class exploitation, and white supremacy.

The meaning of race, gender, class, and other social identities only becomes clear when we understand the historical and site-specific ways in which they converge to position people in different and ever-changing positions of power, privilege, and disadvantage. Taking all of this into account, the main objective of this book is to help redefine parameters of critique around the environmental justice movement in Nova Scotia and Canada by opening a discursive space for a more critical dialogue on how environmental racism manifests within the context of white supremacy, settler colonialism, state-sanctioned racial and gendered forms of violence, patriarchy, neoliberalism, and racial capitalism. In so doing, I hope to address the many limitations inherent to the environmental justice lens in Nova Scotia and Canada — one that seems most concerned with such issues as conservation, wildlife protection, and sustainable development. While these are all important issues, work carried out in these areas by scholars, activists, and environmental organizations tends to be missing an expanded analysis of how the environment is experienced in specific ways by different bodies who hold varying levels of power.

The second objective of this book is to elucidate the ways in which environmental racism operates as a form of racial and gendered violence that is produced and sustained by the state and that works in partnership with other forms of state-sanctioned racial and gendered violence to dehumanize and harm communities that are already dealing with pre-existing vulnerabilities. By using the term "state-sanctioned racial and gendered violence," I am describing the systematic ways in which government and social institutions harm or otherwise disadvantage Indigenous and racialized communities and women, preventing them from meeting their basic needs and rights related to employment, income, justice, housing, food security, and other resources. State-sanctioned racial and gendered violence is subtle, invisible, and often has no specific person who can (or will) be held responsible, in contrast to interpersonal violence where a main perpetrator can be identified. For example, environmental racism is similar to other structurally induced racial and gendered forms of state violence that result in high rates of underemployment and unemployment, income insecurity and poverty, low educational attainment, high rates of incarceration, and other harms common in Indigenous and Black communities. I situate this book as a contribution to a broader dialogue on structural racism, structural violence, structural inequalities, and the myriad other terms we use to characterize policies and decisions that harm (directly or indirectly) historically marginalized communities.

The third objective of the book is to illustrate how environmental health inequities in Indigenous and Black communities are not only outcomes of disproportionate exposure to environmental contamination and pollution but are also worsened by pre-existing and long-standing social and economic inequalities that are products of Canada's colonial legacy. In other words, structural determinants of health — such as low educational attainment, unemployment, income insecurity, and poverty — compromise community members' capacity to fight back against the placement of harmful industries in their neighbourhoods, and they intersect in ways that make these communities more vulnerable to environmental illness and disease.

Throughout this book, I use the term "structural determinants of health" rather than the more commonly used "social determinants of health" because, as Sarah De Leeuw, Nicole Marie Lindsay, and Margo Greenwood (2015: xii) observe,

> the concept of social determinants of health, by definition, tends to exclude or marginalize other types of determinants not typically considered to fall under the category of the "social" — for example, spirituality, relationship to the land, geography, history, culture, language, and knowledge systems.

The authors also argue that colonialism has yet to be fully acknowledged as a significant determinant of health, despite the fact that Indigenous peoples identify colonialism as the most important determinant of health.

Given the dearth of studies on environmental racism and environmental justice issues in Nova Scotia and Canada, the book's fourth and final objective is to document the long history of struggle, grassroots resistance, and mobilization in Indigenous and Black communities to address environmental racism. It is an issue that has yet to be fully explored, particularly from the perspectives of these communities.

Understanding settler colonialism as the framework of the Canadian state, this book describes the material reality of that framework by unpacking how environmental racism operates as a mechanism of erasure enabled by the intersecting dynamics of white supremacy, white settler colonialism, state-sanctioned racial and gendered violence, patriarchy, neoliberalism, and racial capitalism in white settler societies. In other words, the book connects the material reality of environmental racism, as an embodiment of settler colonialism, to settler colonial theory. Rather than being pinpointed to a single encounter, settler colonialism is an ongoing event that can be described as a form of colonial formation and governance involving the invasion of foreigners for the purposes of assimilating, depopulating, or erasing Indigenous populations (Veracini 2011; Wolfe 1999). The temporal and spatial extension of settler colonialism involves the reproduction of power relations between and among settlers and Indigenous peoples. Its central features include profit seeking through land acquisition, resource extraction, and other features of the built environment; denial of any responsibility for dispossession; and the repudiation of Indigenous governance structures. In Canada, legal tools and policies such as the federal *Indian Act* and residential schools, respectively, were the mechanisms through which the assimilation, subordination, and genocide of Indigenous peoples were legitimated and settler political, cultural, and economic hegemony achieved (Veracini 2011; Wolfe 1999).

BUILDING ON THE FOUR PILLARS OF THE CRITICAL ENVIRONMENTAL JUSTICE STUDIES FRAMEWORK

In many ways, this book draws from critical environmental justice studies (CEJ studies), a term coined by David Pellow and Robert Brulle (2005) in their quest to expand the academic field and politics of environmental justice. Extending the Black Lives Matter (BLM) movement's analysis of and mobilization against state-sanctioned racial violence, Pellow (2016) suggests that environmental racism should also be articulated as a form of state-sanctioned violence perpetrated against racialized communities by state agencies and state-regulated companies. BLM is a social movement that emerged in response to the acquittal of George Zimmerman, a man who killed a seventeen-year-old African American, Trayvon Martin, in 2012. It has since become an ideological and political intervention to address the structural harms meted out to Black peoples within various social institutions, including criminal justice, education, employment, and health. CEJ studies grounds its analysis in BLM's intersectional approach to the problem of devalued Black life by acknowledging that this analysis must be inclusive of not just race but also class, gender, sexuality, immigration status, citizenship, age, ability, and other social identities. Therefore, this book's analysis of environmental racism is very much guided by a CEJ studies framework (Pellow 2016; Pellow and Brulle 2005) in that it theorizes environmental racism as a form of state-sanctioned racial and gendered violence through which violent control over Indigenous and racialized bodies, space, and knowledge systems works to harm the economic, political, and social well-being of these communities. It is a framework that is absent from most environmental justice scholarship.

Pellow (2016) challenges us to consider how the focus on anti-Black police violence in the BLM movement creates a discursive space within which to discuss the increasing exposure of Black communities to environmental risks by states and corporations. He points out that while the first generation of environmental justice studies was concerned primarily with analyzing environmental inequalities in low-income, racialized communities, second-generation studies have moved beyond a focus on distributive injustice to a more critical theoretical focus on the ways in which social differences like gender and sexuality, among others, intersect to disproportionately expose certain individuals to exclusion, marginalization, erasure, and discrimination. Following BLM's emphasis on intersectionality, CEJ studies extends its analysis to multiple and intersecting social identities to understand the context-specific ways in which different bodies are subjected to various forms of violence.

In recent years, a BLM movement has emerged in Canadian cities like Montreal and Toronto to challenge anti-Black police violence and other forms of Black criminalization. While the list of demands outlined by BLM in the US includes environmental justice issues such as divestment from industrial multinational use of fossil fuels and investment in community-based sustainable energy solutions (Movement for Black Lives n.d.), the Canadian incarnations of the movement have said little or nothing about environmental racism or environmental justice. For example, in reviewing the websites for Black Lives Matter — Toronto (Black Lives Matter — Toronto n.d.), I note that their list of demands includes directives related to policing and incarceration, education, LGBTQ issues, Islamophobia and white supremacy. The Facebook page for Black Lives Matter — Montreal (Black Lives Matter — Montreal n.d.) does not outline a list of demands, but the Facebook postings clearly indicate a focus on policing. To be fair, the BLM movement is still very much in its infancy in Canada. My hope is that it will evolve to address the many other ways in which state violence harms Black bodies in Canada, such as environmental racism. While these issues may not seem, on the surface, to be salient issues in Toronto or Montreal where Black populations tend to reside disproportionately in urban areas, a more critical analysis and deeper engagement with issues of race, place, space, the environment, and justice by BLM in both cities will most certainly reveal that environmental racism systemically weaves itself into both urban and rural infrastructures in Canada.

CEJ studies is built on four pillars that offer important conceptual tools to address some of the main limitations of environmental justice movements in Canada, which I outline in this book (Pellow 2016). First, while I take the critical stance that race must be foregrounded in understandings of environmental racism, I agree with the argument put forth in the CEJ studies framework that greater attention needs to be accorded to how multiple social identities intersect to produce environmental injustices (Pellow 2016). Second, I engage with the CEJ studies perspective that progressive and transformative change on issues of environmental racism must move beyond addressing entrenched social inequality and power (including state power) through legislation, institutional reforms, and other policy concessions, toward building an unapologetically anti-authoritarian agenda. The most common vision of change articulated by environmental justice studies scholars and activists is to work with the institutions and agencies that are responsible for sanctioning environmental racism violations in the first place. However, this has been largely ineffective because it reinforces the legitimacy of these institutions and agencies and thus leaves intact the power structures within which environmental racism manifests. Therefore, in drawing from CEJ studies, I recognize the need for Indigenous and Black communities to engage with a transformative anti-authoritarian agenda, rather than a reformist one, in addressing the ways in which social inequality is entrenched and embedded in society (Pellow 2016).

Third, I take up CEJ studies' focus on the largely undertheorized notion that marginalized human populations exposed to environmental threats are viewed by states and industries as inferior, lacking in value, and therefore expendable and disposable. In his book *Black–Brown Solidarity: Racial Politics in the New Gulf South* (2014), John D. Márquez introduces the concept of "racial expendability" to advance the argument that racialized peoples are constructed as and rendered expendable because the state and legal system's perceptions of them as deficient, threatening, and criminal suggest that they are deserving of violent discipline and obliteration. Similarly, Charles Mills (2001) asserts that it makes cultural common sense for policymakers and institutions to implement environmental policies that disproportionately expose people of African descent to environmental hazards, since they are perceived as "trash" and associated with filth, waste, and uncleanliness.

Finally, this book reflects the multi-scalar approach espoused by the fourth pillar of the CEJ studies framework, which argues that not only must environmental justice researchers contextualize and examine environmental justice struggles at the local, regional, national, or transnational scales, they must also elucidate how these struggles function at multiple other scales — they must understand the impacts of environmental justice from the cellular or bodily level to the global level and back. In other words, in addition to describing the ways in which environmental racism and environmental justice struggles have been enacted in Nova Scotia, Canada, and the US, this book argues that these issues can't be discussed separately from their impacts on the souls, minds, and bodies of Indigenous and racialized peoples. As a health researcher, my main interest is in highlighting how disproportionate exposure to environmental risks in Indigenous and Black communities operates in partnership with pre-existing health disparities in these communities to produce environmental health inequities.

CEJ studies offers the conceptual tools to theorize environmental racism as a form of state-sanctioned racial and gendered violence — one of several structural forms of violence sanctioned by the state that are perpetrated upon the bodies of Indigenous and racialized communities through policy actions and decision making. The subtle, insidious, and — often — intergenerational manifestations of state-sanctioned racial and gendered violence mask the ways in which white supremacy and structural racism disadvantage and harm racialized and Indigenous peoples. It is important to shed light on the racialized, gendered, and classed nature of state-sanctioned violence that is enacted by the state and its links to white supremacy, capitalism and class exploitation, and heteropatriarchy (Alimahomed-Wilson and Williams 2016). Cecilia Menjívar (2016) provides a multi-faceted analytic lens for understanding state violence that moves beyond a focus on micro forms (including interpersonal forms of violence, such as physical violence) to a consideration of the ways in which micro forms intersect with macro forms of violence (such as state-sanctioned violence) emerging out of broader structural inequalities. Following her analysis, I argue the need to expand the analytic lens of the environmental justice movement in Nova Scotia and Canada in ways that consider how racist environmental policies, as well as other kinds of state policies, have enabled the cultural genocide of Indigenous, Black, and other racialized peoples (Pulido 2017). The state's failure to connect environmental issues to racial capitalism — not simply to capitalism — is an overlooked issue. In other words, the lack of political will and commitment to addressing environmental racism can be linked to the cost the state will incur by intervening in and halting the activities from which industry profits at the expense of Indigenous and Black peoples. Therefore, environmental racism, like many other forms of state-sanctioned violence, drives racial capitalism (Pulido 2017).

The kinds of structural arguments for environmental racism I advance in this book require that readers start from a critical premise that white privilege accords economic, material, social, and psychological benefits and advantages to white people simply based on skin colour. Since whiteness is often construed as an "unmarked" or "normative" category to which "racial others" are compared, many white people view themselves as "race-less" or beyond race. For white people to fully appreciate their privilege, they must move beyond a focus on individual hostile acts to a consideration of how structural and institutional decision making supports and upholds policy actions that protect and benefit white people economically, materially, socially, and psychologically, often at the expense of Indigenous, Black, and other racialized peoples' well-being. Rather than asking if the landfill was sited near the African Nova Scotian community in Lincolnville because the owner was racist (an individual malicious act of racism), it may be more revealing to ask why African Nova Scotian and Mi'kmaw peoples are disproportionately burdened by pollution in Nova Scotia (state-sanctioned racial violence).

White people's silence about racism and those who are impacted by it informs how race gets taken up (or not taken up) and addressed (or not addressed) in Canada. In other words, what Dyson (2016) refers to as "racial procrastination" continues to characterize the approach to racial equity in Canada. Not surprisingly, then, muting social differences and inequalities — particularly as they pertain to race — remains the order of the day in the Nova Scotia government, also characterizing the environmental justice movement in Nova Scotia.

As I took my seat in the balcony at the House of Assembly on April 29, 2015, I was joined by friends and other community members excitedly anticipating the day's events on the floor of the House below. I waved excitedly to Lenore Zann and former acting Nova Scotia NDP leader Maureen Macdonald as they smiled at the community members who had gathered on the balcony. As I patiently waited for members of the House to introduce and discuss various bills, I grew increasingly tense. Zann stood up suddenly, passed a sheet of paper to an individual next to her, and sat down. I was confused about what had just happened. Had Bill 111 just been introduced and approved? "Was it approved?" I asked my friends. None of them seemed to know. As everyone turned to each other with questioning looks, I heard someone suddenly blurt out, "Yes, it was approved!" While I did not expect to hear fireworks go off, I was surprised by what a "non-event" the introduction of the bill had been. As someone who had little knowledge about the process a private member's bill goes through to become legislation, my only hope at that time was that the bill would raise awareness and elicit conversation about environmental racism in the province.

SETTING THE STAGE

The journey to get to this day began in spring 2012, when I responded to an email from Dave Ron about meeting to discuss a proposed project on environmental racism in Nova Scotia. I was struck by how earnest Ron seemed to be about the topic of environmental racism and social justice in general. Ron, a white social and environmental activist and former executive director of the Nova Scotia Public Interest Research Group (NSPIRG), had been involved for some time in the Save Lincolnville Campaign, a community-led initiative for the removal of the landfill located within a kilometre of the African Nova Scotian community of Lincolnville. The campaign was started by the Concerned Citizens of Lincolnville and supported by a broad-based coalition of community groups and individuals, including NSPIRG and the Ecology Action Centre (EAC).

At the meeting, I listened to Ron enthusiastically discuss the impact a research project on environmental racism could have on the lives of Mi'kmaw and African Nova Scotian communities across the province, and I became increasingly aware of how little I knew about the topic. As a professor whose scholarship had focused mainly on the health and mental health impacts of race, gender, and class inequalities over the past ten years, environmental racism had simply never caught my attention. While I did remember reading a few articles on the topic as a doctoral student at the University of Toronto, these articles were based on studies conducted in the United States. Was this truly a problem in Canada as well, I wondered? Noticing my confusion, a bemused Dave smiled in slight disbelief, blurting out, "You've never heard of environmental racism?" I slowly shook my head and smiled, slightly embarrassed.

I have since learned that environmental racism, a subset of the larger environmental justice movement that originated in the United States, refers to environmental policies, practices, or directives that disproportionately disadvantage individuals, groups, or communities (intentionally or unintentionally) based on race or colour (Bullard 2002, 1993). The concept of environmental racism emerged when the Northeast Community Action Group, a group of African American suburban homeowners in a middle-class enclave in Houston, tried to prevent the siting of a landfill near their neighbourhood in 1979. The group launched the civil rights suit *Bean v. Southwestern Waste Management, Inc.* under the legal direction of Linda McKeever Bullard, the wife of professor Robert Bullard who is often referred to as the "father of environmental justice." Findings outlined by Bullard and published in *Sociological Inquiry* in 1983 found that 80 percent of the landfills and incinerators in Houston were built in predominantly African American neighbourhoods. Both the lawsuit and subsequent studies conducted by Bullard to document "ecoracism" cases (Bullard 1983) were groundbreaking moments in making a case for fighting environmental decisions as violations of civil rights (Blades 2016).

Reverend Benjamin Chavis is credited for coining the term "environmental racism" in 1981, when he was with the United Church of Christ Commission for Racial Justice in the United States, although there are reports that he coined the term in 1987 (Commission for Racial Justice 1987). After taking action against a proposed toxic waste site planned for a poor, largely African American community in North Carolina, the Commission launched a regional study that found that hazardous waste sites, landfills, incinerators, and coal-fired plants were disproportionately placed in communities composed mostly of African Americans, Hispanics, Native Americans, and the working poor (Commission for Racial Justice 1987). A few years later, further weight was given to the concept of environmental racism when Bullard's 1990 book *Dumping in Dixie: Race, Class, and Environmental Quality* was released. The book examines the relationship between environmentalism and social justice by tracing the efforts of five African American communities to address facility siting in their communities. He found that the patterns of distribution of facilities were, indeed, linked to race and poverty.

Bullard (1990, 2002) characterizes environmental racism as racial discrimination in environmental policymaking; in the greater exposure of non-white or racialized communities to toxic waste disposal and the siting of polluting industries; and in the implementation of policies that sanction the harmful and, in many cases, life-threatening presence of poisons in these communities. Environmental racism is also characterized by a number of other factors: the history of excluding Indigenous and racialized communities from mainstream environmental groups, decision-making boards, commissions, and regulatory bodies; the lack of political power these communities have for resisting the siting of industrial polluters in their communities; the disproportionate negative impacts of environmental policies that result in differential rates of cleanup of environmental contaminants in these communities; and the disproportionate access to environmental services, such as garbage removal and transportation (Bullard 2002).

The life of the late Nigerian environmental activist Ken Saro-Wiwa has not only been a source of inspiration for environmental and human rights activists globally, but also provides a textbook case for how environmental racism manifests internationally in the context of the increasing globalization of the world's economy. As the president of the Movement for the Survival of the Ogoni

People (MOSOP), Saro-Wiwa led a movement to protect the environmental and human rights of the Ogoni people who live in the Niger Delta by demanding sound environmental practices and compensation for the devastation of Ogoni territories. An estimated $30 billion worth of oil has been extracted by Royal Dutch Shell since 1958, none of which has been provided to the Ogoni people. Instead, they have been left with an environment that is contaminated from oil spills and acid rain (Goldman Environmental Foundation n.d.).

In January 1993, Saro-Wiwa gathered 300,000 Ogoni to march peacefully to demand a share in oil revenues and some form of political autonomy. MOSOP also asked the oil companies to begin environmental remediation and pay compensation for past damage. In May 1994, Saro-Wiwa was abducted from his home and jailed along with other MOSOP leaders in connection with the murder of four Ogoni leaders. The Nigerian military subsequently took control of Ogoniland. Saro-Wiwa was convicted of murder in October 1995 by what many governments and organizations worldwide deemed a fraudulent trial and hanged later that year along with his co-defendants (Goldman Environmental Foundation n.d.).

In yet another example of environmental racism, recent outcries about the water crisis in the predominantly African American and poor city of Flint, Michigan, have garnered considerable public attention. In April 2014, amid a financial emergency, the state temporarily switched Flint's water source from Lake Huron to the Flint River. Residents soon started complaining that their water looked, smelled, and tasted strange. Later, Virginia Tech researchers found the water to be highly corrosive (Hernandez 2016). A class-action lawsuit soon followed, alleging that the Department of Environmental Quality had not been treating the Flint River water with an anti-corrosive agent. Combined with this, approximately half of the service lines to homes in Flint are made of lead pipe, and lead soon began leaching into the water supply (Hernandez 2016). Flint residents were kept in the dark for eighteen months, after the damage had already been done. Little is known at this point about the illnesses and diseases that, most likely, will befall this community. Events such as these have opened a much-needed discussion on not only environmental racism, but also the influence of place on health; the geographical patterning of disease; and the disproportionate environmental health risks experienced by low-income, racialized communities (Hernandez 2016).

Since I began conducting the ENRICH Project in 2012, I have noticed an increasing interest from white environmental activists, journalists, and members of the Nova Scotian public at large in discussing environmental racism, as well as their increased comfort in using the term "environmental racism." While I am pleased that the project has helped to invigorate an interest in the issue, I have to admit that I remain wary of those who simply wish to exploit the environmental concerns of Indigenous and Black peoples to shape the issue according to their own agendas. Those agendas often seek to subsume environmental racism within the broader (and more comfortable) environmental justice lens, in which racism gets displaced from its rightful place at the centre. Brian K. Bullock (2015) argues that, in the United States, environmental racism lost its way when it was either highjacked or subsumed by white environmentalists into the environmental justice movement. I am wary of a similar thing happening in Canada since the "mainstream" or white environmental justice movement in Nova Scotia and Canada has, for some time, been considerably limited in its scope, missing perspectives about the specific and unique ways in which Indigenous and racialized peoples experience a number of environmental issues such as food deserts, transportation, toxic waste sites, and landfills. While the term "environmental racism" is increasingly being used in Nova Scotia and Canada, there is still a preference among environmental activists and researchers for using the term "environmental justice" rather than "environmental racism." This speaks to the discomfort many people in Canada have in discussing race and engaging in a dialogue about the underlying structural factors that produce the need for environmental justice to begin with. However, is it truly possible to achieve environmental justice (the end goal) without discussing and dismantling the structural factors that enable environmental racism (the condition)?

This book is largely based on my experiences leading the ENRICH Project with a team of researchers, scientists, community members, activists, environmental organizations, students, and volunteers. The ENRICH Project is a collaborative, multidisciplinary, community-based research project investigating the socio-economic, political, and health effects of environmental racism in Mi'kmaw and African Nova Scotian communities throughout Nova Scotia. Its main goal is to examine and address environmental racism through research, publications, legislation, community advocacy, community capacity building, and public education. Quotations from community members, presented throughout the book, were taken from community workshops and focus groups the ENRICH Project organized and held in partnership with community members (Waldron 2014a, 2016) over the last several years.

The book traces the colourful but often challenging journey my team and I have taken to examine the legacy of environmental racism in Mi'kmaw and

African Nova Scotian communities. We have worked to draw the limits of the current environmental justice movement in Nova Scotia and Canada; provide the conceptual tools to broaden parameters of critique on environmental racism; and address its social, political, economic, and health effects in Indigenous and Black communities. The book also argues that the politics of race and class shape policies about where polluting industries and other environmental hazards are placed in Nova Scotia, and that environmental racism is emblematic of larger social structures within which race, gender, income, class, and other social factors get inscribed in subtle ways to cause harm to mostly rural, remote, geographically isolated and, therefore, "invisible" communities. Inherent to this analysis is a focus on how race, class, and other social hierarchies are inscribed in environmental policies.

The book makes explicit how the environmental justice lens in Canada mutes race and other social hierarchies, resulting in environmental policies that obscure or negate the centrality of these issues in the spatial patterning of industry. At the same time, the book attributes the long history of indifference and inaction around environmental racism to the ahistorical stance government has taken — one that fails to appreciate how state-sanctioned racial and gendered violence within various institutions has manifested both historically and in the present day to inform environmental policymaking and practices. Taken together, these factors provide fertile ground for environmental racism to manifest and endure.

I locate my analysis of environmental racism in Canada's settler-colonial existence. The theoretical framework offered by settler-colonial studies sheds light on how environmental racism is connected to historical and present-day colonial systems, subjugation, forced displacements, land dispossession, exclusion from the polity, social marginalization, extraction of wealth, destruction of culture, dehumanization, and genocide, primarily in Indigenous and Black communities. Through this analysis, I tease out how race, class, and gender intersect to create spatial arrangements today that are products of a legacy of colonialism in Canada. The book opens the ability to interpret the many manifestations of how spaces and communities are organized by structures of colonialism and racial capitalism. In so doing, the book pushes beyond normative debates about environmental justice in Canada to argue that the environmental justice movement be tethered to profound substantive and structural issues.

Drawing on work by Cheryl Teelucksingh (2002, 2007; Teelucksingh and Masuda 2014), George Lipsitz (2007), and others (McKittrick 2002, 2011; Pulido 1996, 2000; Razack 2000, 2002) on the "racialization of space" and the "spatialization of race," the book unpacks the larger socio-spatial processes of inequality that produce, reproduce, and sustain environmental racism. For example, I unpack Razack's (2000) assertion on the importance of "denaturalizing geography" to question how social spaces emerge, as well as to examine how social spaces are created through ideologies and practices of domination. It's an analysis that is helpful in guiding an understanding of the environment as a product of both the symbolic meaning of space and the materiality of space. It is also useful in helping to advance the argument that the symbolism that characterizes space as innocent, pure, untainted, and natural is in opposition to the materiality of space, which is imbued with a colonial and racial character. This is best illustrated by Indigenous and Black peoples' experiences of state-sanctioned forms of racial and gendered violence.

Not only is environmental racism illustrative of the spatial character of state-sanctioned racial and gendered violence (i.e., spatial violence), it also manifests alongside other forms of violence experienced by Indigenous, Black, and other racialized communities, such as high unemployment rates, income insecurity, poverty, food insecurity, poorly resourced neighbourhoods, poor-quality housing, gentrification, criminalization, police brutality, disproportionate rates of incarceration, the prison industrial complex, and proximity to polluting industries and other environmental hazards. I contend that the lived experience of spatial violence and other manifestations of state-sanctioned racial and gendered violence and toxic exposure live together — it is not possible to understand environmental racism independent of other forms of violence that impact the minds, bodies, cultures, and lands of Indigenous and Black peoples. This speaks to the importance of advancing an environmental justice lens in Canada that encapsulates both environmental justice and civil rights.

CHAPTER OVERVIEW

My hope is that this book will guide readers in thinking through a number of important questions. What would a different conversation about the relationship between race, place, space, environment, and health in Indigenous and Black communities look like if we grappled more seriously with an intersectional framework, a CEJ studies framework, settler-colonial theory, and concepts such as racial capitalism, neoliberalism, and the racialization of space? How can we engage in a more intersectional and inclusive conversation about the social justice dimensions of place, space, environment, and health? How are hierarchies and intersections of race, culture, gender, income levels, class, and other social identities spatialized in rural and urban settings? How do we unpack the larger socio-spatial processes that create disproportionate exposure and vulnerability to the harmful social, economic, and health impacts of polluting industries and other environmental hazards in Indigenous and Black communities? What are the possible public health advocacy responses to existing or proposed industrial projects near these communities?

In Chapter 1, I trace the path that the ENRICH Project has taken over the last six years to address the socioeconomic, political, and health effects of environmental racism in Mi'kmaw and African Nova Scotian communities using an innovative, interdisciplinary, and multi-pronged approach to research, policy development, partnerships, community engagement, community capacity building, as well as community mobilizing, activism, and advocacy. This chapter also offers insight into the many hurdles we have faced in engaging and mobilizing affected communities, advancing a more critical dialogue on environmental racism among academics and the broader community, and addressing environmental racism through policy.

Drawing on the work of prominent theorists who study settler colonialism (Shoemaker 2015; Veracini 2011; Wolfe 1999), Chapter 2 locates debates about environmental racism within settler-colonial studies. In this chapter, I probe the relationship between settler colonialism, racial capitalism, and neoliberalism to unpack the ways in which environmental racism operates as a mechanism of erasure through land dispossession and the accumulation of profit. While this analysis highlights the significance of land to Indigenous peoples, it also points to how land and place are inscribed with racial meanings in ways that enable and sustain unequal relations of power. In situating this consideration within broader discussions about white privilege, "white ignorance," and state-sanctioned racial and gendered violence, I argue that environmental racism is one of several manifestations of state-sanctioned racial and gendered violence that has been informed by policies rooted in a legacy of colonial violence in Canada.

In Chapter 3, I draw on work by Teelucksingh (2002, 2007; Teelucksingh and Masuda 2014), Lipsitz (2007) and others (McKittrick 2002, 2011; Pulido 1996, 2000; Razack 2000, 2002) to contribute to and advance discussions on settler colonialism as a spatial project that makes explicit the territorial nature of power and that is also constitutive of environmental racism. In presenting a socio-spatial analysis of the racial geography of place and space, I give sustained attention to the ways in which race spatializes power by articulating space as both symbolic and material, and by pointing to the ways in which Mi'kmaw and African Nova Scotian peoples experience spatial violence within employment, education, criminal justice, and other systems.

Chapter 4 outlines the main pillars of the environmental justice framework and also makes explicit how procedural forms of justice that create more inclusive, participatory, and democratic consultation processes with affected communities can help address inequities in the distribution or spatial patterning of environmental risks in these communities. This chapter also highlights the many factors and processes that enable and sustain environmental racism and points to specific cases of environmental racism in African Nova Scotian and Indigenous communities across Canada over the last several decades.

The impact of environmental racism on the spirits, minds, and bodies of Indigenous and Black peoples is the main focus of Chapter 5. I present health as rooted in and informed by place. Acknowledging "structural determinants of health," I consider how colonialism, spirituality, relationship to the land, geography, history, culture, and knowledge systems shape health outcomes in Indigenous and Black communities. I invite readers to broaden their interpretation of environmental health inequities in ways that illuminate the relationship between illness and pollutants, out-migration, employment opportunities, labour market structure, land depreciation, income insecurity, poverty, and other structural determinants of health. I also argue that the disposability and expendability of Indigenous and Black bodies are made explicit not only in environmental policy that disproportionately exposes Indigenous and Black peoples to environmental hazards, but also in their greater vulnerability to long-standing social and economic inequalities in Canada that impact their spiritual, emotional, mental, psychological, and physical health and well-being.

Using the accounts of Mi'kmaw and African Nova Scotian community members, environmental activists, journalists, and researchers, Chapter 6 amplifies the voices of those who have opposed environmental racism over the last several decades. This chapter highlights the agency and oppositional politics of Mi'kmaw and African Nova Scotian communities that have been at the forefront of environmental and other social justice struggles, and resistance movements seeking to disrupt various forms of subjugation. The chapter calls attention to the transformative human agency of Indigenous and Black communities by illuminating their rich and varied legacy of solidarity building, organizing, mobilizing, and activism against environmental racism, historically and in the present day.

In the book's conclusion, I note the implications, in the past and for the future, of the *Environmental Racism Prevention Act* (Bill 111) (Nova Scotia Legislature n.d.a) and other activities to address environmental racism in the province. I consider the potential for a *Nova Scotia Environmental Bill of*

Chapter 1

ENVIRONMENTAL NOXIOUSNESS, RACIAL INEQUITIES, AND COMMUNITY HEALTH PROJECT

Blurring the Boundaries between Community and the Ivory Tower

> The ENRICH Project is not seeking to necessarily recreate or replace some of the community-based initiatives that are happening around environmental racism in the province. It's really just about creating a hub, a network so that if any of these campaigns, initiatives, or struggles seem silo-ed — which many of them are — then it's to create a network by which people can also build off one another's success and victories. (Dave Ron quoted in Lypny 2013)

In the spring of 2012, I agreed to direct a project on environmental racism after meeting with Dave Ron, who I hired as the ENRICH Project's first research coordinator and who later became one of its many volunteers. While I was initially hesitant to take on a project about which I knew little, I became intrigued by the prospect of addressing such a politically charged issue. I was thirsty for a new challenge that had the potential to effect real change in racially marginalized communities. In addition, I recognized that the significance of the ENRICH Project lay in its uniqueness; few, if any, studies examine environmental racism in *both* Indigenous and Black communities in Canada. Given the dearth of research on environmental racism in Nova Scotia, particularly from the perspectives of both of these communities, the ENRICH Project serves as a kind of case study for telling a particular story situated in the Nova Scotian context and, in many cases, the Canadian context.

Furthermore, as a professor and researcher interested in social, economic, and political inequalities that shape health outcomes in Indigenous, Black, and other racialized communities, I recognized quickly that I could make a significant contribution to research on environmental health inequities in these communities which, although increasing, is limited. Findings from a study conducted by Jeffrey Masuda, Tara Zupancic, Blake Poland, and Donald C. Cole (2008) suggest that while there has been a significant growth in environmental health research in the last several decades, the research has not focused enough on vulnerable populations.

My rationale for conducting the ENRICH Project was based on a number of other factors. For example, the project is driven by community members' strong need for research that addresses the impacts of polluting industries and other environmental hazards on socioeconomic well-being and health in their communities. Community members have also been concerned about the lack of transparency and accessibility of Nova Scotia Environment's community consultation process. One of the main objectives of the project is to amplify community voices by contextualizing them within all project activities.

From its inception, the mission of the ENRICH Project has been to employ an interdisciplinary, multi-methodological approach that bridges the academy and community to support ongoing and new efforts by Mi'kmaw and African Nova Scotian peoples to address the social, economic, political, and health effects of disproportionate pollution and contamination in their communities. It reflects the principles of the CEJ studies framework in that it is activist–scholar inspired in its quest to bridge and blur the boundaries and borders between academic scholarship, theory, and analysis and grassroots activism or other community-based activities (Pellow 2016). Since 2012, the project's diverse activities have included conducting community-based participatory research; mapping using geographic information systems analysis (GIS); writing peer-reviewed journal articles and research reports; presenting at academic conferences and seminars; training students and volunteers; developing multi-disciplinary partnerships; engaging and mobilizing Mi'kmaw and African Nova Scotian communities and advocating on their behalf; developing and implementing social action campaigns; organizing, hosting, and facilitating community workshops and public engagement events; consulting with government and legal experts; helping to develop policy; granting interviews to media; and sharing information on social media.

The ENRICH Project also validates the histories, cultures, and local contexts of Mi'kmaw and African Nova Scotian peoples through the integration of Indigenous and African-centred knowledges, traditions, and epistemologies into all project activities. In addition to incorporating the expertise and knowledges of these communities into project activities, the ENRICH Project builds on the groundwork already laid by Wayne Adams, a former Canadian provincial politician who was the first Black Canadian member of the Nova Scotia House of Assembly, as well as the first Black cabinet minister to serve Nova Scotia. His message focused on halting the placement of dumps near low-income communities, something he later helped realize as the minister of environment. In this role, he introduced the *Wilderness Areas Protection Act* in 1998 (Nova Scotia Legislature n.d.b) although this bill did not go beyond first reading.

Over the last several years, the ENRICH Project has been addressing the many limitations inherent to the environmental justice movement by mobilizing public understandings of environmental racism. In addition, the project has been improving the flow of research benefits to communities by ensuring that its activities serve as a platform to investigate the socioeconomic and health impacts of environmental racism, while potentially informing provincial regulatory requirements for environmental justice in Mi'kmaw and African Nova Scotian communities. Ultimately, then, the project seeks to create a culturally relevant platform through which community members, particularly in remote areas, can efficiently connect with academics and non-profit organizations to pursue meaningful research and community capacity-building projects that address concerns related to environmental issues in their communities.

Community-based participatory research (CBPR) is an ideal research approach for achieving many of the ENRICH Project's objectives. CBPR is a collaborative approach that involves researchers and communities working in partnership in ways that enable power to be shared among all participants (Israel, Schulz, Parker, and Becker 1998; Minkler and Wallerstein 2011; Minkler, Vasquez, Tajik, and Peterson 2008). It requires the involvement of community members at every stage of the research process, including research design, data collection and analysis, and knowledge dissemination and mobilization. It values mutual respect and co-learning among partners, capacity building, systems change, and balancing research and action (Israel, Schulz, Parker, and Becker 1998; Minkler and Wallerstein 2011; Minkler, Vasquez, Tajik, and Peterson 2008).

Through this approach, partners contribute their expertise to enhance understandings of a given phenomenon and to integrate the knowledge gained through action to benefit the communities involved. Community ownership is an integral aspect of CBPR, particularly for studies that involve vulnerable communities. CBPR must be premised on equitable power sharing in how communities are engaged, how studies are conducted, and how knowledge and resources resulting from these studies are shared (Israel, Schulz, Parker, and Becker 1998; Minkler and Wallerstein 2011; Minkler, Vasquez, Tajik, and Peterson 2008). The ENRICH Project also reflects the principles of advocacy research (Community Toolbox 2014) by providing data to support community members' advocacy and mobilization efforts. It does this in a number of ways, including providing technical information to help community members make their case; providing anecdotes, human stories, and examples that describe and illuminate an environmental issue; positioning community members as experts and authorities on issues affecting their communities; and holding government officials accountable for their policy decisions and actions.

In the fall of 2012, after receiving a Team Development Grant from the Nova Scotia Health Research Foundation, I began building a team composed of faculty and researchers across multiple disciplines, Mi'kmaw and African Nova Scotian community members and leaders affected by environmental pollution and contamination, environmental activists, environmental organizations and other non-profit agencies, health professionals, students, and volunteers. As the team began to take shape, we decided that our next step should be to hold community meetings in different regions across the province where Mi'kmaw and African Nova Scotian communities are most impacted by environmental contamination and pollution. After the meetings, we held a final convergence workshop to bring together community members in different regions to share their experiences. The main objectives of these events were to identify community concerns and priorities about the socioeconomic and health impacts of polluting industries and other environmental hazards, obtain suggestions and guidance from community members about if or how research could support their ongoing efforts to address these issues, and listen to community members' personal anecdotes and stories about the impacts of contamination and pollution in their families and communities.

We understood how crucial it was that we meet with community members to begin the relationship-building process and listen to their suggestions for how we could support them in their efforts to address environmental concerns in their communities. We also recognized that meeting face to face with community members would go a long way in fostering, building, and sustaining collaborative community relationships and partnerships in ways that would enable faculty to work *with* communities rather than *on behalf* of them — a central principle of CBPR.

As planning activities carried over into 2013, and after several discussions about which communities should be selected, we decided that we would hold our regional meetings and final convergence workshop in regions where members of our team had already developed significant relationships and partnerships with key community leaders, Elders, and agencies. These regions included Mi'kmaw communities in Pictou Landing First Nation, Acadia First Nation Reserve in Yarmouth, and Eskasoni First Nation in Cape Breton, as well as African Nova Scotian communities in Lincolnville, North Preston, and East Preston. The convergence workshop brought together Mi'kmaw and African Nova Scotian communities and was held in the Halifax Regional Municipality (HRM).

"IN WHOSE BACKYARD? EXPLORING TOXIC LEGACIES IN MI'KMAW AND AFRICAN NOVA SCOTIAN COMMUNITIES": REGIONAL MEETINGS AND FINAL CONVERGENCE WORKSHOP

Between September 28, 2013 and January 11, 2014, four regional meetings were held, as well as one convergence workshop entitled "In Whose Backyard? Exploring Toxic Legacies in Mi'kmaw and African Nova Scotian Communities." The workshop was also filmed for a documentary by Pink Dog Productions entitled *In Whose Backyard?* (Pink Dog Productions 2014). The community members were open and welcoming during the meetings. The passion and frustrations they shared about their experiences of dealing with environmental racism in their communities were palpable and made us even more committed to finding ways to support them in their advocacy efforts.

For example, I was struck by the relentless commitment of the Lincolnville residents at the regional meeting on September 28, 2013, who have been engaged in efforts to address a landfill near their community since the early 1970s. A visit to the landfill site before the meeting set the context for the ongoing struggle to have their concerns about potential contamination and pollution addressed by government. Interestingly, the ominously serene beauty of the area upon which the landfill is situated masks the potential dangers lurking beneath the surface — dangers that pose risks to the health and well-being of community members in the form of contaminated drinking water and toxic soil. Unfortunately, despite the community's efforts to address the harms from the landfill over the past several decades, government has been largely unresponsive to the community's requests to meet with them or to hold mandatory community consultations.

My heart raced as community members attending the meeting in North Preston on October 5, 2013, expressed outrage about the impact of environmental contamination on the health of their community. This meeting brought together residents from North and East Preston. Likening environmental racism to "another Africville" and "racial genocide," community members expressed the urgency of these issues, as well as how important it was for their communities to become more proactive in mobilizing around environmental racism. More than any of the other meetings, this meeting took on a "call to action" tone that left me feeling encouraged and hopeful that community members were ready to work collaboratively.

I was also encouraged by the quiet passion of community members from the Acadia First Nation Reserve at the meeting held in Yarmouth on October 19, 2013. As the meeting organizer took members of the ENRICH team on a thorny trek near a junkyard full of abandoned car parts located on the Acadia First Nation Reserve, I was reminded of Lincolnville and how the serene beauty of the landfill site there masked potential dangers. While the junkyard on the reserve would have seemed harmless had we visited it before the Lincolnville meeting, the concerns raised at the Lincolnville meeting armed me with a heightened awareness of the many risks the junkyard posed to community members.

I was humbled by the warmth and welcoming nature of community members from Eskasoni at the meeting held in Membertou on November 23, 2013. Although some of the community members at times expressed cautious skepticism that our project would bring about any real change, they showed generosity by sharing their concerns and fears about the many ills affecting Mi'kmaq (loss of language, the need to provide culturally and linguistically relevant education to youth, etc.). This indicated to me that they were entrusting us with a certain level of responsibility that had implications beyond polluting industries and other environmental hazards.

Finally, I was left feeling exhilarated by the insightful contributions made by Mi'kmaw, African Nova Scotian, and other participants at the final convergence workshop held at the Halifax Forum on January 11, 2014. Thankfully, this workshop focused more on the concerns and priorities the communities shared, rather than on issues that had long divided them. Witnessing how the event provided these communities with a rare opportunity to come together in one space to voice their shared concerns about environmental racism gave me hope that the ENRICH Project could be a catalyst for building relationships between them.

Although I have always been hesitant to label myself as a community-based researcher in the strictest sense of the term (since the type of research approach I use is determined by the nature of the topic and the participants involved in each specific project), the ENRICH Project has impressed upon me the real and significant impacts CBPR can have on the lives and well-being of some of the most vulnerable members of the population — if conducted with integrity, authenticity, empathy, sensitivity, and with the needs and priorities of community members always in mind. As many researchers working with racialized and Indigenous communities come to realize, gaining the trust and confidence of community members is often hard-fought, hard-won, and, at times, easily lost and never to be found again. Tales of being burned, mistreated, exploited, and ultimately abandoned by researchers abound as community members are asked to recall their experiences participating in research studies that promised to transform their communities for the better. As the ENRICH Project team marches on under the weight of these disappointments and expectations, we remain committed to ensuring that the integrity of the project and the trust placed in us are not compromised by the many competing demands and priorities that will undoubtedly arise as the project continues to evolve.

THE CASE OF PICTOU LANDING FIRST NATION

Community engagement has not been without its challenges. This was exemplified by the difficulties the ENRICH Project team experienced engaging Mi'kmaw community members in Pictou Landing First Nation, who have long been dealing with broken promises made by the government that it would clean up the contaminated Boat Harbour site. In the last section, you may have noticed that I made no mention of a visit to Pictou Landing First Nation, one of the regions that was originally on our list to visit and hold a workshop. The truth is, we never made it there. Although I made numerous attempts throughout 2012 and 2013 to engage the community by connecting with community leaders and organizations, by the summer of 2013 I came to the realization that engaging Pictou Landing First Nation was not going to be possible at that time. The issues in Pictou Landing are long-standing and complex, and the community needs to be given the time and space to address them in their own way and in their own time. In early fall of 2013, I finally made the decision to move forward without Pictou Landing First Nation after receiving communication from a key leader in the region that they were not interested in participating in a workshop. According to this leader, the number of requests community members and leaders in her community had received over the past several years to participate in research surveys and other research activities had left the community feeling over-researched and burned out.

I learned several important lessons from my efforts to engage Pictou Landing

First Nation. First, it affirmed for me how important it is to build relationships and trust with community members and leaders over the long term, particularly in Indigenous and racialized communities that have long felt exploited by researchers. Researchers that fail to forge organic relationships with communities should not expect to gain entry into these communities; they need to have nurtured reciprocal, collaborative, and trusting relationships with community members over the long term. This issue was brought home to the team when we realized how important it was to hire meeting and workshop organizers who resided in the regions and who, as a result, had developed organic and trusting relationships with community members. Second, these challenges underscored how important it is to be sensitive to the timelines, priorities, and cultural realities in each community. In other words, it is important to "take the temperature" of the community to determine their readiness for engaging in the research process. Despite our disappointment about not being able to engage Pictou Landing First Nation in the workshops, we learned valuable lessons that we carry with us today.

I am pleased to report, however, that in June 2017 I finally visited the community at the invitation of a long-time environmental activist in the community. During the meeting, community members discussed the impact that the contamination of Boat Harbour has had on the health of the community. They also noted the community efforts made since the 1960s to pressure the government to clean up Boat Harbour and the commitment made by the government in 2014 to clean it up by 2020 (Campbell 2014). Although a considerable amount of water sampling has already been conducted there, the community expressed their interest in having scientists test more water samples in partnership with them to determine which specific contaminants are in Boat Harbour. They emphasized that they would like the water tested for all contaminants (not just arsenic, which has already been done), including dioxins, mercury, cadmium, and heavy metals. After the meeting I met with a lawyer, with whom I had been collaborating, to discuss some of the legal remedies available to community members. Then, I shared this information with the activist who had invited me to the community. Based on past missteps, I realized that it would be important to give the community time to move at their own pace, given their long-standing concerns and the many broken promises they have endured over the last several decades as the government failed to clean up Boat Harbour. What's most important is that the lines of communication have now been opened and a new relationship forged between the ENRICH Project and Pictou Landing First Nation.

Although it took me four years to meet with the community, I believe that it happened the way it was supposed to. During my conversation with the activist a few days before the meeting, he mentioned that he wanted to invite me to his community after watching the commitment that the ENRICH Project has shown addressing environmental racism over the past five years and had shared this with his community several times.

THE *ENVIRONMENTAL RACISM PREVENTION ACT*

In the spring of 2014, I disseminated the report on the meetings and final convergence workshop (Waldron 2014a) as well as the documentary film *In Whose Backyard?* (Pink Dog Productions 2014) to community members, government departments, and other agencies and organizations. I then began the long and arduous process of consulting with Nova Scotia Environment and other government agencies and departments to determine if and how they could support community members' ongoing efforts to address environmental concerns. These consultations were documented in a government consultation report that was completed at the end of 2014 (Waldron 2014b). As the year came to a close, I realized that there had been little movement on getting Nova Scotia Environment or any other government department or agency to consult with the communities or address their concerns in any way. I had, for the most part, been chasing my tail. Just as I was ready to throw in the towel, a member of my team suggested that I begin meeting with MLAs, since they tend to have closer relationships with communities they represent.

After sending emails to and leaving voice mail messages for several MLAs between December 2014 and mid-January 2015, I received a reply from Lenore Zann, MLA for Truro-Bible Hill-Millbrook-Salmon River. We agreed to meet on January 21, 2015 to explore how she and the Nova Scotia NDP could support community members in addressing their concerns. Finding ways to protect and clean up our environment, address discrimination, and empower communities are some of Zann's biggest passions. A few minutes into my meeting with Zann, I found her passion to be infectious and authentic. Although Zann admitted that she had never heard of environmental racism before, she did remember from her time as a young girl living in Australia that Indigenous peoples always seemed to live near a dump.

Almost immediately, she declared that she was interested in introducing a private member's bill to address environmental racism before the House finished sitting in spring. This bill would outline government's responsibilities for consulting with Mi'kmaw, African Nova Scotian, and Acadian communities throughout the province to provide them with an opportunity to share their concerns and collaborate with government to devise strategies and solutions for addressing environmental racism in the province. Zann was also interested in organizing a press conference on environmental racism to bring more attention to the issue. While the ENRICH Project had already done considerable work raising awareness about environmental racism through media interviews, social media, workshops, and public engagement events, garnering more attention for the issue could certainly not hurt. A few weeks after our meeting, Zann and I arranged to meet with three law professors at Dalhousie University's Schulich School of Law to receive some guidance on crafting the bill. While they cautioned us that private members' bills rarely, if ever, pass into law, they also encouraged us to move forward with the bill. That same week, I developed a brief report to assist Zann in crafting the bill, which included findings from the ENRICH Project's workshops as well as a literature review of studies on environmental racism and environmental justice in Canada. The bill was eventually named the *Environmental Racism Prevention Act* (Bill 111) (Nova Scotia Legislature n.d.a). The Act reads as follows:

> Be it enacted by the Governor and Assembly as follows:
>
>   1. This Act may be cited as the *Environmental Racism Prevention Act.*
>   2. In this Act,
>
>   (a) "Ministers" means the Minister of Environment and the Minister responsible for the *Human Rights Act;*
>
>   (b) "panel" means the panel established pursuant to this Act.
>
>   3. (1) The Ministers shall establish a panel, as set out in this Section, to examine the issue of environmental racism in the Province, and provide recommendations to address it.
>
>   (2) The panel is to be composed of
>
>   (a) three members chosen by the Minister of Environment from among the members of the Round Table established pursuant to the *Environment Act;*
>
>   (b) two members chosen by the Minister responsible for the *Human Rights Act* from among the members of the Nova Scotia Human Rights Commission; and
>
>   (c) three members chosen by the Minister responsible for the *Human Rights Act,* of whom there must be one member from each of
>
>   (i) the African Nova Scotian community,
>   (ii) the First Nations' community, and

(iii) the Acadian community.

(3) Her Majesty in right of the Province shall pay the members of the panel such remuneration as is determined by the Ministers, together with the members' reasonable expenses.

4. Within one year of the coming into force of this Act, the panel shall consult the public, on a Province-wide basis, about the issue of environmental racism, with special emphasis given to consultation with the African Nova Scotian, First Nations' and Acadian communities, and provide a report to the Ministers that sets out its findings and recommendations.

5. The Ministers shall, within 10 days of receiving the report referred to in Section 4, table the report in the Assembly if the Assembly is then sitting or, where it is not then sitting, file the report with the Clerk of the Assembly.

6. The money required for the purpose of this Act must be paid out of money appropriated for that purpose by the Legislature.

I was now even more excited about the ENRICH Project's turn down a path that could potentially lead to legislative changes.

But, I wondered, would it? Was I being naïve, caught up in Zann's seemingly unbridled enthusiasm? Was *she* being naïve? Was she failing to grasp how challenging it had long been to address environmental racism in this province and how long communities had been fighting the good fight, with little success? As I quietly pondered these questions, I needed to turn my attention to other matters that year.

2015: A BANNER YEAR

The year 2015 was, undoubtedly, a banner year for the ENRICH Project — not only because we were preparing to collaborate on a groundbreaking bill with Lenore Zann, but also because we launched a number of exciting new projects. One of these projects was getting a team of volunteers from the ENRICH Project together to organize a silent auction fundraiser on April 12, 2015 for Elsipogtog warrior Annie Clair's legal fees. In the fall of 2014, we had gathered a team of volunteers late one evening at Dalhousie University's Black Student Advising Centre and hacked out a plan to raise funds, including creating a video, setting up a crowdsourcing site, and organizing a silent auction in 2015 (Arsenault 2015). Clair was attempting to fight six charges laid against her in Elsipogtog in 2013, as she fought to protect her community's unceded land. She was facing charges for protesting Texan oil company Southwestern Energy's (SWN) attempts at fracking exploration in her community, Elsipogtog First Nation. Later that year, all charges against Clair were dropped in a Moncton courthouse (Choi 2015). It felt rewarding to know that the ENRICH Project had inspired and collaborated on a series of activities that lead to justice for a community member who was so committed to protecting her land and community.

On April 11, one day before the auction, the ENRICH Project held the final art showcase for *Time to Clear the Air: Art on Environmental Racism by Mi'kmaw and African Nova Scotian Youth.* This project, which was launched in September 2014 and was coordinated by seven students in Dalhousie's College of Sustainability, engaged African Nova Scotian and Mi'kmaw youth in creating and presenting diverse forms of art to showcase examples and experiences of environmental racism in their communities. I was pleased to learn earlier that week that the project had been awarded the Green Campaign of the Year Award by the Dalhousie Student Union Sustainability Office. A few weeks later, on April 29, 2015, Zann finally introduced Bill 111 in the Legislature, which meant that meaningful consultations with community members could now be a reality — particularly given the fact that community members have long believed that Nova Scotia Environment's citizen engagement and community consultation process has not been sufficiently explicit, transparent, or accessible.

There was little time to rest on our laurels, however, since planning was already underway in May for the ENRICH Project to partner with NSPIRG and EAC on a public engagement event at the end of July, entitled Connecting the Dots: Confronting Environmental Racism in Nova Scotia. While the ENRICH Project had previously hosted several events to raise awareness about environmental racism, Connecting the Dots needed to be different. For example, although the event we held almost one year earlier in October 2014 at Dalhousie's McInnis Room had been a great success, it had been a "heady" affair, requiring attendees to converge at tables in order to brainstorm and strategize effective ways to address environmental racism through education, policy, and community organizing. While this work was crucial in moving the ENRICH Project forward, feedback received from participants after the event suggested that the event was mentally exhausting. I was determined that Connecting the Dots not simply be educational and informative, but also celebratory, fun, and joyous. In June, as we were putting the final touches on event planning activities, I was pleased to receive a voice mail from EAC informing me that the ENRICH Project was set to receive yet another award — second-place prize in EAC's Annual Sunshine Award — that was to be handed out at EAC's annual general meeting on June 22. The award was established to recognize the efforts of an individual or group to protect Nova Scotia's environment.

On July 28, 2015 Connecting the Dots went off without a hitch in the Paul O'Regan Hall at the Halifax Central Library, where it was standing room only. With panelists Mary Desmond (Lincolnville), Dorene Bernard (Indian Brook), Carolanne Wright-Parks (Greater Halifax Partnership), and Lenore Zann providing insight into how they were addressing environmental racism through community organizing and policy, the event proved to be what I had hoped. It was informative, educational, joyous, celebratory, and fun. It was bookended by majestic, jubilant, and rousing musical performances by two drum groups: the Umoja Cultural Diversity Drummers, who opened the event, and All Nations Drummers, an all-female Mi'kmaw drum group, who closed the event.

By the end of 2015, I was exhausted from the many meetings and events the ENRICH Project helped plan that year. Although 2015 had been our most fruitful year up to that point, I promised myself that the next year had to be different; I simply could not keep up the same pace. I decided that in 2016, we would focus less on organizing events to raise awareness about environmental racism and more on research and other community capacity-building activities.

THE WAY FORWARD: CONNECTING SCIENCE WITH COMMUNITY KNOWLEDGE AND THE LAW

The first quarter of 2016 saw the completion of two important mapping projects, which had begun early in 2015: the Africville Story Map and the ENRICH Project Map. The Africville Story Map was developed by a Dalhousie Master of Planning student for her thesis and handed over to the ENRICH Project to use for educational purposes. Using historical maps, it traces the history of environmental racism in Africville by displaying industrial facilities near Africville throughout the nineteenth and twentieth centuries. The ENRICH Project Map, created by a research assistant, is an online, interactive, open-source, community-based map that shows the location of facilities near Mi'kmaw and African Nova Scotian communities across the province.

I was surprised and encouraged by the increasing attention the ENRICH Project was garnering nationally. I received an email in February 2016 from Professor Deborah McGregor at York University's Osgoode Hall Law School, inviting me to speak at York University's Indigenous Environmental Justice Knowledge Sharing Symposium on May 26. She wanted me to deliver the presentation with female activists from the Mi'kmaw community in Nova Scotia. The symposium was a unique opportunity to partner with Nova Scotia–based

Mi'kmaw female activists at a symposium that was for and about Indigenous peoples who were addressing environmental injustices in their communities across Canada.

In 2016, the ENRICH Project moved into unchartered waters with the launch of a water monitoring project in Lincolnville. Work that had begun in fall 2015 by the ENRICH Project's Water Monitoring Working Group forged ahead in a big way. This working group had been collaborating with African Nova Scotian members of the Lincolnville Reserve Land Voice Council on the Lincolnville Water Monitoring Program. The project had three objectives: to determine if there was contaminated water flowing in the direction of the community from the landfill site, to build the community's capacity to test their own water, and to provide community members with basic knowledge about contaminants and groundwater sampling. Since the project's inception, members of the ENRICH Project's Water Monitoring Working Group had engaged in a number of activities, including meeting with members of the Lincolnville Reserve Land Voice Council, developing a historical profile of Lincolnville, and identifying labs willing to conduct inexpensive or free water testing. Since we were unsuccessful in identifying a lab willing to conduct inexpensive or free water testing, working group member Wilber Menendez Sanchez generously gave of his time to conduct water testing in a lab at Nova Scotia Community College, where he teaches. Members of the working group also reviewed reports and other literature on policies and legislation related to environmental impact assessments, water quality monitoring, hydrogeology, and bedrock geology, as well as facility siting regulations from the Municipality of the District of Guysborough (where Lincolnville is located), and maps created by government.

The sampling program conducted by members of the working group involved sampling wells for bacteria and major ions and elements (or parameters) that are normally included in a typical water analysis. Generally speaking, the two main routes for possible contamination by these parameters would be through groundwater contamination. A second, more remote possible source of groundwater bacteria contamination would be liquids leaking out of garbage trucks and trucks delivering and picking up organics as they drive past Lincolnville. There is a possibility of leakage from the trucks that could find its way overland (via the road, then ditches) and then into wells close to roads. Analytical results in the project report (Bonner, Menendez Sanchez, Bonner, Clarke, and Beckett 2016) show that one of the sites tested positive for both coliforms and E. coli, while another site tested positive for coliforms. The wells at two of the sites contain slightly elevated levels of chlorine and sodium, which together produce sodium chloride or common salt. Surface water is most likely entering these wells, which is consistent with coliform contamination (Bonner, Menendez Sanchez, Bonner, Clarke, and Beckett 2016). The project was completed at the end of August 2016, when members of the working group returned to the community to share findings from the project, answer questions, and address concerns.

As the Lincolnville Water Monitoring Project was proceeding during the summer of 2016, I was working behind the scenes to forge a relationship between members of the Lincolnville Reserve Land Voice Council and a lawyer at Ecojustice's Calgary office. Ecojustice, Canada's largest environmental law charity, goes to court and uses the power of the law to defend nature, combat climate change, and fight for a healthy environment. Since the summer of 2016, Ecojustice has been communicating with Lincolnville community members to explore possible legal remedies to address the landfill, including examining overlap between human rights law and environmental law to determine if government has violated residents' human rights and the *Canadian Charter of Rights and Freedoms*. Human rights violations may include the exposure of racialized communities to harm, as well as underprovision of clean drinking water and positive environmental services. Ecojustice is also making considerable use of the findings in the Lincolnville Water Monitoring report since, other than that report, there is little information on water quality in the community. In 2017, the ENRICH Project became an official member of the African Nova Scotian Decade for People of African Descent Coalition (ANSDPAD) following a meeting on October 19 with the United Nations Working Group of Experts on People of African Descent. The group met with coalitions composed of Black Canadian organizations in Halifax, Toronto, Ottawa, and Montreal that year. The objective of ANSDPAD is to examine, reconstruct and mutually strengthen relationships between the African Nova Scotian community and the government. On September 25, 2017, the United Nations Working Group of Experts on People of African Descent submitted its final report on the human rights situation of people of African descent in Canada to the council based on its consultations (Beaumont 2017; *Canadian Press* 2017; United Nations General Assembly 2017).

While that was going on, in spring 2017, Nova Scotia Community College science instructor Dr. Wilber Menendez Sanchez, geologist Fred Bonner, Shelburne community activist Louise Delisle, and I formed Rural Water Watch, a new non-governmental organization that evolved out of the ENRICH Project's Lincolnville Water Monitoring project, which both Menendez Sanchez and

Bonner led. We were later joined by James Kerr, an instructor in Nova Scotia Community College's Environmental Engineering Technology Program. The mission of Rural Water Watch is to equip rural Nova Scotian communities with the knowledge, skills, literacy, and resources to address their concerns about drinking water quality. Its objectives are to build the capacity of homeowners in rural Nova Scotian communities to manage their drinking water resources by becoming knowledgeable about analytical testing, undertaking water sampling, and learning how to identify potential contaminants that could affect water quality; to help homeowners in rural Nova Scotian communities build a community-based drinking water monitoring network; to raise funds for water sampling and water quality testing and improvement; and to train students to address drinking water quality (Jiwa 2017).

In the of summer 2017, the ENRICH Project's team members and volunteers were also planning a two-part public and academic symposium that was held on October 26 and October 27, 2017, entitled Over the Line: A Conversation on Race, Place and the Environment — the first major event the ENRICH Project would host since 2015's Connecting the Dots event. Unlike that event, which focused solely on environmental racism in Nova Scotia from the perspectives of Nova Scotia–based community leaders and activists, Over the Line brought together community leaders, activists, professors, and environmental professionals based in Nova Scotia, Ontario, and the United States to discuss race, place, and the environment more broadly. Along with environmental racism, the event focused on how other socio-spatial processes and projects impact well-being and health in Indigenous and Black communities in North America, including renewable energy, climate change, the built environment, and urban planning.

The event was particularly thrilling for me because it featured presentations by scholars whose work I have long followed and who are cited in this book, including Robert Bullard, George Lipsitz, Cheryl Teelucksingh, Michael Mascarenhas, and Deborah McGregor. A few days after the event, I received an email from George Lipsitz expressing his interest in connecting the ENRICH Project with the work he and others have been undertaking at the Center for Black Studies Research at the University of California, Santa Barbara. Since I have been interested in creating more national and international exposure for the ENRICH Project, I accepted his invitation. I also relished the opportunity to work with George Lipsitz, whose work has been foundational to the issues and arguments made in this book and to the ENRICH Project over the years.

Chapter 2

A HISTORY OF VIOLENCE

Indigenous and Black Conquest, Dispossession, and Genocide in Settler-Colonial Nations

> The successful settler colonies "tame" a variety of wildernesses, end up establishing independent nations, effectively repress, co-opt, and extinguish indigenous alterities, and productively manage ethnic diversity. (Veracini 2011: 3)

Environmental racism is violence — one of several forms of state-sanctioned racial violence perpetrated upon the lands, bodies, and minds of Indigenous and Black communities through decision-making processes and policies that have their roots in a legacy of colonial violence in Canada and other white settler nations. Environmental racism is also constituent of settler colonialism. In this book, I understand the reality of settler colonialism through recent theoretical approaches to the various aspects of it (Veracini 2011; Wolfe 2006). The framework of settler-colonial studies calls attention to the ways in which environmental racism operates as a visible manifestation of white supremacy, racial capitalism, neoliberalism, possession and dispossession, and the erasure and genocide of Indigenous and Black peoples.

One of the many limitations of the environmental justice lens in Canada is its failure to fully grapple with how land value is deeply inscribed with ideologies about race in ways that illuminate how we value or don't value certain bodies, providing fertile ground for environmental racism and other place-based injustices to manifest and flourish over time. I agree with Deborah M. Robinson's assertion (2000 n.p.) that environmental racism is "old wine in a new bottle" — another manifestation of historical racial oppression that produces, reproduces, and sustains racial and other social inequalities by disproportionately affecting already-vulnerable communities in the present day. It is important to make explicit, however, that environmental racism harms Indigenous and Black communities in very specific and unique ways. For example, while both experience racism, land sovereignty is also a key variable for Indigenous peoples and one that settler-colonial studies and struggles against settler colonialism have tended to foreground.

Lorenzo Veracini, one of the leading theorists on the topic of settler colonialism, differentiates between colonialism and settler colonialism in his article "Introducing Settler Colonial Studies" (2011), published in the founding issue of the journal *Settler Colonial Studies*. For Veracini, colonialism describes the late nineteenth-century European conquest and colonization of Africa and Asia, characterized by uneven structural power between areas of a nation state as well as unequal social relations, exploitation, and enslavement for the purposes of creating technological progress and improved infrastructure, among other factors. Settler colonialism, on the other hand, is conceptually distinct from other types of colonialism because it describes contemporary forms of colonialism in British-descended "settler colonies" such as Canada, the United States, and Australia, focusing specifically on the elimination of Indigenous peoples and their relationships from and with the land (Shoemaker 2015; Veracini 2011). Whereas in colonial states, the colonizers go out to the colonies and then return home in a circular movement, there is no return home in the case of settler colonialism. Rather, the goal becomes the transformation of the new colony into "home" — a process that lasts indefinitely.

While there are many different historical, political, theoretical, and practical definitions of colonialism, they all share one key feature: uneven power relations between individuals indigenous to the land and newcomers or "settlers." These relations of power are shaped by hierarchies of race, culture, gender, and class, and lead to the political, social, cultural, and material subordination of the less powerful group through domination and exploitation. Therefore, settler colonialism relies on the intersecting logics of white supremacy, capitalism, the reproduction of uneven power relations between and among settlers and Indigenous peoples (Veracini 2011).

European colonization began in 1492, when Christopher Columbus sailed west from Spain to the Americas, sparking large-scale exploration, colonization, and industrial development in the Caribbean, North America, and South America. In 1497, English explorer John Cabot landed on the North American coast, followed a year later by Columbus's third voyage, which reached the South American coast. France also colonized Eastern North America, several Caribbean islands, and small coastal parts of South America; Portugal colonized Brazil, the coasts of present-day Canada, and the northwest bank of the River

Plate, a river and large estuary between Argentina and Uruguay (Wolfe 1999).

Ugo Mattei and Laura Nader (2008) employ the concept of "plunder" to describe different historical processes of colonization and domination used by the Global North around the world. The goal was enrichment from plunder through exploitation of resources found in the colonized territories (extractable natural, human, and mineral resources) and the destruction of life. Mattei and Nader also distinguish between colonial practices of extraction and environmental colonialism. While the extraction of resources (raw material, natural history specimens, and ethnographic artifacts) imposed by colonialism is characterized by violent strategies where colonized peoples receive nothing in exchange, environmental colonialism is an ideological system of exploitation that operates with the consent and participation of the national elites. These elites are promised a reward (e.g., development, modernization, etc.) in exchange for implementing a system of management of natural and mineral resources that allows for the extraction, contamination and destruction of the environment. Thus, environmental colonialism involves both the exercise of biopower over the colonial territory and a sociopolitical and legal structure that allows for the exploitation of resources with the consent of the parties concerned.

Rob Nixon (2011) observes that neoliberalism upholds the legal-political structure of environmental colonialism because it interprets natural resources as "consumer products" included in the market economy. In fact, the new neoliberal geography suggests that natural resources have now become ecological commodities that reinforce environmental colonialism. These ecological commodities give rise to new strategies for control and domination, such as biopiracy, the mass purchase of agricultural lands, carbon emissions trading, and other contemporary enrichment practices (Atiles-Osoria 2014; Nixon 2011).

The colonialism practised by imperial powers focused on expansion and aggrandizement, motivated by imperial rivalries between France and Britain to amass territory in eighteenth-century North America. Postcolonial colonialism is primarily characterized by the inability of former colonies to distance themselves from the "colonial imprint," or in other words, the legacy of economic dependency and other entanglements that ensue from colonial relations and affinities (Shoemaker 2015). The enforcement of colonial institutions and laws upon Indigenous and Black peoples in Canada has been enabled, perpetuated, supported, and sustained by racist ideologies and practices that characterize Indigenous nations as uncivilized dependents. Colonial institutions refused to interpret nation-to-nation treaty relationships as agreements between two independent powers; they did not view Crown promises in treaties with Indigenous peoples as legally enforceable obligations under international or domestic law (Coates 1999; Macklem 2001). These interpretations of the law, and the legal tools used to support these interpretations, have enabled Canada to continue to claim ownership of Indigenous lands and territories.

Legislation directed at Indigenous peoples was informed by the European belief that Indigenous peoples were racially and culturally inferior, and it was used to justify their exploitation and oppression. For example, the 1857 *Act to Encourage the Gradual Civilization of the Indian Tribes in the Province* was premised on assimilationist ideology that provided for individuals of good character to have voluntary enfranchisement or be released from Indian status; they would no longer be considered "Indians" and would obtain the rights held by non-Indigenous settlers. This assimilationist policy attacked the integrity and land base of Indigenous communities and was used as a tool to move educated Indians away from the "backward" culture of the reserves. The *British North America Act* of 1867 represented a legal enactment of colonial domination, conferring on the colonial government unilateral powers to control Indians and lands reserved for Indians under section 91(24). This colonial piece of legislation provided a legal apparatus with which to advance and support the social and cultural genocide of Indigenous peoples. The 1869 *Gradual Enfranchisement Act* interfered with tribal self-government in various ways, including privileging bureaucratic authority over traditional leaders and distinguishing between registered status Indians and non-registered, non-status Indians (Gosine and Teelucksingh 2008; Henry and Tator 2006).

Finally, the 1876 *Indian Act* sought to further assimilate Indigenous peoples by instituting elected rather than traditional Band Councils and making Indigenous peoples "wards" of the federal Department of Indian Affairs (Henry and Tator 2006). The Chief and Council system created by the *Indian Act* also stripped Indigenous women of their political powers, stipulating that only men could be elected as Chiefs and Councillors. These legislative decisions instigated and cemented inequalities between Indigenous women and men, thereby shaping the negative perception and treatment of Indigenous women. The government began to establish residential schools across Canada in the 1880s, in conjunction with other federal assimilation policies. In 1920, under the *Indian Act*, it became mandatory for Indigenous children to attend a residential school, making it illegal for them to attend any other educational institution. The removal of Indigenous children from their homes by authorities, as well as their placement in the care of strangers, was perceived as an effective resocialization strategy that would culturally transform Indigenous children by creating a bridge from the Indigenous world to the non-Indigenous world and alienating them from their families, surroundings, and culture (Truth and Reconciliation Commission of Canada 2015).

Legislation directed at Black peoples in Canada from the seventeenth century to the nineteenth century was primarily focused on slave ownership. The first shipload of African slaves arrived at Jamestown on August 20, 1610, and the first named enslaved African to reside in Canada was a six-year-old boy who was the property of Sir David Kirke in New France. The *Code Noir* of 1685 permitted slavery for economic purposes only. It was officially limited to the West Indies and was never proclaimed in New France. It was used in customary law, however. On May 1, 1689, King Louis XIV gave slavery limited approval in New France, giving permission to the colonists of New France to keep Black and Pawnee Indian slaves. In 1709, he formally authorized slavery in New France, permitting his Canadian subjects to own slaves "in full proprietorship" (Historica Canada n.d.a). June 19, 1793 saw the passing of the *Anti-Slave Trade Bill*, which was developed by John Graves Simcoe, the first lieutenant governor of Upper Canada. The bill was a gradual prohibition on slavery rather than a total ban, however. On August 28, 1833, the *Act for the Abolition of Slavery throughout the British Colonies* abolished enslavement in most British colonies, including Canada, formally freeing nearly 800,000 slaves, although there were probably fewer than fifty slaves in British North America by that time (Historica Canada n.d.a).

Patrick Wolfe (1999), another leading theorist of settler colonialism, argues that, as a key feature of settler colonialism, white sovereign domination must be regarded as an ongoing encounter in which the main incentive is wealth and opportunities gained from the acquisition of land. Inherent to capitalism is the creation, consumption, and transformation of spaces and places; the assimilation, depopulation, removal, and erasure of Indigenous peoples; and the dispossession, expropriation, and territorial occupation of Indigenous resources, land, property, homes, and other physical structures — all toward the end goal of profit. Settler society operates on two levels: on the practical level, it seeks to eliminate Indigenous peoples to establish itself on their territory, and on the symbolic level, it needs to demonstrate its difference and independence from the mother country through the recuperation of indigeneity. As Wolfe (2006) and Glen Coulthard (2014) both argue, in settler-colonial societies economic, gendered, racial, and state power operate structurally and in tandem to dispossess Indigenous peoples of their lands and self-determination and turn the land into property, laying the foundation for colonial state formation and capitalist development.

Heteropatriarchy is also a key feature of settler-colonial societies. Heteropatriarchy and racism operate as two interrelated, intersecting, and mutually supporting systems of domination that subordinate, marginalize and oppress women. In other words, not only do Black and Indigenous women experience both racism and sexism, they also experience patriarchy differently than white women, since racism is patriarchal, and patriarchy is racist. As Cindy Courville (1993: 33) observes, "The study of African women's exploitation and oppression requires an understanding of the transhistorical nature of patriarchy as an ideology and how patriarchy as an ideology shaped the construction and reproduction of African women's oppression." Kelly Macias (2015) notes that slavery and colonialism exposed African cultures to patriarchal values and norms, such as European father-led societies, male-centred control over women, the erosion of mother-centred values, and the marginalization and devaluation of women.

Tiffany King (2013) observes that the "othering" and "sexualization" of the Black female slave body ushered in sexual violence as a tool of settler colonialism. In settler-colonial nations, the intersection of race, gender, and sexuality shaped ideological representations of Indigenous and Black women as non-human and, therefore, legitimated and ensured their violation through genocide and rape. The sexualities of Black and white women became polarized during slavery based on a highly romanticized image of the ideal woman as a pure, passive, submissive, and dependent mother and housewife. These stereotypes placed Black and white women at opposite ends of a hierarchy, casting white women as fragile, modest, and sexually repressed and Black women as strong, resilient, and sexually immoral (Waldron 2002).

White women have played a significant role in the racial subordination of Black women. White feminists often obscure how they have long been implicated in the oppression of Black people at the same time that they have been oppressed by white men. Colonialism accorded the white woman a multiplicity of roles that allowed her to occupy a subordinate status in relationship to white men, as well as a dominant one in relation to Black people in her newly constituted role as an oppressor. In other words, white women occupied a position in which they were simultaneously privileged and oppressed. Anne McClintock (1995) argues that the shifting identities of white women accorded them an ambiguous status in which their dominance was masked by patriarchal systems of domination that placed them in a subordinate position to white men. White women's role as oppressor has been constituted historically and contemporaneously since they benefitted from the exploitation of Blacks during and since slavery (Knowles and Mercer 1992; Waldron 2002).

Although white men were responsible for the creation of slavery, white women helped foster racial hostility, encouraging hierarchical relations between the colonizers and the colonized (hooks 1981; Stoler 1991; Waldron 2002). For example, many white women were involved in the ownership of Africans as chattel during slavery, as well as in the abuse of slaves in their homes. White women failed to dismantle the system of slavery, because it benefitted them (Olsen 1995). The subjugation of Black women encouraged white women's allegiance to patriarchy. This is a critical lesson about the relationship between racism and patriarchy: racism did not perfect patriarchy only by allowing slave masters the possibility of unrestrained control of Black women. It also secured the compliance of white women by promising them the privileges denied to slaves and threatening them with the punishments meted out to slaves.

Since the abolition of slavery, white women's role in oppressing Black women has evolved in less conspicuous ways. Despite their involvement in the abolition movement, the first white women's rights advocates in the 1830s had wished to maintain the racial caste system and seek social equality solely for white women (hooks 1981; Waldron 2002). Many of these women resisted alliances with Black women, fearing that it would undermine their status as morally pure ladies (hooks 1981). Sojourner Truth, a Black abolitionist and women's rights activist demonstrated the schism between white and Black women during this time. In the following quote, Miriam Schneir (1972: 94) documents how Truth identified the different relationships that each had with men and the white power structure:

> That man over there say that women needs to be helped into carriages, and lifted over ditches, and to have the best place everywhere. Nobody ever helps me into carriages, or over mud-puddles, or gives me any best place! .... And ain't I a woman? .... I have ploughed, and planted, and gathered into barns, and no man could head me! And ain't I a woman? I could work as much and eat as much as a man — when I could get it — and bear the lash as well! And ain't I a woman.

It would be misleading however, to suggest that white men and women have been the only oppressors of Black women. Despite Black men's status as a subordinate group victimized by racism, they have participated in the sexist oppression of Black women. Gender hierarchies among Black people were firmly in place long before the institutionalization of slavery and were reinforced by the sexist politics of colonial America. Black men exercised their belief in their "natural" ability to lead by dominating leadership roles during the early Black liberation movement, consequently participating in the patriarchal system alongside white men (hooks 1981; Waldron 2002). They used the Civil Rights Movement of the 1950s as a forum to denounce racism, as well as to announce their support of patriarchy. The concept of matriarchy was used as an ideological tool to confine Black women to rigid ideals of womanhood that were based on a traditional Western viewpoint. The Black men who joined Black Muslim groups in the 1960s and 1970s constructed a "feminine ideal" in which their wives were prescribed roles that were seen as naturally befitting women and that relegated them to a subordinate status (hooks 1981; Waldron 2002).

RACIAL CAPITALISM: ADDRESSING
ENVIRONMENTAL RACISM'S PROFIT MOTIVE

Canada was founded on enslavement and dispossession. Canada in the eighteenth and nineteenth centuries was characterized by assimilationist ideologies, practices, and policies; displacement, discrimination, subjugation, and oppression of Indigenous and Black peoples and cultures by Europeans; and the expropriation of Indigenous lands. In Canada, "the primitive accumulation of capital through the colonial theft of land is foundational to both current capitalist wealth and to state jurisdiction" (Solidarity Halifax 2017: 1). The potential for Europeans to access sources of new wealth prompted the expansion of European colonization in North and South America, as well as the creation of a global economy that was dominated by Spain, Portugal, Holland, France, and Britain. European settlers engaged in a number of activities to ensure their access to these newly settled lands, such as negotiating treaties, waging wars to extinguish Indigenous peoples, and eliminating and disrupting Indigenous landholding traditions (Truth and Reconciliation Commission of Canada 2015). Therefore, colonialism is by its very nature capitalist because it dispossesses Indigenous peoples of their land and resources and subjugates their communities.

The concept of race as an ideology and discourse emerged at approximately the same time that colonization began, and when Indigenous and Black peoples were considered "racial others." However, while colonialism employed the organizing grammar of race as a means to foster unequal relationships between Europeans and racial others, anti-Semitism, Islamophobia, Negrophobia, and other European xenophobic traditions are considerably older than the discourse of race, which emerged in a significant way late in the eighteenth century. By the mid-nineteenth century, the discourse of scientific biological differences between groups of humans was in full effect and informed characterizations of racial others as heathen, uncivilized, and barbaric (Hier and Singh Bolaria 2007).

As Audrey Kobayashi argues (2000), the racialization process involves the application of stereotypical traits to racialized groups, leading to the social and spatial segregation of these groups; the hierarchical organization of society based on race, class, gender, and other social differences; and the creation of racialized spaces that are characterized by disproportionate rates of unemployment, income insecurity, poverty, policing, incarceration, and other racialized and gendered forms of state-sanctioned violence. As Michael Omi and Howard Winant (1994) observe, the state is inherently racial because it organizes space based on its interpretation of race, and instead of addressing conflicts emerging from racial hierarchies and inequalities, it is a driving force in sustaining those hierarchies and inequalities. The antithetical roles that Indigenous and Black peoples have played in the formation of settler-colonial societies reflect the unique ways they have been racialized and implicated in the landscape of white settler nations and in capitalist expansion. For example, while the reproduction of Black slaves expanded the wealth of owners, the increase of Indigenous populations was viewed as a threat because it hindered settlers' access to the land.

Racism drives and sustains capitalism, which is a racial, gendered, and patriarchal regime (Kelley 2017). Racial capitalism describes the commodification of racialized peoples for the purposes of acquiring social and economic value that benefits white people and white institutions through the surplus value and worth tied to racialized peoples' identities. Ultimately, racial capitalism harms racialized peoples through the reinforcement of social and economic inequalities that have the most disadvantageous impacts on racialized peoples whose economic well-being is determined by their market value. Capitalism is preserved through the ongoing salience and resilience of racism and substandard wages provided to racialized peoples, immigrants, and women (Leong 2013). It relies on the possession of Indigenous land, the perceived expendability of Indigenous peoples, and the perceived value of gendered and racialized labour (Goldstein 2017). Similarly, historical and contemporary forms of racialized dispossession have been shaped by chattel slavery and the legacy of inequality it left in its wake (Goldstein 2017).

Although environmental racism has not been sufficiently incorporated into anticapitalist traditions, environmental racism is "a distinct category of capitalist strategy and an example of how capitalist exploitation exacerbates racial oppression" (Solidarity Halifax 2017: 1). The capitalist economic structure has led to the commercialization of industrial facilities and the waste disposal industry, which are considerably profitable. Therefore, it is a challenge to foster sustainable environmental practices in a capitalist economy based on consumption, especially when there is no sign that this consumption is slowing down. Capitalism can be defined as the profit that accumulates from an economic system in which the means of production is privately owned, and the distribution of goods is mainly driven by market competition. Capitalism's main tenets include private property, wage labour, voluntary exchange, competitive markets, mass consumption, and capital accumulation. Fundamental to capitalism is technological progress and sophistication, the replacement of "the old" with "the new," higher levels of productivity, and increased wealth (Robinson 2015).

Canadian capitalist expansion emerged out of a transformation from a primarily mercantile to an industrial form of capitalism that required lands to settle large incoming European populations. As state policy shifted at the turn of the nineteenth century, the objective of the colonial regime — as documented in the *Indian Act* — was settling treaties with Indigenous peoples, assimilating them, and extinguishing their land rights. Over the past few decades, globalization has restructured world capitalism to the degree that it has become distinct from earlier forms of capitalism. For example, all nations have been incorporated into a new global production and financial system as transnational capital has ascended. Whereas in the past a world economy linked countries and regions to each other through trade and financial flows, today nations are linked more organically in a global economy where the transnationalization of the production process, finance, and the circuits of capital accumulation are dominant features. (Robinson 2015).

Neoliberalism, which emerged in the 1970s, is a central component of racial capitalism and is itself a racial and class-based project that has increased race-based inequalities and normalized racism globally. Mardi Schmeichel (2011: 108) asserts that neoliberalism is a process of transformation whereby the administrative state that was previously responsible for the economy and human well-being became more concerned with treating people as "productive economic entrepreneurs of their own lives." The main objective of neoliberalism is to turn the "nation-state" into a "market-state" to facilitate global capital accumulation. Since environmental racism manifests within economic relations and exploitation inherent to capitalism, class systems, and the neoliberal agenda, those communities that are the most marginalized, the poorest, and the most lacking in political clout will pay a disproportionate price for various forms of capitalist exploitation such as economic development, resource extraction, and industrialism. Furthermore, given that the impacts of resource extraction and industry on the health and well-being of communities are of minimal concern to a capitalist agenda, these communities will also bear the greatest environmental burdens and health risks. However, the communities most impacted by environmental harms also lack the power, information, resources, and global strategies to address and resist the actions of powerful multinational corporations and oppressive governments.

The neoliberal agenda is focused on economizing everything, from viewing human beings as market actors and every field of activity as a market to ensuring unrestricted accumulation of capital through fiscal and monetary discipline, flexible labour markets, liberalization of trade and capital flows, and the elimination of workers' rights. Its objective is to liberate private enterprise from government-imposed restrictions, regardless of negative impacts on citizens. The neoliberal agenda is much more concerned with individual responsibility and basic market logic that produces subjects who are self-interested entrepreneurs than it is with the public good and legal regulations that protect the welfare of citizens. Therefore, citizens — and not the state — are held responsible for addressing the lack of health care, education, and social security. Consequently, one of the main criticisms of neoliberalism is that it eliminates shared and equal access to public goods, fosters social and economic inequalities, and creates disposable populations (Martinez and Garcia n.d.; Shenk 2015).

Global capitalism had its origins in slavery and also impacted the lives of indentured servants, prisoners, or other coerced persons. Racism remains one of the most significant pillars of capitalism because racial ideologies are used to justify labour and employment hierarchies that distribute rewards unequally (Robinson 2015). The long history of assigning value to race in the Americas means that property is inherently inscribed with racial meaning: whiteness has historically legitimized possession of property, and non-whiteness was valued only to the extent that a non-white person could be possessed as property. Capitalism was founded on the acquisition of social and economic value through the degradation and commodification of an individual's racial identity (Leong 2013). Katherine McKittrick (2011) observes that capitalism is greatly enabled by the exploitation of Black geographies in the Americas where uneven development, underdevelopment, and poverty remain central features.

Furthermore, the relationship between gender, feminism, and neoliberalism highlights the interplay between patriarchy and neoliberalism, the gender blindness of neoclassical economics, and the negative impacts of neoliberal policies on women (Cornwall, Gideon and Wilson 2008; Elson 1992; Sparr 1995). The cultural strand of feminism was complementary to neoliberalism in the context of cultural changes that equated women's self-worth with work outside the home, leading to women's increased presence in the labour force and their greater financial independence. However, the perceived advancement of women obscured their economic exploitation in the labour force. Referred to as the "feminization of labour," neoliberal policies contributed to the deterioration of working conditions that impacted women in specific ways, including the violation of international labour standards and low wages (Smith 2008). Although neoliberalism values individual agency, it is rooted in liberal theory that has always excluded women from this notion of individuality in favour of ideologies that characterize women as protective mothers whose main concerns are personal and economic gain and making personal sacrifices for the betterment of the household. Neoliberalism re-embeds women within the domestic sphere, stripping them of their individuality (Smith 2008).

Neoliberalism's meritocratic view of women's advancement in the labour force obscures the fact that these achievements are experienced by a small group of women and, consequently, compromises the work being carried out by collective movements for equity. Neoliberalism is also less willing to critique the political and economic structures that produce inequalities between women and men and among women (Schmeichel 2011). Feminist interventions that have the potential to become radical grassroots efforts are often sidelined because the women who work in women-oriented non-governmental organizations are hired to provide basic human services. While the technical professionalization of these women as gender experts and service subcontractors means that they can compete effectively in the neoliberal social policy arena, they also experience barriers building relationships and solidarity with disadvantaged women (Hawkesworth 2006; Smith 2008).

The ongoing debate as to whether race or class is the main determinant of environmental injustice has been challenged by a body of environmental justice scholarship that argues racism should never be separated from class, capitalism, gender, or other social relations and is, instead, an intrinsic feature of state apparatus that works to structure other social differences (Cutter 1995; Kurtz 2009). For example, Laura Pulido (1996) contends that rather than extricating race from analyses of the capitalistic economic structure, environmental justice scholarship should pay attention to the racialized nature of the economy and how this shapes environmental injustices. The notion that racism can be subsumed within or reduced to class fails to consider the ways in which racism operates discursively and materially to assign different values to individuals. Therefore, Pulido (2016) argues the importance of rethinking capitalism as racial capitalism.

Environmental racism, then, is a visible manifestation of racial capitalism because the pursuit and accumulation of power and profits for elites through the placement of harmful industries in isolated and poor Indigenous, Black, and other racialized communities relies on ideological notions about the expendability and disposability of Indigenous, Black, and other racialized bodies residing in racially devalued places. Given that Indigenous and Black peoples residing in rural areas in Nova Scotia experience high rates of precarious employment, they are seen as having little value to capital, lacking in worth, value, and political clout, and therefore expendable and disposable. Consequently, it makes cultural common sense, as Mills (2001) argues, to place harmful industries in these communities. Racial capitalism remains the main obstacle to addressing environmental racism, since the main goal of industry owners is to benefit themselves by creating surplus value, producing and maximizing profit, allocating resources, and accumulating wealth in areas where the population is most marginalized and less able to fight back.

EPISTEMOLOGIES OF IGNORANCE

Decisions about where to locate a waste facility involve complex interactions among government, legal actors, and commercial actors, which are informed by historically constituted racist policies that ultimately sustain white privilege by protecting the social well-being and health of white people and the economic elite (Bullard 1993). In a study that the ENRICH Project conducted about environmental health in African Nova Scotian communities, an African Nova Scotian participant residing in Lucasville illustrates how white privilege confers a sense of entitlement to white industry owners, who come into her community and engage in activities without any consideration for how it affects the community:

> Well, I find, myself personally, that things are done in a Black community without the knowledge of the people of the community a lot more than if you were in a white community because they could care less about what we feel, you know, about what's being done in this

community. You know, like you can't go into a white community and do whatever you want. If a Black man went into a white community, he'd be arrested and locked up. A white man comes in our community, he does what he wants, and he's backed up to do whatever he cares to do in our community with the knowledge of the people of Halifax Regional Municipality. You know, they grant him the permits he needs to do what he wants to do. And, even if he doesn't get the permits, he still does whatever he wants, and nothing's said to him. If a Black man builds a house or puts a garage up without the permits, they want him to tear it down … Memento Farm [a horse farm that was built in the community] comes in here, built the house, and that's all they had a permit for. Then they put up barns and stuff without permits, and did what they want. And, nothing happens to them. (Waldron 2016)

The situation in Lucasville demonstrates how deeply embedded white privilege is. Even in spaces where racialized communities disproportionately reside, the taken-for-granted nature of whiteness confers to white people a sense of entitlement and ownership that is often not questioned by policymakers.

Mills (2007: 48) observes that "an epistemology of ignorance" characterizes the many ways in which white blindness is actively reproduced to inform knowledge, practices, and policies that uphold white privilege. For Mills (15), white people's main cognitive handicap is their ignorance of the ways in which white people as a group are recipients and beneficiaries of an epistemological legacy and logic that drives and informs racist acts. It is important at this juncture to distinguish between innocent forms of ignorance and structural forms of ignorance in articulating epistemologies of ignorance that convey whiteness as a form of capital. Whereas innocent forms of ignorance characterize white people's lack of knowledge about the privileges they benefit from based on skin colour, structural ignorance refers to white people's lack of understanding about how these privileges are embedded within laws, policies, and institutions in ways that confer to them social, economic, and political advantages. As Richard Dyer points out, "White power secures its dominance by seeming not to be anything in particular" (1988: 44). For white supremacy to be maintained, there must be a deep investment by whites in a universal narrative that denies the humanity of the enslaved and colonized, and that characterizes these individuals as not fully human, as Paulo Freire points out in his book *Pedagogy of the Oppressed* (2000: 56):

Whereas the violence of the oppressors prevents the oppressed from being fully human, the response of the latter to this violence is grounded in the desire to pursue the right to be human.

Lipsitz (1998: 2) argues that a contributory factor to racialized hierarchies in society is a "possessive investment in whiteness" created by both public policy and private prejudice. The cash value inherent to whiteness confers advantages to whites, who are more likely to profit from housing acquired in discriminatory markets, receive quality education, access employment opportunities through insider networks, and inherit wealth through intergenerational transfers conferred to successive generations. In asserting that the accumulation of resources, power, and opportunity rely on an investment in whiteness by white people, Lipsitz (1998) encourages us to rethink our understanding of white supremacy. Rather than an ideology that merely signifies contempt for racial others, white supremacy is a system that aims to preserve the privileges of whites by restricting access to opportunities for asset accumulation and upward mobility by Indigenous and racialized communities. This universal narrative of whiteness as being most worthy conveys whiteness as valuable and white people as most deserving of benefits and rewards, resulting in policy decisions that benefit whites, often at the expense of Indigenous, Black, and other racialized communities (Lipsitz 1998).

Andrea Smith (2005) observes, however, that it is important to complicate the concept of settler colonialism beyond notions of whiteness and white privilege, since it is a multi-dimensional phenomenon that is shaped by and shaping interactive relations of capitalism, coloniality, racism, gender, class, sexuality, and ableism. She argues that hierarchies impacting Indigenous peoples and settlers are naturalized by sexual, gendered and racial power, often influencing how place, culture, and power relations are understood, and disrupting intersecting power relations culminating from colonialism, capitalism, and heteropatriarchy (Smith 2005). The historical manifestation of race coincided with capitalism. A spatial imaginary that splits the world into white/Black is inherently patriarchal in origin, as is bifurcation along class and gender lines, which are, themselves, redefined and filtered through class exploitation and racism. Since heteropatriarchy and the gendered and racial division of labour operate through relations between settlers and the colonized, it is not possible to understand the colour line as separate from gender.

Drawing on these and other analyses, this book situates environmental racism within broader discussions on state-sanctioned racial and gendered violence to unmask the multiple forms of inequality disproportionately compromising the social, economic, and political well-being of Indigenous and Black communities in Nova Scotia and Canada. In so doing, the book aims to contribute a different conceptualization of environmental racism and environmental justice in Nova Scotia and Canada by highlighting the relationships among environmental racism, other forms of state-sanctioned racial and gendered violence, settler colonialism, racial capitalism, neoliberalism, patriarchy, and health.

I recognize, however, that the reason these kinds of critical discussions have yet to be had in Canada is because there is still a dearth of studies on environmental justice in Canada, and because environmental racism has yet to be fully problematized in the environmental justice literature in this country. Moreover, both environmental racism and environmental justice have been largely divorced from the literature on contemporary urban geography and the social science literature on race (particularly in sociology). In the next chapter, I attempt to converge insights from contemporary urban geography and sociology to provide a critical analysis of environmental racism as a spatial project, as well as to call attention to the ways in which spatial violence and other forms of state-sanctioned racial and gendered violence are embodied in both the symbolic meaning of space and the materiality of space.

Chapter 3

RETHINKING WASTE

Mapping Racial Geographies of Violence on the Colonial Landscape

The racial demography of the places where people live, work, play, shop, and travel exposes them to a socially shared system of exclusion and inclusion. Race serves as a key variable in determining who has the ability to own homes that appreciate in value and can be passed down to subsequent generations; in deciding which children have access to education by experienced and credentialed teachers in safe buildings with adequate equipment; and in shaping differential exposure to polluted air, water, food, and land. (Lipsitz 2007: 12)

Lipsitz's (2007) assertion that the racial imaginary is racially marked characterizes well how racially marked spatial imaginaries are imbued in hierarchical social relations. A "white spatial imaginary," he argues, is one that is premised on white privilege because it confers to white people advantages in the form of valued opportunities, life chances, and goods and resources. As McKittrick (2002) observes, the perception of Canada as rational, white, and homogenous needs to be interrogated since nationhood, citizenship, and belonging are not experienced by Black Canadians in the same way that it is experienced by white Canadians. Differences such as race and gender are spatially organized in ways that create hierarchies and relations of domination and subordination among various groups within the home, the workplace, and the city (McKittrick and Peake 2005). This results in spatial forms of state-sanctioned racial and gendered violence within spaces (i.e., spatial violence), such as labour market inequalities, poverty, and over-policing, among others.

The racialization of space manifests in a number of ways: in the expropriation of Indigenous lands through legal means; in the formation of neighbourhoods segregated by income, class, and race; in so-called neighbourhood revitalization projects that gentrify low-income and often racialized areas by bringing in businesses and housing that ultimately push out long-term residents; and in the disproportionate placement of polluting industries and other environmentally dangerous projects in racialized communities. These examples shed light on the ways in which industry owners carve out spatialities of profit that ultimately lead to possession, dispossession, and displacement. They also reveal the extent to which our lived experience of race, gender, and other factors has a spatial dimension, as well as how our lived experience of space has a racial and gendered dimension, among other factors (Lipsitz 2007). As Henri Lefebvre (1976: 31) explains, space is an inherently political concept:

> Space is not a scientific object removed from ideology and politics; it has always been political and strategic. If space has an air of neutrality and indifference with regard to its contents ... it is precisely because it has been occupied and used, and has already been the focus of past processes whose traces are not always evident on the landscape. Space has been shaped and molded from historical and natural elements, but this has always been a political process ... It is a product literally filled with ideologies.

In other words, space can never be divorced from past and present-day processes and ideologies, even when those processes and ideologies are not apparent because they have become taken for granted within each socio-historical moment.

In his book *The Production of Space* (1991), Lefebvre describes two distinct types of produced space — abstract space and social space. Social space characterizes citizens' understandings and lived experiences of their everyday spaces; abstract space, on the other hand, describes the spaces that are imagined by industry owners, planners, and other members of the elite whose objective is economic gain. Cheryl Teelucksingh and Jeffrey R. Masuda (2014) observe that a socio-spatial analysis highlights the ways in which space embeds into cities the inequalities of power and decision making, as well as injustices, including environmental injustices. A consideration of the socio-spatial dynamics of power, the politics of space, and environmental knowledge helps us to think through the role that race, income, and class play in environmental racism. Building on the Lefebvrian socio-spatial approach, Teelucksingh and Masuda contend that space is more than a geographical area, but a socially constructed and highly contested product bound up in political, cultural, and economic meanings.

Teelucksingh (2002) also challenges the notion put forth in the environmental justice literature that space is fixed, neutral, ahistorical, and physical, rather than an embodiment of power relations that are fluid and ever-evolving. Doreen Massey (1992: 81) asserts that space is never apolitical but imbued with "a complex web of relations of domination and subordination, of solidarity and cooperation." Similarly, McKittrick (2011) understands space as an inherently historical and political construct in her observations about the ways in which spaces inhabited by Black peoples before and after slavery have been deliberately harmed by practices of domination and racialized relations of power. For McKittrick, "urbicide" is a term that characterizes the ongoing destruction of a Black sense of place in the Americas through environmental, social, and infrastructural deterioration and surveillance. Urbicide is defined as the deliberate murder, annihilation, and death of the city, particularly in areas of a city experiencing poverty and other forms of state-sanctioned racial violence. These analyses help us gain insight into the structural inequalities deeply embedded in federal, provincial, and local governments' decisions related to housing and infrastructure issues, such as where we put our highways, our streets, and our waste in and out of cities.

Discriminatory practices in housing and lending, school district boundaries, transit design, zoning regulations, and policing all play a role in relegating people to different geographical and physical locations where they experience varying levels of exclusion and inclusion based on race and other identities. Opportunities to access and acquire such goods and resources as home ownership, good education, and clean, high-quality air, water, land, and food are determined by these differences. Since it is policy that designs and drives a system that creates places, and since Indigenous and racialized peoples experience disproportionate rates of low-income and poverty, they often don't have a choice of where they live. Consequently, they are often confined to some of the poorest neighbourhoods with the greatest environmental risks.

In thinking through the significance of social inequities to spatial theory as it relates to environmental racism and other forms of spatial violence, the following issues must be considered: How do socially constructed ideologies about race, class, gender, and other identities shape the constitution and perception of space? How are these ideologies spatialized in rural and urban settings? How are spatial configurations of Indigenous and racialized bodies enabled through boundary-making practices supported by policy and law? How does the spatialization of race, class, gender, and other social identities inform the spatial segregation and containment of certain bodies in spaces associated with poverty, crime, and waste and pollution?

Lipsitz (2007: 12) observes that shared cultural ideals and moral geographies that are premised on a "romance with pure spaces" help inform the policies that enable racially and economically dominant and privileged communities to gain access to valued resources and goods, while simultaneously excluding "undesirable populations" from these same resources and goods. The "imagined community" promulgated by colonizers and white settler communities today is one that is characterized as pure and homogenous and that requires that "impure populations" be eradicated. Lipsitz (2007: 15) also asserts that policy actions that seek to create racially exclusive neighbourhoods free from "undesirable others" are imbued with the "privileged moral geographies of the contemporary national landscape." This is best exemplified by the removal of Indigenous peoples from their lands through conquest, expulsion, and genocide, as well as by the gentrification of racially and economically segregated neighbourhoods. In other words, the racial demography of spaces is a sound predictor of who will and will not have access to valued resources.

IN YOUR PLACE: SPATIALITIES OF CONTAINMENT
AND EXCLUSION IN INDIGENOUS AND BLACK COMMUNITIES

It is important at this juncture to distinguish between the symbolic meaning of space and the materiality of space. The former is concerned with how identities shape space, as well as with how the white spatial imaginary is premised on an imagined community where space is conceived of as abstract, pure, innocent, untainted, orderly, empty, unoccupied, and free of racial others. The latter refers to how the white spatial imaginary produces Indigenous and Black peoples' lived or material realities, such as low income and poverty, neighbourhoods with poor infrastructures, over-policing, and disproportionate exposure to environmental risks.

These material realities are created by policies that are informed by the spatial imaginaries of powerful elites, such as planners, architects, and policymakers and that seek to create boundaries between "white spaces" and racialized spaces. These elites often envision and implement "spatial projects" that are premised on the fears and anxieties that white people have about racialized peoples, concerns about the preservation of white spaces that are perceived as respectable and civilized, and the containment of racialized peoples within "undesirable" neighbourhoods.

A socio-spatial analysis of the ways in which race, income, class, and other social differences come to be imbued in the places where we live, work, and play must be premised on what Razack (2002: 5) describes as a "denaturalizing of geography" that interrogates "white settler innocence." White settler innocence interprets social space as a naturally occurring phenomenon, rather than a social construction. The project to denaturalize geography is concerned with illuminating the ways in which social space is imbued with a colonial and racial character that convey hierarchies of difference, practices of domination, and ultimately the spatial violence that underpins socio-spatial relations. As Razack (2002) argues, the freedom that white people — particularly white men — have to move back and forth between perceived "respectable" and "degenerate" spaces, and to do whatever they wish within those spaces without being questioned can be characterized as a transgression that speaks to race and gender privilege. The following statement by an African Nova Scotian community member in Truro who participated in a study the ENRICH Project conducted on environmental health in African Nova Scotian communities exemplifies Razack's analysis:

> As white people move into the communities, whether it's the Island, the Hill or the Marsh, they start to do things to enhance ... perception, to enhance the area. Whereas, as long as it was predominantly a Black area, they just left it as it was and figured, you know, we don't do anything to enhance the area or to improve the area. But, as soon as one white person moves into the area, then all of a sudden, "okay, let's see what we can do." (Waldron 2016)

This sentiment reveals how policy is used to support perceptions of place that enable spatial projects that benefit powerful white elites.

In pushing toward a rethinking of environmental racism in Nova Scotia and Canada, I wish to open up a discursive space that maps the racially violent encounters that Indigenous and Black peoples have long experienced in this country. This requires, as McKittrick argues (2002, 2011), an understanding of and appreciation for how "the complex geographies" of racialized peoples have been shaped by colonialism, transatlantic slavery, contemporary practices of racism, and resistance to white supremacy. Following McKittrick, who argues that Black Canadian geographies are permanently linked to the Canadian landscape through racial violences of the past and present, I examine instances of environmental racism in Canada to elucidate the symbolic and material ways in which the complex geographies of Indigenous and Black communities have been characterized by erasure, domination, dehumanization, destruction, dispossession, exploitation, and genocide.

As McKittrick (2002, 2011), Razack (2000, 2002), and others (Lipsitz 2007; Massey 1992) observe, it is not possible to understand space as separate from the social processes that play out within spaces and which enable the production and reproduction of spatial violence. As McKittrick (2002: 28) puts it, "geography materially structures, marks and spatializes difference" since spatial processes are, themselves, social relations that inform material social practices that have taken on a geographical form. Therefore, while space (like race) is a social construct, its materiality lies in how it maps inclusion and exclusion by organizing social life based on racial, gendered, and other differences. Its materiality also lies in how it produces and reproduces hierarchical social relations and manifests violence by creating and sustaining inequalities in ways that harm Indigenous and racialized peoples. Understanding the spatial nature of state-sanctioned racial and gendered violence (i.e., spatial violence) on the lands, cultures, bodies, and spirits of Indigenous and Black peoples in Canada, and Nova Scotia in particular, requires a historical, place-based, site-specific, and context-specific analysis of the multiple incarnations of state, gendered, and racial violence within such institutions as criminal justice, employment, labour, education, health, and the environment.

I situate my analysis of spatial violence within discussions that seek to disrupt traditional notions of "the environment" that are primarily premised on harmonizing cities and nature. Instead, I wish to engage readers in a conceptual reimagining of the environment as a product of both symbolic meanings of space and the materiality of space. In this reimagining, I argue once again that race must be a fundamental analytical entry point for understanding the racialized workings of spatial violence in urban and rural contexts, as well as the "slow death" (McKittrick 2011: 956) of non-white communities through possession, dispossession, expropriation, urbicide, and genocide.

SPATIAL VIOLENCE AND GENOCIDAL "SLOW DEATH"

Mi'kmaw communities across Nova Scotia experience spatial violence in a number of ways, including in education, jobs, criminal justice, and of course through environmental racism. The Mi'kmaq or Lnu are the founding people of Mi'kma'ki (what is now known as Nova Scotia), having existed there over 11,000 years (Sipekne'katik n.d.a). The Mi'kmaw land stretches from the Canadian Maritimes to the Gaspé Peninsula in Quebec (Sipekne'katik n.d.a). It is composed of thirteen Bands/First Nations, each of which is governed by a Chief and Council. The largest of the thirteen Bands in Nova Scotia are Eskasoni (4,314 members) and Sipekne'katik (2,554 members) (Indigenous and Northern Affairs Canada 2014; Sipekne'katik n.d.b).

The majority of Indigenous peoples in Nova Scotia are Mi'kmaq (Office of Aboriginal Affairs n.d.). There is a total of 16,245 Mi'kmaw people residing in

Nova Scotia. The median age of the First Nation population in Nova Scotia is 25.4, compared to 41.6 for the population as a whole, making them significantly younger than the rest of the population (Indigenous and Northern Affairs Canada 2014; Statistics Canada 2011a, 2011b). An increasing proportion of the Mi'kmaw population resides in Halifax (5,666) (Indigenous and Northern Affairs Canada 2014; Statistics Canada 2011a, 2011b).

A self-government agreement accorded responsibility for on-reserve educa-tion to the Mi'kmaq (Office of Aboriginal Affairs n.d.; Statistics Canada 2011a). While 27 percent of Mi'kmaw people between ages 25 and 64 did not complete high school (compared to 19 percent in the general population), high school graduation rates in Mi'kmaw Kina'matnewey schools are increasing, reaching 87 percent in 2012–13 (Office of Aboriginal Affairs n.d.; Statistics Canada 2011a). In addition, 12 percent of the Mi'kmaw population between the ages of 25 and 64 held a university degree, compared to 20 percent in the general population (Office of Aboriginal Affairs n.d.; Statistics Canada 2011a). The unemployment rate for Mi'kmaw people living on reserve in the 2006 census was 24.6 percent, compared to 9.1 percent for all Nova Scotians (Office of Aboriginal Affairs n.d.; Statistics Canada 2011a). Only 50 percent of people living on-reserve participated in the labour force, compared to 63 percent for the total Mi'kmaw population, the same rate as the general population (Office of Aboriginal Affairs n.d.; Statistics Canada 2011a).

Although not indigenous to Nova Scotia, Black people have been residing in Nova Scotia for almost three hundred years, making them the oldest Black population in Canada. They are descendants of African slaves and freedmen, Black Loyalists from the United States, the Nova Scotian colonists of Sierra Leone, the Maroons from Jamaica, and the refugees of the War of 1812. In Acadia, from the early to mid-1700s, there were more than three hundred peo-ple of African descent in the French settlement of Louisbourg, Cape Breton. Between 100 and 150 people of African descent were among the new settlers, now known as Planters, who came from New England after the British gained control over Nova Scotia in 1763. The Planters were slaves who were used by plantation owners to do field work and other jobs (Waldron 2010b, 2015b). Between 1783 and 1785, over three thousand Black people left New York and other ports for Nova Scotia, as part of the Loyalist migration at the close of the American Revolution. They settled in Annapolis Royal and other areas such as Cornwallis/Horton, Weymouth, Digby, Windsor, Preston, Sydney, Fort Cumberland, Parrsboro, Halifax, Shelburne, Birchtown, and Port Mouton. In New Brunswick, Black Loyalists were settled in Saint John and along the Saint

John River. They were promised freedom in exchange for fighting for Britain. However, once in the Maritimes, they were denied equal status, cheated out of land, and forced to work on public projects such as roads and buildings. They were also taken to the West Indies, Quebec, England, Germany, and Belgium (Black Cultural Centre for Nova Scotia n.d.; Maddalena, Thomas Bernard, Etowa, Davis-Murdoch, Smith, and Marsh-Jarvis 2010; Nova Scotia Museum n.d.; Waldron 2010b, 2015b).

In 1796, 550 people known as the Maroons were deported from Jamaica to Nova Scotia and were then relocated to Sierra Leone in 1800. Approximately two thousand escaped slaves came from the United States during the War of 1812 (under conditions similar to those of the Black Loyalists) and were offered freedom and land in Nova Scotia. They moved into the Halifax area to settle in such areas as Preston, Hammonds Plains, Beechville, Porter's Lake, Lucasville Road, and the Windsor area. During the 1920s, hundreds of Caribbean immigrants, referred to as the "later arrivals," flocked to Cape Breton to work in coal mines and the steel factory. The majority of African Nova Scotians continue to reside in rural and isolated communities as a result of institutionalized racism during the province's early settlement (Black Cultural Centre for Nova Scotia n.d.; Maddalena, Thomas Bernard, Etowa, Davis-Murdoch, Smith, and Marsh-Jarvis 2010; Nova Scotia Museum n.d.; Waldron 2010b, 2015b).

There are 21,915 African Nova Scotians residing in Nova Scotia (Statistics Canada 2017a). They represent the largest racially visible community, constituting 2.4 percent of the total Nova Scotian population (Statistics Canada 2017b). Forty-four percent of the population is below the age of twenty-five (Statistics Canada 2017c). Two general categories of people of African descent can be identified in Nova Scotia: those who were among Nova Scotia's earliest inhabitants, and those immigrants that have arrived more recently from African and Caribbean countries (Maddalena, Thomas Bernard, Etowa, Davis-Murdoch, Smith, and Marsh-Jarvis 2010). In addition, there are Canadian-born Black people residing in Nova Scotia (such as the author) who have come from other provinces, a category that is often not highlighted in the literature or statistics. In terms of birthplace, 80.7 percent of Black people in the province were born in the province, while 6.7 percent were born elsewhere in Canada. Ten percent are new Canadians, having immigrated from Africa, the Caribbean, and the United States (African Nova Scotian Affairs n.d.; Statistics Canada 2011a).

Like the Mi'kmaq, African Nova Scotian people experience inequality in every sector of society, including education, jobs, income, and criminal justice. For example, in 2011, African Nova Scotians had a rate of unemployment higher

(14.5 percent) than the rest of Nova Scotia (9.9 percent) and African Canadians (12.9 percent) across Canada (Statistics Canada 2017d). The employment gap was greater among males, with African Nova Scotian males experiencing an unemployment rate of 17.2 percent, compared to 10.7 percent for Nova Scotians and 12.9 percent for African Canadian males across Canada. According to the 2016 Census, the average total incomes for African Nova Scotian men and women are $33,456 and $29,622, respectively. In comparison, the average total income for other Nova Scotians is $41,479 (Statistics Canada 2017d).

With respect to educational attainment, African Nova Scotians are less likely to finish high school or attend university (African Nova Scotian Affairs n.d.; Statistics Canada 2011a); of African Nova Scotians aged 25–64 years, 77.7 percent have some sort of certificate, diploma or degree compared to 85.3 percent of all Nova Scotians (African Nova Scotian Affairs n.d.; Statistics Canada 2011a); and 18 percent of African Nova Scotians have a university degree, compared to 22 percent of all Nova Scotians aged 25–64 years (African Nova Scotian Affairs n.d.; Statistics Canada 2011a).

Processes of criminalization informed by racist stereotypes result in the spatial management of race within prisons, as well as racial punishment and violence meted out to both African Nova Scotian and Mi'kmaw peoples at every stage of the criminal justice system. For example, a January 2017 report by the Halifax RCMP found that in the first ten months of 2016, 41 percent of 1,246 street checks involved African Nova Scotians (Auld 2017). In Nova Scotia, statistics collected by the provincial Department of Justice show that between 2014 and 2015, African Nova Scotians and Mi'kmaw peoples were over-represented in the province's jail system, particularly youths in custody (Luck 2016). These numbers indicate that about 16 percent of youth sentenced to a youth correctional facility were African Nova Scotian and 12 percent were Mi'kmaw (Luck 2016). Fourteen percent of adults sentenced to jail were African Nova Scotian, while 7 percent were Mi'kmaw (Luck 2016).

The *Annual Report of the Office of the Correctional Investigator* (Correctional Investigator Canada 2013) found that growth in the inmate population in Canada is almost exclusively driven by growing incarceration rates of ethnically and culturally diverse offenders. For example, over the past ten years, the Indigenous incarcerated population increased by 46.4 percent, while other racialized populations (e.g., Black, Asian, Hispanic) increased by almost 75 percent. The population of white inmates actually declined by 3 percent. Black and Indigenous populations were disproportionately over-represented in federal penitentiaries. Black offenders comprise 9.5 percent of federal inmate population, which is an increase of 80 percent since 2003–04, despite the fact that Black Canadians account for less than 3 percent of the total Canadian population. Four percent of Black inmates are women. Indigenous offenders comprise 23 percent of federal inmate population, although they comprise 4.3 percent of the total Canadian population. One in three women under federal sentence are Indigenous.

Children from Indigenous, Black and other racial minority groups in Canada have historically been over-represented in child welfare settings and among children and youth in care (Blackstock 2010; Gilbert, Fluke, O'Donnell, Gonzalez-Izquierdo, Brownell, Gulliver, Janson and Sidebotham 2012; One Vision One Voice Steering Committee 2016; Trocmé, Knoke, and Blackstock 2004). The inequities experienced by families whose children have been taken into state care are linked to intersecting factors, such as gender, race, colonialism, citizenship, immigration, and socioeconomic status (Johnson 2014). For example, the Children's Aid Society of Toronto reports that 40.8 percent of the children and youth in care as of September 23, 2013, were African Canadian. This results in a racial disproportionality rate of 4.8 (One Vision One Voice Steering Committee 2016). A report by the Black Community Action Network of Peel (2015) in Ontario identified eight key risk or causal factors that contribute to racial disproportionalities in child welfare: anti-Black racism, racialized poverty, immigration stress, biased decision making, agency-system factors, placement dynamics, policy impacts, and lack of culturally relevant services.

A preliminary report from the restorative inquiry into abuse at the Nova Scotia Home for Colored Children orphanage found that African Nova Scotians continue to be over-represented in the child welfare and correctional systems, and that parents and children from these communities have been traditionally excluded from Canadian society and are experiencing marginalization and vulnerability (Ujima Design Team 2015). As of March 2016, there were 1,034 children who were in the care of the state or of Mi'kmaw Family and Children's Services; of that number, twenty-four identified as African Nova Scotian (2.3 percent) and eighty-six identified as mixed race (African Nova Scotian and other) (Province of Nova Scotia 2016).

Public policy decisions designed to contain and control perceived "troubling" populations are also evident in spatial projects such as "urban renewal" or gentrification that aim to "clean out" perceived immoral, impure, and contaminated spaces inhabited by racial others. This is a form of spatial violence that can be defined as a dynamic process that seeks to restore a less affluent or working-class neighbourhood through migration of and reinvestment by middle- and upper-class individuals, including local government, business groups, artists, academics, and activists. Often, old industrial buildings are converted into residences and shops. New businesses, which can afford increased commercial rent, cater to a more affluent base of consumers, further increasing the appeal to higher-income migrants and decreasing accessibility to low-income and poor individuals (Waldron 2015b).

David Harvey's (2003: 115) conceptualization of a "spacio-temporal fix" sheds light on how geographical expansion and urbanization provide solutions to capitalist accumulation. Gentrification can be viewed as a manifestation of spatial, social, and power relations in the context of neoliberal urbanism, which is itself rooted in capital accumulation resulting from the production of the city. In this context, space is a direct product of the need to absorb surpluses generated from capital accumulation and profit. Gentrification is a visible incarnation of how income and class inequalities, as well as relations of domination, reconfigure and transform urban space. Gentrification reveals the "geographies of exclusion" (Sibley 1995) that are enabled by local media and planning and development advocates and officials. It also helps to drive public discourse that demonizes original residents as undeserving and lazy minorities who are dependent on public assistance, castigating them for the perceived misuse and abuse of their spatial area (Hetzler, Medina, and Overfelt 2006).

In understanding gentrification as a form of spatial violence leading to slow death, or in this case, urbicide, we must consider the relationship between neoliberalization, the production of the city, and spatial justice (Vives Miro 2011). This type of analysis calls attention to the despatialized nature of neoliberal urban transformation and the ways it is abstracted from the cultural and ecological contexts in which it takes root. For example, it helps us to unearth racialized peoples' experiences of displacement by unpacking ongoing debates that, on one hand, argue that residents must live where they can afford, and on the other hand defend the notion that neighbourhoods belong to residents who have long lived there — a stance that speaks to the protection of individual and community rights (Recoquillon 2014). However, those who argue that residents must live where they can afford often don't consider the fact that redevelopment is rarely, if ever, accompanied by social interventions that address outcomes for low-income residents who may not be able to afford new rents, may experience challenges subsisting, and who may not have anywhere else to go or the means of transportation to move out if they are unable to subsist.

Lucasville, a 200-year-old, rural African Nova Scotian community near

Lower Sackville, has been witnessing the gradual geographical extermination and erasure of their community over the last several years. This kind of "rural gentrification" (Devet 2017b) has been accompanied by the presence of a horse farm in their community, a busy road without sidewalks, and a lack of public transit. Mapping conducted by city bureaucrats shrunk the community boundaries of Lucasville in half, resulting in the exclusion of a large trailer park on Lucasville Road, considered to be part of Hammonds Plains (Devet 2017b). There have long been concerns that the community is being purposely squeezed out, according to a Lucasville resident who participated in a study the ENRICH Project conducted on environmental health in African Nova Scotian communities:

> Historically, this is the type of action that has been taken in African Nova Scotian communities. Our communities are being eradicated because of councillors and governments developing zoning and by-laws that are totally contrary to the way of life of African Nova Scotian communities. And in saying that, our community here in Lucasville is another example of how communities are being wiped off the face of the Earth. African Nova Scotian communities are being just totally taken over by industry, big businesses, developers who want to come in. They see the value of our land without seeing the historic purposes or historic content of us being here for over two hundred years. The first land grants in Lucasville were handed out in the late 1700s. So, our community was established. And now because the land is cheap and close to the city, people feel like they can come and do what they want. That is a problem. And that's a historic injustice that needs to be changed. (Waldron 2016)

Lucasville residents' concerns highlight how gentrification operates as a form of spatial violence to ensure the pushing out and erasure of "troublesome" communities without any consideration for the historical value of these places. On December 12, 2017 Halifax Regional Council voted to restore the original boundaries of the Lucasville, a change that African Nova Scotian residents and the Lucasville Community Association had been fighting for many years (Devet 2018). As McKittrick (2002) observes, Black geographies and racialized geographical struggles in Canada are produced both through the visibility of a Black or Indigenous body that is perceived to be inherently troublesome, threatening, and expendable and their impending or forced geographical erasure as their communities are demolished through redevelopment and gentrification processes. Lipsitz (2007) echoes these sentiments when he asserts that the plantation, the prison, and the ghetto have been visible manifestations of white supremacist use of space, thereby highlighting how race, class, gender, and other identities work to regulate the occupation of space.

What has been less obvious are the ways in which white supremacist use of space manifests in the disproportionate placement of polluting industries in Indigenous and Black communities. While more subtle because of its systemic nature, environmental racism allows us to unmask how white supremacy and the accompanying legal tools that support it enable the boundary-making practices that create social hierarchies. Using the analyses on criminal justice, redevelopment, and gentrification I have highlighted in this chapter, I contend that environmental racism must be theorized and articulated as a form of spatial violence in the way that it enacts authoritarian control over knowledge systems, bodies, and spaces.

Over the past few years, I have encountered a few people who expressed their skepticism about the reality of environmental racism in Nova Scotia. These people require proof of intentionality and a clear motive for the siting of environmentally harmful activities in Mi'kmaw and African Nova Scotian communities to believe that it is an issue that is actually taking place. In their communication with me, they also questioned which came first: Were the environmentally hazardous activities purposely located in certain communities because they were poor and composed of residents who had minimal political clout, or did race and economic status have no bearing on where these industries were placed, so that over time these communities became disproportionately racialized due to white flight, land depreciation, depressed housing prices, and other social problems (Pulido 2000)? Questions about causation are important, but they fail to consider the larger and more important issue of how racial differences are spatially organized, and how environmental racism is a material consequence of social processes and relationships that are racially marked in all white settler nations. This speaks to the importance of ensuring that both spatial theory and racial theory come into view simultaneously when understanding environmental racism and environmental justice.

Chapter 4

NOT IN MY BACKYARD

The Politics of Race, Place, and Waste in Nova Scotia

> For a colonized people the most essential value, because the most concrete, is first and foremost the land: the land which will bring them bread and, above all, dignity. (Fanon 1963: 44)

On October 24–27, 1991, delegates at the First National People of Color Environmental Leadership Summit gathered together in Washington, DC, to begin building a national and international movement of racialized peoples to challenge the many forms of environmental injustice that had been impacting their communities. They began drafting seventeen principles of environmental justice (see Appendix D) that would define the growing grassroots environmental justice movement and drive future initiatives that would address the following issues: the destruction, possession, and control of Indigenous lands and communities; spiritual interdependence that acknowledges the sacredness of the earth; respect for and celebration of the cultures, languages, and worldviews in Indigenous and racialized communities, as well as their role in healing themselves; promotion of economic alternatives that would foster environmentally safe livelihoods; and political, economic, and cultural liberation.

In the decades following the 1991 Summit, a cohesive framework on environmental justice developed that was grounded in a number of tools, strategies, and policies focused on eliminating unfair, unjust, and inequitable conditions and decisions that contribute to and produce differential exposure to environmental hazards and result in unequal protection. This framework highlights such ethical and political questions as "who gets what, when, why, and how much?" (Bullard 2002: 38) and, in so doing, places the responsibility for failing to give equal protection to racialized and low-income people on government and industry owners, regardless of intent (Bullard 2002). In general, an environmental justice framework adopts a public health model of prevention that seeks to eliminate the threat before harm occurs and targets resources where environmental and health problems are greatest (Bullard 2002).

Bullard (2002) observes that a sound environmental justice framework should be based on three main principles: procedural, geographic, and social equity. Procedural equity makes explicit the extent to which rules, regulations, evaluation criteria, and enforcement are applied fairly, uniformly, and in a non-discriminatory way in all communities. Several factors may account for why communities may not experience equal protection from environmental hazards. These include non-scientific and undemocratic decisions, exclusionary practices, public hearings held in remote locations and at inconvenient times, and the use of English-only material when communicating and conducting hearings for a non-English-speaking public (Bullard 2002). Geographic equity describes the geographic location and spatial configurations of communities, including their proximity to polluting industries and other environmental hazards. Finally, social equity focuses on how sociological factors (race, ethnicity, class, culture, life style, political power, etc.) influence environmental decision making. This relates to the disproportionate location of poor and racialized peoples in the most dangerous jobs and in the most polluted neighbourhoods, as well as the exposure of their children to a variety of environmental toxins in playgrounds and in homes (Bullard 2002).

While a race analysis has increasingly and gradually been a focus of the environmental justice movement in the United States for over thirty years, environmental activists, organizations, and scholars in Canada have engaged in a kind of "racial procrastination" (Dyson 2016), showing considerably more reticence in grappling with the structural factors underlying environmental decision making and policy. As the environmental justice movement evolved in Canada, it was increasingly being appropriated by white environmentalists. Not surprisingly, their concerns about the right to clean air and water and climate change has rarely extended to Indigenous, Black, racialized, and low-income communities that are more vulnerable to these and other environmental hazards (Deacon and Baxter 2013; Fryzuk 1996; Waldron 2015a; Wiebe 2016).

While Canadian studies on environmental injustices experienced by Indigenous populations have been emerging over the last few years (Booth 2017; Huseman and Short 2012; MacIntosh 2007; Riahi and McSorley 2013; Wiebe 2016), considerably more research needs to be conducted regarding the impacts on African Nova Scotian and other racialized communities in Canada. Cheryl Teelucksingh (2002, 2007) is one of few researchers in Canada whose work demonstrates a deep engagement with race and racialized communities experiencing environmental contamination and pollution. Her study (2002) found that racialized, immigrant, and low-income people residing in a mid-Scarborough neighbourhood in the Greater Toronto Area were affected by pollution and health problems associated with nearby industrial companies. Teelucksingh asserts that changes in immigration settlement patterns, as well as deindustrialization in Toronto, have led to the disproportionate allocation of undesirable industries in this neighbourhood.

Both Teelucksingh (2007) and Randolph Haluza-Delay (2007) use the concept "environmental racialization" rather than environmental racism to characterize the proximity of racialized communities to polluting industries. Both authors argue that while the pattern of racial and class inequity in the siting of polluting industries in the United States is highly correlated with large-scale patterns of racial segregation, Canada's racial history has been more associated with ethnicity, immigration status, language competency, income, and other forms of differentiation, rather than with patterns of racial segregation. However, I would argue that patterns of racial segregation have indeed been a feature of Nova Scotia's racial history — a history that is unique compared to the rest of Canada. One only need to point to the spatial segregation, containment, and marginalization of Indigenous and African Nova Scotian people on reserves and in isolated rural communities, respectively, to understand that these spatial arrangements are a product of Nova Scotia's unique racial and colonial history.

Susan L. Cutter (1995) examines the ways in which environmental policy creates, upholds, and sustains inequities in the spatial patterning of polluting industries and in the consultation process. She conceptualizes environmental justice as having two components: distributive/spatial and procedural. The first is concerned primarily with the inequitable distribution or spatial patterning of environmental burdens or risks; the second focuses on inequitable and non-inclusive consultation and decision-making processes related to the siting of industry, as well as inequitable toxic waste management regulatory practices, evaluation criteria, and enforcement.

PROCEDURAL AND DISTRIBUTIVE JUSTICE

Leith Deacon and Jamie Baxter (2013) conducted a study on the first- and second-generation landfills in the African Nova Scotian community of Lincolnville and conclude that conceptualizations of environmental justice in recent years have paid more attention to its procedural components than its distributive/spatial ones. They argue that the procedural process has not been inclusive and that the public consultation process, in particular, remains limited. The environmental assessment process in Nova Scotia allows members of the public to submit comments and review project proposals for various industries that are planned for certain communities. Although the process for determining whether a landfill will be situated within a municipality may involve some level of public consultation, the level and scope of that consultation will vary depending on the municipality. The importance of consultation and collaboration with Indigenous communities is emphasized throughout the report *Water for Life: Nova Scotia's Water Resource Management Strategy* (Nova Scotia Environment 2010).

This requirement stems from both obligations and treaty rights under section 35 of the *Constitution Act* (Government of Canada 1982), as well as a recognition of the long connection Indigenous communities have with water. A study (Waldron 2016) and a series of regional meetings and a convergence workshop (Waldron 2014a) conducted and organized by the ENRICH Project in Mi'kmaw and African Nova Scotian communities indicate that Nova Scotia Environment has excluded these communities from fully participating in consultation and decision-making processes related to the environmental assessment process. Members of these communities contend that a more equitable and inclusive system of public participation should be instituted to ensure that there is clear communication with residents who wish to participate in these processes (Waldron 2014a, 2016).

Given that more attention has been paid over the years to the procedural components of environmental justice (decision making, consultation processes, etc.) rather than its distributive components (the spatial patterning and distribution of industry), as Deacon and Baxter (2013) observe, it is important to shed light on the factors that collectively enable inequitable distribution of industries and other environmental hazards in Mi'kmaw and African Nova Scotian communities across Nova Scotia. Over twenty years ago, Lori Fryzuk (1996) did just that when she isolated African Nova Scotian and Mi'kmaw population variables to conclude that environmental racism was indeed a reality in Nova Scotia. She found that thirty out of sixty-five waste sites (46.2 percent) were located near communities where African Nova Scotian and Mi'kmaw communities were higher in number than the provincial average. She also found that 5,230 (28.5 percent) of 18,355 African Nova Scotian residents lived within geographic areas canvassed by a census representative (enumeration areas) that hosted a waste site or within an impact zone of 5 kilometres.

Fryzuk (1996) identified the following three cases where waste sites were located in enumeration areas or impact zones where African Nova Scotian and Mi'kmaw populations were high in numbers: 1) Truro, which is 3.42 percent

African Nova Scotian and 2.33 percent Mi'kmaw; 2) Sydney, which is 8.84 percent African Nova Scotian and 3.74 percent Mi'kmaw; and 3) Wellington, which is 4.66 percent African Nova Scotian and 1.60 percent Mi'kmaw. All three of these waste sites were located in areas where African Nova Scotian and Mi'kmaw communities had settled before the siting of the waste facilities. Fryzuk emphasizes, however, that environmental racism is more easily demonstrated by focusing on specific areas and communities rather than on relying on statistical data.

Fryzuk (1996) focuses attention on the sociopolitical factors that combine to enable environmental racism in Nova Scotia, including poverty, environmental blackmail, lack of political power and representation, lack of protection and enforcement, and neoliberal policy reform. First, and not surprisingly, she asserts that industries choose impoverished areas with lower property values because they are able to reduce business costs, and because these areas are industrial wastelands. They are able to offer low-paying and potentially hazardous jobs to residents in low-income and poor communities that are experiencing high unemployment and have few options to leave polluted neighbourhoods and move into more environmentally desirable ones (Fryzuk 1996).

This economic trade-off, the second factor that enables environmental racism according to Fryzuk (1996), is illustrative of a kind of "environmental blackmail" that occurs when low-income and poor communities agree to host hazardous waste sites and are subsequently promised compensation in an amount such that the perceived benefits outweigh the potential risks. Compensation represents an economic inducement for communities experiencing high unemployment. Many of these communities don't lobby for reforms in environmental policies or oppose toxic facility sitings because they fear that this will lead to plant closures and layoffs. Therefore, residents in these communities are more susceptible to environmental blackmail (Fryzuk 1996).

Third, Mi'kmaw and African Nova Scotian communities are also disproportionately lacking in resources, political power, and representation compared to white communities, making them targets for the siting of potentially hazardous industries. Lawmakers and decision makers are more likely to be responsive to opposition from vocal middle- and upper-income communities with the greatest political influence. Compounding this issue is the fact that communities lacking political leadership and representation are less likely to participate in decision-making processes related to facility siting or in the political process, since they are less likely to be aware of policy decisions affecting their community (Fryzuk 1996).

The fourth factor that facilitates and sustains environmental racism in Nova Scotia is lack of protection and enforcement. Fryzuk (1996) observes that environmental policy is less concerned about distributional effects that could potentially lead to unequal environmental protection than with determining acceptable levels of pollution and the legal guidelines required for reducing pollution to acceptable levels. The burdens of environmental protection, including the economic costs of poisoning and contamination, are not equally distributed among all groups. The fifth and final factor Fryzuk (1996) attributes to the disproportionate location of polluting industries and other environmental hazards in Mi'kmaw and African Nova Scotian communities is neoliberal policy reform. She contends that neoliberalism further marginalizes already-vulnerable communities because it is rooted in specific forms of unsustainable production that create the conditions for environmental racism to flourish. It does so by making cuts to social services, exploiting marginalized communities, and rolling back environmental regulations and funding. These factors and processes deepen the sense of powerlessness these communities already have, further compromising their ability to challenge and oppose disproportionate distributional environmental effects in their areas.

ENVIRONMENTAL RACISM IN INDIGENOUS COMMUNITIES

Studies conducted over the last several years in Nova Scotia and Canada (Booth 2017; Cryderman, Letourneau, Miller, and Basu 2016; Huseman and Short 2012; Riahi and McSorley 2013; Scott, Rakowski, Harris, and Dixon 2015; Waldron 2014a, 2015a; Wiebe 2016) show that Indigenous communities are more likely than other communities to be located near polluting industries. The remote nature of these communities, along with their unique jurisdictional status has led to a failure by government to address environmental risks and their health impacts (Senate of Canada 2007). It is important to contextualize environmental racism in Indigenous communities within long-standing forms of oppression and abuses resulting from colonialism and resultant government policies seeking to eradicate or assimilate Indigenous peoples. The impacts of colonization also manifest in the federal and provincial government's failure to acknowledge its responsibilities to address land management and environmental protection issues, despite the fact it has a legal duty to do so under the *Indian Act*. Nova Scotia has no legislation, regulation, policy, or program in place that directly addresses environmental injustices. While the province's *Environmental Goals and Sustainable Prosperity Act* (Nova Scotia Environment 2007) acknowledges Indigenous concepts of environmental health, it does not implement them or require the use of an environmental justice lens. Municipalities alone have the responsibility to develop waste management plans, which include the location of landfill sites, as well as the power to control whether a landfill is located within its boundaries.

Environmental racism in Indigenous communities manifests in several ways, including abrogation of treaty and land rights, devaluing of their resource management efforts, poor water quality, and water contamination. The *Report of the Commissioner of the Environment and Sustainable Development* (Office of the Auditor General of Canada 2005) does address the discrepancy between on-reserve and off-reserve drinking water quality and safety in Indigenous communities, conceding that these communities do not benefit from a level of protection comparable to that of people who live off reserves. This can be partly attributed to the fact that there are no provincial laws or regulations governing the provision of drinking water in Indigenous communities, unlike in other communities.

To promote collaboration, Indigenous representatives have been included in the Nova Scotia Water Advisory Group. The Advisory Group partners with government to implement the Integrated Watershed Management approach, a comprehensive approach to managing water resources that focuses on human activities and their effects on watersheds and ecosystems. Its objective is to ensure sustainability of water resources and their functions today and into the future. There is limited room for involvement from the provincial government in managing water supplies for Indigenous communities, since reserve lands are formally under the jurisdiction of the federal government. Therefore, the provincial government is relegated to playing a more passive role by engaging Indigenous communities in water management decisions and fostering collaboration between these communities and nearby municipal governments. On June 19, 2013, the *Safe Drinking Water for First Nations Act* (Government of Canada 2013) was passed into law. It empowers the Minister of Aboriginal Affairs and Northern Development to make regulations regarding drinking water systems, waste water systems, source water protection, and the collection and treatment of waste water, among other things. However, despite the policies and administrative guidelines that have been implemented to ensure access to safe drinking water, the water in many of these communities remains contaminated.

Studies examining water insecurity in Indigenous communities in Canada have been emerging over the last decade (Chalifour 2013; MacIntosh 2007; Mascarenhas 2007; McGregor 2012). Deborah McGregor (2012), in particular, provides an Indigenous perspective on further steps that need to be taken to increase recognition of traditional knowledge in addressing the water crisis. She observes that taking care of water is a core principle within Anishinaabe knowledge, despite the fact that legal, financial, social, cultural, and economic factors associated with water management in Indigenous communities have prevented them from exercising this responsibility. McGregor also urges Canadian government officials to restore and maintain Indigenous access to traditional territories and ways of life, as well as a mutually respectful collaboration between Indigenous and Western knowledges.

McGregor (2012) also contends that Indigenous peoples have sought to fulfill their responsibilities toward water, despite seemingly insurmountable hurdles. For example, the Chiefs of Ontario were involved in drafting the *Water Declaration of Anishinaabek, Mushkegowuk and Onkwehonwe* (Chiefs of Ontario 2008), which highlights the importance of exercising Indigenous peoples' caretaking role with regard to water and the environment. The *Water Declaration* also recognizes the unique role of women and traditional knowledge in decision making regarding water and denounces the lack of state recognition and respect for the authority and responsibility of Indigenous peoples to care for water. It also calls into question the authority and jurisdiction of governments in making decisions about water.

Similarly, Michael Mascarenhas (2007) attributes poor water quality in Indigenous communities in Ontario to neoliberal reform, reduction of industry monitoring and reporting requirements, the inability of provincial ministries and local agencies to regulate and monitor environmental conditions, and the inability of Indigenous communities to control the mechanisms that ensure access to safe water. Mascarenhas also observes that water resources represent an important aspect of Indigenous culture; within Indigenous knowledge, water is not only thought to shape the future but is also considered to represent social, cultural, economic, and ecological well-being. He argues that it is considerably important that Indigenous communities manage water resources in a culturally meaningful way.

In another study on the topic, Constance MacIntosh (2008) attributes disparities between water quality on Indigenous reserves and the majority of other Canadian communities to a number of factors, including the government's failure to legislate standards, regulatory abandonment of reserve lands, inapplicability of jurisdictional legislations to reserve lands, and inadequate distribution of power in Indigenous governance. She points out that, although Canada has jurisdictional authority over Indigenous peoples, their lands, and reserve communities, this jurisdictional assignment precludes the operation of provincial water regimes over reserve lands. Furthermore, there are no lines of statutory accountability, despite the fact that Canada has introduced agreements, contracts, and protocols that make Indigenous peoples responsible for maintaining capital facilities on their reserves. Therefore, reserve communities have no decision-making power about the enforcement of water quality standards and how their well-being fits into the government regime. MacIntosh proposes that a legislative approach be taken that would require Canada to harmonize standards on reserves with each province and identify a line of accountability, an overseer, and remedial mechanisms.

Building on this, Nathalie Chalifour (2013) points out that, unlike other Canadians who enjoy water security (piped water that is monitored and treated by government authorities), Canadian law, policy, and practice do not provide a legislative framework for safe drinking water for Indigenous on-reserve populations, resulting in unreliable sources of safe drinking water on reserves as well as physical, financial, psychological, and cultural burdens for these residents. Ongoing lack of access to clean water is discriminatory under section 15 of the *Canadian Charter of Rights and Freedoms,* which constitutes the first part of the 1982 *Constitution Act* (Government of Canada 1982) and guarantees protection for Canadians. Section 15 of the Charter is meant to promote a society in which all human beings are equally deserving of concern, respect, and consideration. This section has been used to help numerous claimants address discrimination in different contexts, as well as advance equality in Canada. In the following sections, I discuss some of the most egregious examples of environmental racism in Canada.

Sydney

The Sydney Tar Ponds, often referred to as "Canada's Love Canal," was a hazardous waste site on Cape Breton Island that sparked some of the first concerns about environmental injustice in Canada. The estuary at the mouth of the Muggah Creek where it joins Sydney Harbour used to be a hunting and fishing ground for Mi'kmaq who are indigenous to the island of Cape Breton. From 1901 through 1988, Sydney Steel Corporation's now decommissioned steel mill operated in the area with no pollution controls. Over a million tons of particulate matter were deposited and several thousands of tons of coal tar were released into the estuary over that period, including polychlorinated biphenyl (PCBs), which are known to cause cancer (Lambert, Guyn, and Lane 2006). As a result, Sydney area residents experienced a local cancer rate 45 percent higher than the Nova Scotia average, and the highest rate in Canada (Nickerson 1999).

The Cape Breton coal that was used to produce coke was of poor quality, producing significant amounts of toxic waste and contributing to the production of poor-quality steel. Very little money was invested to modernize the facilities or to address the health and safety concerns of the workers (Campbell 2002). In 1974, Environment Canada found that air pollution from the coking operations was 2,800 to 6,000 percent higher than national standards allowed (Barlow and May 2000). As Robert A. Campbell (2002) documents, there were several attempts over the years to remediate this former industrial site. Genuine concerns were raised in 1980 about the need to address the environmental risks of steelmaking in Sydney after the federal fisheries department discovered that lobsters in Sydney Harbour contained high levels of PCBs and various toxic metals such as mercury, cadmium, and arsenic (Campbell 2002).

In May 2004, the governments of Canada and Nova Scotia announced that they would commit $400 million over the next ten years to remediate the Sydney Tar Ponds site to reduce the ecological and human health risks to the environment (Walker 2014). The cleanup was completed in 2013 with the opening of Open Hearth Park, which is situated on the site of the former steel plant (Morgan 2015).

Pictou Landing First Nation

Despite repeated promises, the provincial government also failed to address contamination in Boat Harbour until recently. Boat Harbour is a quiet estuary near Pictou Landing First Nation, an Indigenous reserve connected by a narrow channel to the Northumberland Strait. It was once a fertile hunting and fishing ground. It was also a sacred burial ground until 1967 when an effluent waste water treatment facility for the Northern Pulp mill was built and operated by the provincial government in nearby Boat Harbour. The treatment facility has been discharging pulp and paper mill effluents into Boat Harbour ever since, under a provincial agreement. The mill has been a significant player in the local and provincial natural resource economies since it was established (Hoffman, Bernier, Blotnicky, Golden, Janes, Kader, Kovacs-Da Costa, Pittipas, Vermeulen, and Walker 2015). Boat Harbour subsequently turned into a highly toxic site, which has resulted in environmental degradation (Hewitt, Parrott and McMaster 2006; Hoffman et al. 2015; Lindholm-Lehto, Knuutinen, Ahkola, and Herve 2015; Pokhrel and Viraraghavan 2004).

Some of the most significant societal concerns related to pulp and paper mills include impacts to air, water, soils, and sediments in the surrounding environments (Munkittrick, McMaster, and Servos 2013). Pollution within aquatic receiving environments can result from poorly treated pulp and paper effluents (Newcombe and MacDonald 2011; Pokhrel and Viraraghavan 2004). Years of Northern Pulp's mill dumping billions of litres of untreated effluent and other industrial contaminants into Boat Harbour has had considerable ecological and human health costs, including the third-highest cancer rates per capita in Canada's health districts (Idle No More 2014; Mirabelli and Wing 2006; Soskolne and Sieswerda 2010; Thomas-Muller 2014). Daniel S. Reid (1989) studied the link between the mill and potential adverse human health effects and found that there were higher proportions of respiratory disease in Pictou Landing compared to provincial averages for three consecutive years. Although the findings were inconclusive, the mill is most likely a causal factor of the high rates of respiratory disease in Pictou Landing.

The massive contamination of Boat Harbour continued uninterrupted due to an agreement Nova Scotia entered into fifty years ago during the logging sector boom. In June 2014, the pipeline that carries effluent from the Northern Pulp mill to Boat Harbour ruptured, which triggered a road blockade by Mi'kmaw community members. Chief Andrea Paul ended the blockade after the Liberal government promised to introduce legislation within a year to close the provincially owned waste treatment facility. In a historic announcement in April 2015, the province introduced a plan to close the facility and clean up Boat Harbour by January 2020, setting aside $52.3 million for remediation. This deal guaranteed a $1 million payment to Pictou Landing First Nation if the government failed to introduce legislation and action on the burial ground where the pipeline ruptured (Idle No More 2014; Thomas-Muller 2014; Withers 2015).

Sipekne'katik Band of the Mi'kmaw First Nation

The Sipekne'katik Band of the Mi'kmaw First Nation, other local Mi'kmaq, and Millbrook First Nation are currently opposing the development of a brine discharge pipeline next to the Shubenacadie River (Hubley 2016). Sipekne'katik First Nation is located in Hants County near Shubenacadie, Nova Scotia, and includes the communities of Indian Brook, New Ross, Pennal, Dodd's Lot, Wallace Hills, and Grand Lake. Eight years ago, Alton Natural Gas Storage applied to the Nova Scotia government to implement a project that would allow natural gas to be stored in underground salt caverns near the Shubenacadie River. Failure rates for salt cavern liquid natural gas projects have been high in the United States, and are considered to be dangerous because of risks of explosion, leaks, and emissions of poisonous chemicals like methane (Howe 2016; Hubley 2016). According to the Council of Canadians, underground salt cavern storage of liquid natural gas has a 65 percent failure rate in the US and 40 percent globally (Howe 2016; Hubley 2016).

In the fall of 2014, Alton Gas began developing the brine discharge pipeline, but halted the project as local resistance grew. The project resumed in January 2016, after Alton Gas was given environmental approvals for several permits by the Government of Nova Scotia. These approvals include an industrial approval provided by Nova Scotia Environment to operate the brine storage pond, the lease of submerged Crown land to complete the discharge channel from the Department of Natural Resources, and an agreement to construct a dyke on Crown lands from the Department of Agriculture (Nova Scotia Canada 2016).

Throughout 2016, resistance to the project grew stronger, with Sipekne'katik and Millbrook Nations arguing that they were not adequately consulted, that they had never given consent for the project to resume, that they were not given enough time to review project proposals and environmental impact assessments, and that they were provided with little to no notice about public meetings where they could express their concerns about the project before it resumed (Howe 2016; Hubley 2016). Community members also contend that the government has ignored the treaty rights and title of the Mi'kmaq, which they possess through treaties signed between themselves and early settlers. In response, the government has argued that it received approval for the project from the Mi'kmaq Rights Initiative (KMKNO), which claims to represent twelve of thirteen Mi'kmaw Bands as a consulting authority. However, both Sipekne'katik and Millbrook Nations maintain that the government failed to properly consult with the community, an issue that has polarized them and the KMKNO (Howe 2016; Hubley 2016).

In addition to concerns about the Alton Gas project, the Sipekne'katik Band has been concerned for some time about contaminated water in their community. The community had been blessed with clean water until 2012, when the community's water table was contaminated by digging at the nearby Nova Scotia Sand and Gravel Pit. During a meeting the ENRICH Project held several years ago (Waldron 2014a), residents in Indian Brook spoke about the environmentally hazardous methods used by the Nova Scotia Sand and Gravel Pit to dig up and clean sand in the area. This involved digging down to the level where the community's water table flows, resulting in the water table flowing into their site, as well as huge reservoirs of water the community was no longer able to use. The community was subsequently issued a do-not-drink advisory, after which the Department of Indian Affairs began shipping water into the community. Despite this, the root cause of the problem — the pit located in the community's backyard — was never addressed, resulting in ongoing issues with water contamination (Donovan 2015; Waldron 2014a, 2014b).

Eskasoni First Nation, Millbrook First Nation, and Acadia First Nation

Other Mi'kmaw communities in Nova Scotia who have concerns about contamination include Eskasoni, which is nestled alongside the beautiful Bras d'Or Lake in eastern Cape Breton Island; Millbrook First Nation, which is located within the town of Truro and positioned as the transportation hub of Nova Scotia; and Acadia First Nation Reserve in Yarmouth, located in the southwestern region of Nova Scotia. Eskasoni is less than five kilometres away from a recycling centre, which poses a risk of possible contamination to the community's drinking water and fish. Millbrook First Nation shares a waste disposal site with the African Nova Scotian communities of Cherry Brook, Lake Loon, and East and North Preston. At a meeting the ENRICH Project held in 2014, residents of Acadia First Nation in Yarmouth expressed their concerns about the health risks associated with the junkyard:

> Well, in our community our reserve is actually built on a dump, over a dump. So, when they were digging it up, trying to loosen up all of the soil, so that I could put fertilizers on it and what not, we actually dug up car parts that are underneath us and I was getting some history on this. So, when the band bought that land, they bought toxic land. I don't know what they paid for it at the time, probably three-quarters of a million dollars, I don't know, but anyway, all that land the band bought was used for a dumping zone, for cars, it was hundreds of cars where all the housing is right now. (Waldron 2014a)

This junkyard has been used as a dumping ground for car parts for over sixty years and is a source of anxiety for residents who believe it is associated with high rates of cancer in their community (Waldron 2014a, 2014b).

INDIGENOUS COMMUNITIES IN OTHER PROVINCES

Elsipogtog First Nation

In 2011, David Alward's Progressive Conservative government welcomed hydrofracking in New Brunswick, despite many New Brunswick residents being opposed to the use of this technique. Along with the Elsipogtog First

Nation, residents opposed to this method believe the possible negative impacts of hydrofracking on the environment outweigh the potential royalties from the development of the shale gas. A suite of fracking companies, including Southwestern Energy (SWN), Corridor Resources, and Windsor Energy obtained licenses from New Brunswick's Department of Natural Resources to initiate exploration activities to determine if natural gas could be extracted at various sites in the Frederick Brook shale play (Simon 2016).

Hydraulic fracturing — or fracking — involves horizontal drilling techniques using high-volume pressure and explosive charges. This is done to break up shale rock formations in order to release shale-trapped methane or oil deposits. The hydrocarbons are then captured for processing and distribution. It is a form of energy extraction that is considered to be invasive and high risk due to the toxicity of the chemicals (lubricants, biocides, and germicides) that are injected into the ground through the high-pressure water flush that occurs when the shale is being broken up. The extraction process is also toxic to human health and wildlife, since it involves the release of radioactive, heavy elements from the fractured shale (e.g., uranium, strontium, radon) (Simon 2016).

The Elsipogtog First Nation, in particular, feared that hydrofracking on their traditional lands would pose a risk to the water and wildlife. Their opposition is noteworthy since the Frederick Brook shale formation underlies its traditional land, and the area surrounding its reserve land had previously been under lease for shale gas exploration by SWN (O'Brien and Hipel 2016). As Derek Simon (2016) points out, opponents of shale gas industrialization in New Brunswick also had additional concerns, including the threat to water quality; the absence of demonstrable local economic benefit; the long-term fiscal burden of deferred costs and negative externalities placed by the industry on public infrastructure and the public health care system; the absence of provincial capacity to monitor and enforce the regulation of industry behaviours; a weak regulatory regime, coupled with a weak royalty regime and no funds committed to financing regulation costs in the provincial budget; the loss of business opportunities in agricultural, technological, and tourist sectors; the loss of property values for homeowners; and the implicit denial of climate change driven by fossil fuels.

A coalition network of opposition was formed by the New Brunswick Anti–Shale Gas Alliance in partnership with independent Wabanaki partners. In June 2013, as part of a nationwide Idle No More campaign, Elsipogtog First Nation protested legislative abuses of Indigenous treaty rights. The protests involved damage to SWN property, seizure of SWN property by protestors, arrests, and a road blockade on September 30, 2013. On October 17, armed RCMP officers moved in on the Elsipogtog protestors to enforce the court-ordered injunction that prohibited protesters from interfering with SWN's shale gas exploration work. According to reports, this resulted in RCMP officers firing rubber bullets, pepper-spraying demonstrators, and spraying demonstrators with high pressure water. In retaliation, the protestors threw Molotov cocktails at RCMP officers and burned five police cruisers. At least forty protestors were arrested. On October 21, 2013, the injunction was overturned on the grounds that, in the absence of the blockade, the injunction was no longer necessary (O'Brien and Hipel 2016).

First Nations in British Columbia

There are numerous other examples of environmental racism in Indigenous communities across Canada. For example, Annie L. Booth (2017) examines the impacts of industrial developments on Indigenous peoples in northeastern British Columbia, including West Moberly First Nations, Halfway River First Nation, Doig River First Nation, Saulteau First Nations, and Prophet River First Nation. She argues that the failure of the Canadian government to recognize Indigenous title and rights to traditionally used public lands and natural resources is an example of systemic environmental injustice. In 2009, the West Moberly First Nations filed a challenge against the British Columbia government and First Coal Corporation over what they believed to be a failed provincial environmental assessment regarding the potential impact of mining on caribou habitat and the extent to which the First Nations' concerns had been acknowledged. The court ruled in favour of the First Nations, noting the need to meaningfully engage the First Nations and the failure of the environmental assessment process to accommodate the First Nations' concerns about impacts to caribou (Udofia, Noble, and Bramand Poelzer 2016).

While industrial development in the form of oil and gas development has provided employment opportunities to residents, it has also resulted in health risks in the form of polluted, toxic, and contaminated air, land, and water, as well as the loss in quantity and quality of fresh water, the loss of use of private lands adjacent to extraction sites, and the loss of employment from other resources. Construction of the Site C hydroelectric dam was recently approved by the British Columbia government. With 1,100 megawatts of capacity, the Site C dam will provide enough energy to power the equivalent of about 450,000 homes a year. However, it will also flood 55 square kilometres of river valley, which will negatively impact wildlife, agricultural land, and First Nations communities, according to an environmental review. It will be built with new hiring requirements that will seek to increase the number of apprentices and workers from First Nations. Some of the revenues generated by the dam will be used to support farming. The West Moberly and Prophet River First Nations plan to proceed with court action, believing that the dam's construction infringes on their treaty rights to hunt, trap, and fish, and that the flooding of the valley will swallow ancestral graves (Hunter and Bailey 2017).

Kashechewan First Nation

In 2005, the First Nation community in Kashechewan (formerly Fort Albany) near James Bay, Ontario, was exposed to toxic E. coli bacteria in their water supply. The Ontario government was forced to evacuate nearly a thousand community members after the federal government refused to take responsibility (Dhillon and Young 2010; Jacobs 2010). A boil water advisory was subsequently issued, and it lasted for two years (Basdeo and Bharadwaj 2013; Dhillon and Young 2010). Other problems affecting the community's water system include broken treatment plant equipment, malfunctioning safety alarms, funding shortages, and water sampling deficiencies (Jacobs 2010).

Complicating matters was the fact that the community sat on a flood plain. These factors combined to produce poor water quality that resulted in a number of health problems, such as severe rashes and infections in children (Jacobs 2010). The federal government failed to take responsibility for and address these issues (whether intentional or unintentional), despite its responsibility to this community under the *Indian Act*, Environment Canada's responsibility under the *Canadian Environmental Protection Act*, and Health Canada's awareness of the health issues affecting this community (Gosine and Teelucksingh 2008; Jacobs 2010).

Athabasca Chipewyan First Nation,
Mikisew Cree First Nation, and the Métis Nation

Similarly, the federal and provincial governments failed to take responsibility for poor water quality in Fort Chipewyan, a remote urban community composed mostly of Athabasca Chipewyan, Mikisew Cree, and Métis peoples. This community is located downstream from Alberta's tar sands, near Saskatchewan's Uranium City, and is considered to be the largest industrial project on the planet (Jacobs 2010). The term "tar sands" refers to bituminous sands that constitute a mixture of sand, clay, water, and bitumen — a considerably dense form of petroleum that has been referred to as "tar" since the late nineteenth century because of its similar viscosity, odour and colour. However, since naturally occurring bitumen is chemically more similar to asphalt than to tar, the term "oil sands" is now more commonly used by industry and in the producing areas (Huseman and Short 2012). Environmental, human rights, and Indigenous activists consider Canada's oil sands the most destructive industrial project on earth.

Residents of Fort Chipewyan expressed concerns that they were no longer able to swim, fish, or drink from the nearby water supply and that they were being poisoned by contaminated water (Riahi and McSorley 2013). They were also angered by the provincial and federal governments' refusal to take action, whether it be conducting an empirical study to determine a potential link between water quality and high mortality rates in the community or testing the water for polycyclic aromatic hydrocarbons (PAHs), which are linked to cancers and other illnesses (Huseman and Short 2012; Jacobs 2010).

Aamjiwnaang First Nation

Aamjiwnaang First Nation near Sarnia's "Chemical Valley" has long had concerns about air pollution from industrial facilities in the area, such as oil refineries, power generating stations, and landfills (Jacobs 2010; Riahi and McSorley 2013). Chemical Valley is located in southwestern Ontario and is Canada's largest petrochemical complex, grouping over sixty petrochemical facilities within a 25-square-kilometre area (Riahi and McSorley 2013). Aamjiwnaang carries Ontario's highest air pollution load, placing a disproportionate environmental burden on the community (Jacobs 2010; Riahi and McSorley 2013). Between 1974 and 1986, the area experienced thirty-two major spills and three hundred minor ones, contributing approximately ten tonnes of pollutants to the St. Clair River, which flows through Chemical Valley (Jacobs 2010).

As a result, air pollution has been a major concern in the community, resulting in high rates of eye and skin irritations, central nervous system disorders, digestive problems, high blood pressure, anemia, chronic severe headaches, and respiratory problems (Jacobs 2010; Wiebe 2016). Approximately 22 percent of children on the reserve have asthma, compared to 8.2 percent in the neighbouring Lambton County, including the city of Sarnia. The area also has high rates of cancer and increased incidences of reproductive and developmental disorders (Riahi and McSorley 2013). In addition, 88 percent of mothers and 64 percent of children reported experiencing anxiety or fear associated with contaminants released by surrounding facilities (Cryderman, Letourneau, Miller, and Basu 2016). There has also been a dietary and cultural shift among the Aamjiwnaang

First Nation, with residents eating fewer locally grown foods and fish in recent years (Cryderman, Letourneau, Miller, and Basu 2016). Despite high rates and increasing incidences of these illnesses and diseases, the government health authorities maintain that the lifestyle choices of Aamjiwnaang residents are to blame for these adverse health effects (Wiebe 2016).

Asubpeeschoseewagong Netum Anishinabek/ Grassy Narrows First Nation

Asubpeeschoseewagong Netum Anishinabek (also known as Grassy Narrows First Nation) is an Ojibway reserve located north of Kenora, Ontario, that has long been concerned about the health effects of contaminants from mercury that was dumped into the Wabigoon-English River from Reed Paper's chemical plant in Dryden, Ontario, in the 1960s and again in the 1970s. In the community, this resulted in mercury poisoning from fish (Basdeo and Bharadwaj 2013; CBC News 2016; Dhillon and Young 2010; Free Grassy Narrows n.d.). The Ontario provincial government subsequently advised the community to stop eating fish and closed their commercial fishery, which meant economic disaster for a reserve that had been considerably reliant on tourism and had been experiencing an unemployment rate of over 90 percent in 1970. High unemployment subsequently led to high rates of alcoholism, personal withdrawal, negative self-evaluation, and routine violence (Clement 2003). After twenty-four years of operations, both the paper and chemical companies ceased operations in 1976. Asubpeeschoseewagong Netum Anishinabek subsequently received a settlement in 1986 from the federal and provincial governments, the Reed Paper Company, and its successor company Great Lakes Forest Products (Historica Canada n.d.b).

Despite these steps forward, the mercury was never removed from the water and continued to affect the health of residents. On June 27, 2016, Environment Minister Glen Murray and Indigenous Relations and Reconciliation Minister David Zimmer visited the community to announce that the Ontario government would work with the community on remediation efforts on the Wabigoon-English River system. This includes committing $300,000 to support water, sediment, and fish sampling in a stretch of river that has been identified as top priority (CBC News 2016; Free Grassy Narrows n.d.).

ENVIRONMENTAL RACISM IN AFRICAN NOVA SCOTIAN COMMUNITIES

Africville

Perhaps no other African Nova Scotian community has served as more of a classic example and symbol of segregation, racism, inequality, profits at all costs, and environmental racism than Africville. The community was located just north of Halifax on the shore of the Bedford Basin and was first settled in the mid-1800s by Black refugees who came to Nova Scotia following the War of 1812 (Allen n.d.; Fryzuk 1996; Nelson 2001). Some Africville residents ran fishing businesses and farms and owned small stores toward the end of the nineteenth century (Historica Canada n.d.c).

The community was subjected to injustices on many levels. For example, although the City of Halifax collected taxes in Africville, they did not provide the community with basic utilities and infrastructure offered to other parts of the city, such as paved roads, sanitary water, sewage, public transportation, garbage collection, recreational facilities, fire protection, street lights, and adequate police protection (Allen n.d.; Fryzuk 1996; Halifax Regional Municipality n.d.; Historica Canada n.d.c; Nelson 2001; Tavlin 2013).

As early as 1912, the City had decided to use Africville's land for industrial development, and in 1947 it rezoned Africville as industrial land. By 1965 the City had embarked on an urban renewal campaign, resulting in the expropriation and bulldozing of homes and the forcible displacement of Africville residents. Some residents were moved to derelict housing or rented public housing. The final property was expropriated and demolished in 1969, when the last of Africville's four hundred residents left. One resident, Eddie Carvery, remains in Africville after returning to the site in 1970 and pitching a tent in protest (Historica Canada n.d.c).

Africville became host to a number of environmental hazards, including a fertilizer plant, a slaughter house, a tar factory, a stone and coal crushing plant, a cotton factory, a prison, two infectious disease hospitals, and three systems of railway tracks (Allen n.d.; Fryzuk 1996; Nelson 2001). In the 1950s, the City built an open-pit dump in Africville, which many considered to be a health menace (Historica Canada n.d.c).

In 2010, some former Africville residents reached a multi-million dollar settlement with the City. While no individual compensation was paid out, the settlement included an apology, a hectare of land on the former site to rebuild the Seaview African United Baptist Church, and $3 million to help build it. African Nova Scotian Affairs was also established by the municipality. In

November 2016, up to three hundred former residents of Africville and their descendants joined a lawsuit against the City of Halifax over the loss of their land four decades ago, if the Supreme Court of Nova Scotia certified the case as a class-action lawsuit for former residents of Africville (Borden Colley 2016).

Lincolnville

Lincolnville represents another important example of environmental racism in Nova Scotia. Lincolnville is a small African Nova Scotian rural community situated in Guysborough County in northeast Nova Scotia. It was settled by Black Loyalists in 1784. Driven from their promised land, they were forced to move inland away from the white population and to become squatters on a barren, rocky piece of land (NSPIRG n.d.). In 1974, a first-generation landfill was opened one kilometre away from the community.

In 2006, the Municipality of the District of Guysborough closed the first landfill and opened a second-generation landfill that accepts waste from across northern Nova Scotia and Cape Breton. The decision to develop this landfill was based on the provincial government's need to decrease spending and generate needed tax revenues. Although Guysborough County determined the suitability of the landfill site and conducted extensive testing of surface water and groundwater, they did not consider the negative social impacts of their decision to site the landfill in the area. The Council proceeded with approvals and the construction of the landfill because the public did not substantively oppose the project through the official environmental assessment process. In the second-generation landfill's first month of opening, 55,780 tonnes of solid waste was received (Save Lincolnville Campaign n.d.).

In accordance with the province's waste management strategy, as of 2006 all municipalities are required to dispose of waste in second-generation landfills, which incorporate special liners designed to prevent runoff into the surrounding environment. According to regional environmental organizations, hazardous items such as transformers and refuse from offshore oil spills have been deposited at the landfill. In light of this, the African Nova Scotian community in Lincolnville has long been concerned about traces of carcinogens — including cadmium, phenol, and toluene — being above acceptable limits in the community's surface water and groundwater, from which residents drink (Benjamin 2008).

Deacon and Baxter (2013) contend that Lincolnville was unfairly chosen as a site for the landfill, and that the proponents used intimidation tactics throughout the siting process. Residents believe that the mandatory community

consultation period for sharing their concerns about the environmental assessment process was neither accessible, nor inclusive; that they were not adequately
notified about the process or consulted about how the landfill project would
affect residents; that they were denied the opportunity to reject the development; that they did not have a clear understanding of the terms used during the
siting process; and that the process reinforced residents' sense of powerlessness
in the decision-making process. Residents perceived the consultation process
as mere "lip service," because the decision to site the landfill in Lincolnville
had already been made by the Minister of Environment. Although residents
were only provided with one public drop-in session, government officials from
the municipality alleged that residents failed to participate in the process or
voice their concerns.

The fact that there were considerable differences in the way the landfills in
Lincolnville and Upper Sackville (a mostly white, low-income community)
were handled provides further weight to the arguments made in this book
about how environmental racism illuminates the greater value placed on white
lives. For example, while both communities had first-generation landfills built
before strict regulations came into place, the Upper Sackville site was retro-
actively lined to catch leachate — potentially toxic garbage water — before it
entered the groundwater, while the Lincolnville landfill was simply closed and
buried. Second, while the Upper Sackville landfill was located farther away
from the community than the Lincolnville landfill, Upper Sackville residents
received financial compensation for the environmental damage the landfill
caused in their community (Boon 2015; Bundale 2015; Lindsay 2011). In fact,
twenty-five families were bought out of their homes and relocated because of
foul odours at the landfill, and the community was paid $5 million under the
Community of Sackville Landfill Compensation Act (Nova Scotia Legislature
2015). Furthermore, the Act was ratified to protect the health and welfare
of residents and prevent the placement of a landfill in the community in the
future. After the landfill was closed in 1996, a multi-million dollar leachate
collection system was installed to protect the groundwater from leachate, and
regular monitoring of the landfill was conducted. To this day, Lincolnville is
still dealing with a degraded liner and waiting to be compensated (Boon 2015;
Bundale 2015; Lindsay 2011).

The Prestons

North and East Preston, located in eastern Halifax Regional Municipality, represent yet another example of environmental racism in the African Nova Scotian community. During the summer of 1991, the Metropolitan Authority was in search of a new landfill site for Halifax and Dartmouth. Included in the top choices were four areas that were close to historically African Nova Scotian communities: the East Lake and Wood Lake sites were near the Preston area; the third area was close to Beechville; and a fourth area was near Pockwock. When the Metropolitan Authority eventually settled on East Lake as the new landfill site, African Nova Scotian residents in East and North Preston were outraged (Fryzuk 1996).

The Prestons opposed the decision to site the landfill in East Lake by launching a formal complaint against the landfill site selection process, arguing that the Metropolitan Authority failed to consider social, cultural, and historical factors in their decision-making process. The Prestons also argued that East Lake had great historical significance for African Canadians in Nova Scotia and Canada. They pointed out that, in the 1700s, the King of England granted the community (including East Lake) as common land to residents (Fryzuk 1996). Political and public pressure subsequently led to the Authority conducting an investigation into the historical significance of the area, as well as the validity of the claims put forward by Preston residents. However, their studies found that there were no historical or archeological resources at the East Lake site or in the Preston community, and that East Lake did not qualify as a national historic site (Fryzuk 1996).

Shelburne, Cherry Brook, Lake Loon, Truro, and Lucasville

Several other African Nova Scotian communities across the province are located near waste facilities or have other environmental concerns. Shelburne, located in southwestern Nova Scotia, had a landfill nearby until the community succeeded in getting it closed in late 2016. Cherry Brook, located near Lake Major in Dartmouth, and Lake Loon, also located in Dartmouth, are approximately two kilometres and four kilometres from a recycling facility, respectively (Waldron 2016). African Nova Scotian residents in Truro, the shire town of Colchester County on the south side of the Salmon River, have been concerned for some time about flooding and a dump near their community (Waldron 2016). Truro has three main communities comprised of African Nova Scotian and other communities: the Marsh, the Island, and the Hill. Today, the Marsh is a primarily white community since many African Nova Scotians left the community; a primarily African Nova Scotian community lives on the Island; and finally, the Hill is comprised mainly of African Nova Scotians and low-income and poor people.

Over the last fourteen years, the primarily African Nova Scotian community of Lucasville, a small community between Lower Sackville and Hammonds Plains in Halifax Regional Municipality, has been dealing with the smell of horse manure, dust, and manure runoff when Memento Farm, a large commercial equestrian farm in the community, moved to the area in 2002 (Devet 2015a, 2015b, 2016, 2017a, 2017b; Waldron 2016). For the next thirteen years, Memento Farm failed to comply with zoning regulations, offering riding lessons and equestrian events that were illegal. Recognizing the illegal nature of their activities, the farm initiated a development agreement process that would have allowed the community to put some constraints on the operation, including setting limits on the number of horses boarding at the farm, imposing a storm water management regime, ordering more intense rodent controls, and setting conditions around manure storage and removal (Devet 2017a; Waldron 2016). Facing considerable pressure, Memento Farm abruptly discontinued its riding lessons and equestrian events and withdrew its application for the development agreement. Consequently, residents were left without a mechanism to lodge complaints. As of July 2017, very little has changed, and the farm continues to board horses (Devet 2017a).

Chapter 5

SACRIFICIAL LIVES

How Environmental Racism Gets Under the Skin

> Everything connected to the land is connected to our bodies. (Konsmo
> and Kahealani Pacheco 2015: 60)

Environmental racism is not only about a concern for profit and wealth, but
also about how the bodies of "racial others" get taken up within the "white
gaze." Policy decisions that lead to the disproportionate placement of polluting
industries and other environmental hazards near Indigenous and Black communities highlight how little value these bodies hold in the white imagination. Joe R.
Feagin and Hernan Vera (1995: 16) aptly point out that "white racism involves a
massive breakdown of empathy, the human capacity to experience the feelings of
members of an out-group viewed as different." This lack of regard for the humanity of Indigenous and Black peoples speaks to enduring perceptions of them as
disposable and lacking in humanity and value and simultaneously invulnerable,
strong, "superhuman" and, therefore, able to endure inconceivable harms inflicted
on their spirits, souls, minds and bodies. Combined, these perceptions perpetuate
enduring pathologizing myths about Indigenous and Black peoples' capacity to
withstand all hurt and pain.

Harriet A. Washington (2007) examines pathologizing myths about the Black
body during the colonial era in her groundbreaking book *Medical Apartheid: The
Dark History of Medical Experimentation on Black Americans from Colonial Times
to the Present.* She reveals that slaves were exploited and abused by physicians by
way of ad hoc experimentation in medications, dosages, and spontaneous surgi-
cal experiments. The powerlessness and legal invisibility of slaves enabled their
neglect and abuse by a court system that had little concern for their safety and
health. Real (skin colour, hair texture, etc.) and imagined (elongated penises,
distended labia, etc.) physical differences between Blacks and whites during the
colonial era contributed to ideologies of Black biological primitivism and, consequently, the pathologization of Black bodies. According to Washington (2007),

physicians advanced theories about the greater immunity of Black people to malaria and yellow fever during the colonial era, although there was no evidence that they had an innate, absolute resistance to malaria. Scientists also claimed that the primitive nervous systems of Black people made them immune to physical and emotional pain and to mental illness. These and other stereotypes highlighted contradictions about the Black body in two main ways during the colonial era: theories about real and perceived physical differences between Blacks and whites were developed and myths about the Black body as inherently stronger, more resilient, or impervious to most illnesses were generated (Washington 2007). These controlling images of Black people were used to justify slavery and various forms of torture endured by slaves, such as branding and whipping.

At the end of the nineteenth century, a popular topic up for debate was the apparent relative absence of "madness" among African, Asian, and Native American people. Henry Maudsley (1879), a prominent British psychiatrist, espoused the idea of the "noble savage," attributing Black people's relative immunity to mental illness to their lack of civilization. As cited by Suman Fernando (1991: 39) in his book *Mental Health, Race and Culture*, the following comment by the clinical director of Georgia State Sanitarium about the apparent rarity of depression among Blacks in the American South is typical of the general views among psychiatrists at the time:

> It appears that the Negro mind does not dwell upon unpleasant subjects, he is irresponsible, unthinking, easily aroused to happiness, and his unhappiness is transitory, disappearing as a child's when other interests attract his attention ... Depression is rarely encountered even under circumstances where a white person would be overwhelmed.

Sentiments such as these infantilized Black people in the American South and contributed to stereotypes and theories that characterized mental illness as a product of the more complex, sophisticated, and advanced European culture. Higher rates of mental illness among whites were thought to result from the stresses they experienced living in a civilized society, as well as their greater creativity and sensitivity. This theory attributed the relative absence of mental illness among Black people to the primitiveness of African society. In other words, Black people were considered to too mentally infantile and their culture too underdeveloped for them to be at risk for developing mental illness (Carothers 1940, 1951, 1953).

Interestingly, myths about Black imperviousness to pain have endured since slavery, as a recent study by Kelly M. Hoffman, Sophie Trawalter, Jordan R.

Axt, and M. Norman Oliver (2016) found. This study quizzed white medical students and residents and found that African Americans are systematically undertreated for pain compared to white Americans because of a perception that their skin is thicker than white Americans. The participants also held other false beliefs about biological differences between African Americans and white people, such as perceptions that African Americans have less sensitive nerve endings than white people. Consequently, they rated African American patients' pain as lower than that of white patients, resulting in physicians making less appropriate recommendations for how African American patients should be treated. These representations convey that Black bodies have long been sites of trauma that carry the weight of the past, as well as dehumanizing present-day stereotypes, facilitating and justifying their brutalization and exploitation by the state.

Several authors (Carrington 1980; hooks 1993; Mays, Caldwell, and Jackson 1996; Schreiber, Noerager, and Wilson 1998, 2000) note that societal stereotypes of Black women as nurturing, strong, self-sufficient, assertive, resilient, and invulnerable "superwomen" ignore the racialized physical and mental trauma that Black women have long had to endure, often leading to Black women minimizing, ignoring, and denying the many challenges they face. Black women are also perceived to be pillars of the Black family by other family members and partners who often hold high and unfair expectations for them to be the physical, emotional, and economic mainstay of their families. Mays et al. (1996) point out that African American culture stresses early in life the ability to "do it," which emphasizes the importance of actively managing difficult situations without showing stress.

Despite these and other enduring myths about Black people's invulnerability and imperviousness to mental and emotional pain, the reality is that both Black and Indigenous communities are more vulnerable than are other communities to illness and disease associated with their greater exposure to environmental risks and other structural determinants of health, such as unemployment and underemployment, income insecurity and poverty, food insecurity, neigh-bourhoods with poor infrastructures, poor-quality housing, criminalization, and a legacy of oppression. Taken together, these environmental, social, and economic inequalities represent different but intersecting forms of "environ-mental violence" (Konsmo and Kahealani Pacheco 2015) impacting well-being and health in Indigenous and Black communities. This chapter highlights one of the more significant limitations of the environmental justice lens in Nova Scotia and Canada: the failure to acknowledge the physical and mental health effects of environmental violence in Indigenous and Black communities, and how it facilitates disproportionate vulnerability and susceptibility to negative environmental exposures.

ENVIRONMENTAL VIOLENCE:
FRAMING THE COMPLEX WEB OF INEQUALITIES

Until recently, frameworks in medicine and health research attributed racial disparities in illness and disease to biological, genetic, cultural, or lifestyle choice differences between racial groups. However, it is now believed that an analysis of the social context of inequality is important for understanding why social, economic, political, and environmental inequalities represent different but intersecting manifestations of environmental violence impacting health and well-being. In other words, health inequalities that are outcomes of disproportionate negative environmental exposures (i.e., environmental health inequities) can't be understood independent of the complex web of inequalities (poverty, food insecurity, poor-quality housing, etc.) that combine to create greater exposure and vulnerability to environmental risks, particularly in Indigenous and Black communities.

Understanding the complex web of inequalities that impact health in Indigenous, Black, and other racialized communities requires an appreciation for structural or distal determinants of health. As I mentioned earlier in the book, an approach that acknowledges the structural — rather than the social — determinants of health is better able to capture colonialism and the many other structurally rooted factors impacting health beyond simply the social. Structural or distal determinants are deeply embedded, representing historical, political, ideological, economic, and social foundations (including Indigenous worldviews, spirituality, and self-determination) from which all other determinants evolve (Reading 2015).

Distal determinants of health interconnect with proximal and intermediate determinants to impact health. Proximal determinants influence health in the most direct ways. They include early child development, income and social status, education and literacy, social support networks, employment, working conditions and occupational health, the physical environment, culture, and gender. Proximal determinants produce various physical, emotional, mental, spiritual, and social challenges. Intermediate determinants facilitate or hinder health through systems that connect proximal and distal determinants. They include health promotion and health care, education and justice, social supports, labour markets, government and enterprise, kinship networks, relationship to the land, language, ceremonies, and ways of knowledge sharing. While these determinants may have a less direct impact on the health of individuals, they have a significant influence on proximal determinants of health (Reading 2015).

As a structural determinants of health approach highlights, there is a need for a more holistic view of environmental health inequalities that recognizes the complex web of inequalities that renders Indigenous and Black communities more vulnerable to environmental risks. Researchers in environmental studies, environmental science, and environmental health must move beyond quantitative assessments of physiological health effects resulting from environmental pollution and contamination and begin to grapple with the multiple, overlapping, and intersecting challenges and stressors that burden vulnerable communities. One of the main stressors burdening the African Nova Scotian community in Lincolnville is the economic fallout of the first- and second-generation landfills, according to one resident who participated in a study the ENRICH Project conducted on environmental health in African Nova Scotian communities:

> When we started getting into the nitty-gritty of saying that because of the amount of revenue being generated by this here facility, that some of the revenue should be going into an economic development fund. Since we're putting up with the fallout, we should be benefitting from it. Money should be put into an economic development fund that would help economic development in the communities. Also, we talked about compensation for the people in the community. (Waldron 2016)

For many in the community, Lincolnville's faltering economy can be attributed to the presence of the first- and second-generation landfills in their community over the last forty years, which has led to a general reluctance by residents in the Municipality of Guysborough County to invest in businesses near the community, hesitance to build homes in the area because of depreciating property values, few available job opportunities, significant out-migration of young adults looking for jobs and opportunities elsewhere, an aging population that is no longer in the labour force and, consequently, a small and dwindling workforce. Lori M. Hunter (1998) found that environmental risk impacts out-migration in neighbourhoods near polluting industries. Lori M. Hunter, Michael J. White, Jani S. Little, and Jeannette Sutton (2003) also observe that populations with higher socioeconomic status that are near polluting industries tend to move out, while lower-income populations remain. This suggests that low income and poverty are significant factors in why Black householders are less likely than white householders to leave environmentally hazardous neigh-bourhoods — it is less expensive to buy homes in environmentally hazardous neighbourhoods.

In their research report "Violence on the Land, Violence on Our Bodies: Building an Indigenous Response to Environmental Violence" (2015), Erin Marie Konsmo and A.M. Kahealani Pacheco characterize environmental violence as both the biological reproductive *and* social impacts of industry on Indigenous women, children and future generations. They argue that it is not possible to foster healthy families, communities, and nations when people's bodies continue to be violated by industry. They list several forms of environmental violence occurring in Indigenous communities, including reproductive health issues; cancer and other illnesses; sexual, domestic, and family violence; missing and murdered Indigenous women; human trafficking for both labour and sexual exploitation; HIV and other sexually transmitted infections; increased crime; increased rates of incarceration; increased drug and alcohol use; alcohol-related traffic fatalities; suicide (particularly among young people); trauma and dispossession; loss of culture and self-determination; divisions in families and communities; child removal; mental health concerns; and poverty.

Over the past fifteen years, a number of other Canadian studies (Access Alliance Multicultural Community Health Centre 2007; Jackson, McGibbon, and Waldron 2013; Johnston, Angelucci, Howey, Waldron, Townsend, and Lawlor 2009; Kisely, Terashima, and Langille 2008; McGibbon, Waldron, and Jackson 2013; Raphael 2007; Waldron 2002, 2003, 2005, 2008, 2010b, 2010c, 2015a; Wilkins, Berthelot, and Ng 2002) have shown that the main determi-nants of health are, in fact, not rooted in medical or behavioural factors. Rather, they stem from a number of structural determinants, such as Indigenous status, race, immigrant and refugee status, early life experiences, education, employ-ment insecurity, unemployment, working conditions, availability of social safety net, food security, quality of neighbourhood, quality of housing, access to health services, access to transportation, access to formal or informal child care, exposure to violence, criminalization and racial profiling, racial or cultural stereotyping, unequal access to information, and social exclusion. For example, Patricia Rodney and Esker Copeland (2009) and Russell Wilkins, Jean-Marie Berthelot, and Edward Ng (2002) observe that higher rates of chronic disease, substance consumption and abuse, prolonged stress, anxiety, depression, and suicide in marginalized communities in Canada can be attributed to high rates of poverty, poor-quality education, poor-quality housing, poor working conditions, and other structural determinants of health. Generational poverty continues to harm Indigenous communities even though these communities are home to the most resource-rich territories in North America and the greatest extractive industrial development (Konsmo and Kahealani Pacheco 2015).

In a study I conducted on health risk perception in African Nova Scotian communities near environmental pollution and contamination (Waldron 2016), participants asserted that good health is dependent on a number of structural determinants, such as access to health care (e.g., medical centres, homecare), services (e.g., stores), jobs, healthy and affordable food, high-quality and low-rent housing; exercise; access to reliable and low-cost transportation; accessibility of sidewalks, crosswalks, and parks (i.e., the built environment); community safety community cohesiveness; and spirituality. The challenges these communities experience accessing various goods and resources highlights how low a priority these communities are to government and would explain why hazardous facilities tend to get placed in Black and other "expendable" communities.

For example, a participant from Lincolnville discussed the relationship between health and poverty, food security, employment, and access to health services in a study the ENRICH Project conducted on environmental health in African Nova Scotian communities:

> Income makes you healthy. Because I notice when you live in low poverty, you tend to not be able to eat well or afford your prescrip-tions. And, that happens a lot with the seniors in the community. So, if there's no jobs available, how are they going to eat tomorrow or how are they going to support their families and themselves and make sure they have okay health if they can't get their medicine? And that also causes depression and it causes anxiety and stress. And stress does bother you and it does kill you. (Waldron 2016)

A participant in East Preston in that same study (Waldron 2016) dis-cussed the importance of accessible and reliable transportation for the elderly population:

> I also think that because of, I guess, people getting older and you don't have the money to do what you want to do, or some people don't have the vehicles to get to town when they want to get to town. We have a bus that runs, what, on the hour, every hour. And, some people can't

take the bus. So, there should be some kind of shuttle bus around here that can pick up these elderly people that may want to go to the doctor, may want to go to a medical centre, they may want to go have a checkup, or maybe they want to go shopping for some food. And we don't have that. There's a lot of things in this community that we don't have that we should have. The rest of the community got them, but we don't have them. And they just say, "oh, it's off the map, it doesn't matter." And there should be more. East Preston should be looked at more as a place like any other place around. Every other place has got buses that are running twenty-four hours, every fourteen minutes. North Preston, Cherry Brook, the buses are running constantly. Here we got a bus that runs every hour. I'm one of the elderly people myself. And, if I didn't have means of getting around and [staying] healthy, I don't know what I would do. (Waldron 2016)

The sentiments expressed by these participants highlight how important income, transportation, and the availability of other resources are to health and well-being.

Another study (McGibbon, Waldron, and Jackson 2013) notes that cardiovascular disease in racialized communities is an outcome of racism-related stress and intergenerational forms of trauma, often referred to as historical trauma, even in the absence of other risk factors. The stress of racism results in the body's physiological stress-handling systems becoming overtaxed, resulting in cardiovascular disease and a number of other health problems. Historical trauma is a concept that is often used to describe the relationship between colonialism, present-day forms of state-sanctioned violence experienced by Indigenous and racialized communities, and poor health outcomes experienced intergenerationally in these communities. In *Wretched of the Earth*, Frantz Fanon (1963: 36) discusses the enduring impacts of colonialism on both the environment and mental well-being, stating that "Imperialism leaves behind germs of rot which we must clinically detect and remove from our land but from our minds as well."

The stressors resulting from colonialism and the intergenerational transmission of other social, economic, and political stressors are contributory factors to high rates of suicide among Indigenous peoples in Canada (Evans-Campbell 2008; First Nations Information Governance Centre 2012; Kirmayer, Brass, Holton, Paul, Simpson, and Tait 2007; Walls and Whitbeck 2012). Suicide rates for Indigenous youth around the world are considerably higher than for non-Indigenous populations (Campbell, Balaratnasingam, McHugh, Janca, and

Chapman 2016; Orellana, Balieiro, Fonseca, Basta, and Souza 2016; Sumarokov, Brenn, Kudryavtsev, and Nilssen 2014). A national representative sample of First Nations adults living on reserve found that 22 percent experienced suicidal ideation at some point in their life and that 13 percent had attempted suicide between 2008 and 2010 (First Nations Information Governance Centre 2012). In 2009, 9 percent of non-Indigenous Canadians reported suicidal ideation in their lifetime (First Nations Information Governance Centre 2012).

It is important that the concept of historical trauma serve as a conceptual lens for understanding and articulating the cumulative social and health impacts of enduring inequalities and oppressions experienced by Indigenous, Black, and other racialized peoples in white settler nations. Through various mechanisms (forced acculturation, residential schools, the reserve system, forced relocation, defilement of land), colonialism disrupted socio-cultural activities and economic systems that were important to the development and maintenance of social networks and to the relationship that Indigenous peoples had with their land. Colonialism also resulted in shifting patterns of health, as the colonizers brought with them new diseases and as traditional or Indigenous practices and beliefs were replaced by Western health practices. In a meeting the ENRICH Project held in 2013 (Waldron 2014a), a Mi'kmaw Elder from Eskasoni discussed the importance of connecting to traditional ways by embracing an Indigenous health perspective that values holism:

> When we're talking about health, do we really mean we're just talking about our physical health or are we going to be also including that most of the society are literally spiritual, spiritually starving and to make a complete person those things have to be kept in a balanced and harmonious way? The spiritual aspect and the physical aspect ... I think it has to be somehow included into these discussions, not just the physical or the emotional. (Waldron 2014a)

This participant's discussion on the importance of embracing a holistic understanding of health that includes spiritual, emotional, and physical well-being is one that is predicated on both Indigenous and African-centred worldviews.

The legacy of colonialism has also had enduring health impacts in African Nova Scotian communities, contributing to higher rates of heart disease, cancer, high blood pressure, diabetes, and death relative to white Nova Scotians (Saulnier 2009). For example, Winnie Benton and Sandra Loppie (2001) found that African Nova Scotians had a higher cancer mortality rate than the general population, which they attributed to systemic forms of racism within various social institutions, including the health care system. The unavailability of medical care in rural African Nova Scotian communities until the late 1930s, the tendency to use medical services only in cases of emergency, a legacy of diseases contracted by early African settlers (tuberculosis, cancer, heart disease), and racial discrimination dating back to slavery in Nova Scotia are also contributing factors in ongoing health disparities between African Nova Scotians and other populations.

Cancer Care Nova Scotia (2013) conducted a study that followed up Benton and Loppie's (2001) study and found that African Nova Scotians continue to face barriers to accessing cancer care health services. These barriers include delays accessing cancer specialist services; challenges communicating with health professionals; transportation barriers; medication costs and other financial issues; geographic isolation; delays in screening and in obtaining a definitive diagnosis of cancer while in the care of a primary care practitioner; lack of access to family physicians in some rural communities, which may contribute to poor screening participation and late diagnoses; racism; and lack of cultural awareness and sensitivity among health professionals.

In her article, "Globalization as Racialized, Sexualized Violence: The Case of Indigenous Women," (2008) Rauna Kuokkanen offers a much-needed gendered analysis to explain the ways in which land exploitation dislocates racialized women from their social roles and positions. Industry brings with it increased social and economic insecurity and instability, resulting in a shift in gender dynamics, a disruption of the social fabric, women's diminished social status, and increased marginalization and exclusion of women. Taken together, these factors increase women's vulnerability and susceptibility to violence within families and in society.

Konsmo and Kahealani Pacheco (2015) emphasize how important it is to understand trauma through an intersectional framework, arguing that Indigenous women have a unique experience of trauma because their gender and Indigenous identity shape how they are impacted by environmental violence, the legacy of colonialism in their communities, and the dispossession and exploitation of their land. Indigenous women in Canada experience poor health outcomes resulting from inequities, including lower life expectancy rates, lower quality of housing, poor physical environment, lower educational levels, lower socioeconomic status, poor access to health services, fewer employment opportunities, and weaker community infrastructure (Hunt 2015). Gendered health inequities experienced by Indigenous girls and women are also evident in their frequent experiences of spousal, sexual, and other violence, as well as their inability to access safe, secure housing both on and off reserve (Hunt 2015).

Environmental violence illustrates that place matters to health and that, consequently, health outcomes and disparities are products of where we live, the resources we have access to or don't have access to (jobs, housing, food, health services, public transit, etc.), historical trauma, and exposure to environmental risks. Sarah De Leeuw (2015) observes that place and geography are fundamental determinants of health in Indigenous communities in Canada and around the world. She suggests that a structural determinants of health framework can more fully encapsulate the physical and material aspects of geography that includes place, earth, land, space, ecology, territory, landscape, water, ground, and soil. Human health (or lack thereof) manifests within and is determined by its geographic context, or where its existence occurs.

In her discussion on the connection between people, land, and health, Chantelle Richmond (2015) points out that there are considerable concerns about the health effects of environmental dispossession in Anishinaabe communities on the north shore of Lake Superior, as well as in other Indigenous communities in Canada and elsewhere. The practice and transfer of Indigenous knowledge across generations has been compromised by environmental dispossession, leading to negative impacts on community health, well-being, and cultural identity. Decreased access to the cultural determinants of health in Anishinaabe communities, such as participation in hunting, fishing, and trapping, and other activities is a result of limited control over and reduced quality of their local environmental resources. The notion that actions taken on the land will have important repercussions for the wellness of the Anishinaabek is central to their belief systems. Anishinaabe knowledge and other Indigenous knowledges are premised on the relationship between the Anishinaabek and the land — a land in which the spiritual, sentient, and physical are connected.

This holistic understanding of health is one that understands the interrelatedness between the physical body and intimate, spiritual relationships with the land. This includes all of the medicines the land provides, as well as social relationships with family members and the wider community. Consequently, the health of the Anishinaabe people is vulnerable as a result of processes of environmental dispossession, including colonial policy and regulations such as the *Indian Act*, and industrial development, because these factors have fundamentally altered the relationship between the Anishinaabe people and their lands. Water, food, and medicine are the most direct link between the health of the Anishinaabe people and the land. Colonialism changed the eating patterns of the Anishinaabek, resulting in significant health impacts, including high rates of obesity, early onset diabetes, and other chronic diseases (Richmond 2015).

These compounded inequalities provide a conceptual framework for articulating the multiple, overlapping, and intersecting social, economic, political, and environmental determinants impacting health and well-being in Indigenous, Black, and other racialized communities. It is a strong challenge to those who insist that environmental inequities can only be confirmed if a causal relationship between a specific environmental contaminant and a specific disease outcome is identified. Researchers must begin to move beyond a focus on the health effects of residents' residential proximity to industrial facilities toward a more critical and inclusive examination of the health effects of place and all its associated inequalities.

ENVIRONMENTAL HEALTH INEQUITIES

Environmental health inequities have been defined as the health impacts associated with the disproportionate location of industries that emit pollutants and contaminants and other environmental hazards in racialized and low-income communities (Deacon and Baxter 2013; Pritchard 2009; Pulido 1996; Scott, Rakowski, Harris, and Dixon 2015; Walker 2009). Environmental health inequities across racial dimensions have been well documented in the literature, which provides strong evidence that Indigenous and racialized communities in Canada are exposed to greater health risks compared to white communities because they are more likely to be spatially clustered around waste disposal sites and other environmental hazards (Atari, Luginaah, and Baxter 2011; Atari, Luginaah, Gorey, Xu, and Fung 2012; Maantay 2002; Mascarenhas 2007; Masuda, Zupancic, Poland, and Cole 2008; Sharp 2009; Teelucksingh 2007). For example, epidemiological studies are increasingly examining the relative risk of cancer, upper respiratory disease, congenital anomalies, cardiovascular disease, skin diseases, and allergies in racialized communities compared to white communities (Bharadwaj, Nilson, Judd-Henry, Ouellette, Parenteau, Tournier, Watson, D. Bear, Ledoux, and A. Bear 2006; Crouse, Peters, Villeneuve, Proux, Shin, Goldberg, Johnson, Wheeler, Allen, Atari, Jerrett, Brauer, Brook, Cakmak, and Burnett 2015; Cryderman, Letourneau, Miller, and Basu 2016; Rowat 1999). Toxins produced by environmental activities may be released into air, water, or land, posing a long-term risk to health and the environment due to direct exposure to environmental contamination. Waste disposal sites house and release harmful chemicals, heavy metals, volatile organic compounds (vocs), fine particulates, and a variety of dangerous gases that harm the environment and human health. The health risks associated with solid waste contamination of fresh water resources and soil contamination include eye irritation, skin rashes, abdominal pain, incontinence, temporary liver dysfunction, seizures, respiratory diseases, and skin rashes (Vrijheid 2000). A Shelburne resident that participated in the study the ENRICH Project conducted on environmental health in African Nova Scotian communities attributes high rates of cancer and liver and kidney disorders in her community to the landfill near her community, which was finally closed in late 2016:

> Everyone knows that in all surrounding communities the dump can be seen in the south end of the community. A significant amount of people in close proximity to the dump has died from cancer and has or is suffering from an array of other health problems such as various forms of cancer, increased blood pressure, changes in nerve reflexes, brain, liver, and kidney disorders. Immune system ... digestive system. (Waldron 2016)

A North Preston resident who participated in a meeting the ENRICH Project held in 2013 also shared her concerns about the relationship between water and air pollution from the waste disposal site near the North Preston Community Centre and high rates of cancer, diabetes, heart disease, respiratory illnesses, and skin rashes in the community:

> For years, part of the community was on a water system which was not flushed out for several decades and because the chemical treat-ment of that water supply was monitored ... but I believe that there was too high concentrations of chlorine in the system. So, I think that accounts for the high cancer rate over the last several decades. I also believe that in terms of environmental health, that it's poor because of our community being associated with a local dump. And therefore, a lot of the fly ash in the air contributed to the high rate of respiratory illnesses. (Waldron 2014a)

While the relationship between air pollution and high rates of respiratory ill-nesses discussed by this North Preston resident has been a focus in the literature on environmental health over the years (Bharadwaj et al. 2006; Crouseet et al. 2015; Cryderman et al. 2016; Rowat 1999), rarely discussed is the relationship between mould and respiratory illnesses in Indigenous communities. Michael Optis, Karena Shaw, Peter Stephenson, and Peter Wild (2012) examine the conditions that allow for mould growth in 50 percent of the homes located on Indigenous reserves in Canada. According to the authors, there are several factors that cause mould growth, including increased moisture levels as a result of environmentally inappropriate construction, structural damage to buildings, a high percentage of overcrowded homes, insufficient use of ventilation systems, and insufficient federal funding for on-reserve housing and socioeconomic improvements. The authors point out that a commitment by the federal government to improving the socioeconomic and housing conditions of Indigenous peoples, as well as long-lasting government initiatives to educate homeowners in mould remediation, control, and prevention techniques would help to address mould growth in homes on reserves. The relationship between high rates of asthma and black mould in homes is a concern in Acadia First Nation in Yarmouth, according to one resident who participated in a meeting the ENRICH Project held there in 2013:

> I know there's a lot of people on the reserve that, especially their basements, I mean when we're talking about cement foundations and toxins and things like that … a lot of the basements have been covered with mould. And, black mould is very hazardous, I mean as you all know, to your health … or breathing it in and I mean it would be interesting to see how many kids do we actually have that have asthma on that reserve. We all have like allergies on the skin. I take Reactin every day because my skin … I could just rip it apart right. (Waldron 2014a)

This resident's account of the health impacts of mould in her community must be contextualized within the broader literature (Optis et al. 2012) that suggests that Indigenous communities are disproportionately impacted by mould and that this often leads to asthma and other respiratory illnesses (Waldron 2014a).

Other scholars argue the importance of looking at gender when examining disproportionate rates of environmental exposures and illness. For example, Nadine Scott, Lauren Rakowski, Laila Zahra Harris, and Troy Dixon (2015) note that structural determinants of health such as race, income, education, class, social support networks, and geographic location influence a woman's vulnerability to chemical exposures, the extent to which she can avoid or address these exposures, and her access to the resources, education, and support systems needed to do so. Exposure to environmental contaminants are influenced by gendered relations of power that manifest in gender-specific roles, responsibilities, expectations, opportunities, and constraints. For example, the gendered division of labour operates in such a way so as to expose women to contaminants in their daily environments. The gendered dvision of labour is also very much present in paid work, which exposes men and women to occupational exposures in different ways depending on the nature of their work (Scott et al. 2015).

Konsmo and Kahealani Pacheco (2015) assert that the generational inheritance of toxic contamination impacts the psychological, relational, emotional, cultural, and economic well-being of communities, and that Indigenous women's reproductive and other bodily health systems bear the brunt of environmental violence across North America. Similarly, Rachel Morello-Frosch, Miriam Zuk, Michael Jerrett, Bhavna Shamasunder, and Amy D. Kyle (2011) observe that poorer health outcomes in racial or ethnic minority and low-income communities in the United States can be attributed to the convergence and cumulative effects of disproportionate levels of exposure to environmental hazards, as well as social stressors like poverty, poor housing quality, and social inequality in these communities. They found an elevated risk of illness and disease in communities near industrial and hazardous waste sites, including adverse perinatal outcomes, respiratory and heart diseases, psychosocial stress, and mental health impacts.

Psychological stress

In addition to the negative effects of pollution and contaminants on well-being and health, several scholars (Dawson and Madsen 2011; Downey and Van Willigen 2005; Kondo, Gross-Davis, May, Davis, Johnson, Mallard, Gabbadon, Sherrod, and Branas 2014) assert that industry and other environmental hazards are often appraised as stressful by residents and may also represent chronic psychological stressors. For example, Liam Downey and Marieke Van Willigen (2005) observe that those who live closer to industrial activity perceive greater neighbourhood disorder, personal powerlessness, and depression, which in turn accounts for greater symptoms of psychological distress in these neighbourhoods. A resident in Lucasville who participated in the study the ENRICH Project conducted on environmental health in African Nova Scotian communities spoke to this issue, describing the emotional toll the equestrian farm has taken in her community:

> And, then talking about these physical industries, there's also a mental cost to that as well — to our mental health and well-being. When we know that all this is happening around us and nobody is concerned enough to do anything about it, that takes a toll on your mental health. So, it's not only your physical health that's being affected here, it's also our mental well-being. (Waldron 2016)

The sentiment expressed by this resident reveals the psychological toll nearby industry takes on a community, particularly when that community feels abandoned by a government that fails to respond to environmental concerns. This suggests that government must acknowledge the public's identification with a place or industry and address immediate environmental stressors such as abandonment, public perceptions about lack of social control, and fears about displacement (Kondo et al. 2014).

Focusing specifically on employees that were involved in uranium work in the past, Susan E. Dawson and Gary E. Madsen (2011) found a link between exposures associated with uranium mine wastes and/or uranium mill tailings and present and possible future health problems, such as emotional stress, depression, and anxiety. Describing the traditional Indigenous worldview in which the land, animals, and elements are perceived as constituting aspects of the self, Laurence Kirmayer, Gregory M. Brass, Tara Holton, Ken Paul, Cori Simpson, and Caroline Tate (2007) found that damage to the land, appropriation of land, and spatial restrictions constitute assaults on the individual and collective sense of self. They also suggest that environmental violence represents an attack on collective and personal identity, self-esteem, and well-being in Indigenous communities and may also have psychological consequences, such as the loss of social role and status in a large-scale urban society.

Cancer

The link between waste disposal sites and cancer has been considerably investigated in the literature. For example, Martine Vrijheid (2000); Pearl Moy, Nikhil Krishnan, Priscilla Ulloa, Steven Cohen, and Paul W. Brandt-Rauf (2008); and Mark S. Goldberg, Jack Siemiatyck, Ron DeWar, Marie Desy, and Helen Riberdy (1999) found that these sites are associated with increased incidences of adult cancers, such as leukemia and brain, stomach, liver, lung, rectum, prostate, and bladder cancers. Cancer rates among the Athabasca Chipewyan First Nation in Fort Chipewyan, a primarily Indigenous community, was found to be 30 percent higher than average for all types of cancers, according to a study by Yiqun Chen (2009). The impacts of oil sand deposits near this community over the last several decades include caustic changes to river water quality, meat quality, and to the availability of wild fish and game. It has also led to an increasing incidence of cancers and other serious illnesses (CBC News 2010; Huseman and Short 2012).

Cancer is a particular concern in Lucasville, according to one resident who expressed her concerns about the link between cancer and the equestrian farm in her community in a study the ENRICH Project conducted:

> It does probably have more of an effect on our physical health. But like I said, we don't know what we're breathing in. We don't know the moment when that reaches our well water, if there's E. coli. We don't know when we breathe that air in or that smell, which smells like it's a smell you shouldn't be smelling ... But we don't know when we breathe it in how harmful it is in our lungs. You know, every time we breathe that in, we're breathing something into our body that's going to manifest into a cancer five years down the road. And you keep remembering all these uncles and cousins and grandfathers and people that died from cancer over the years. And when you compare it to another sector down the road or over there in the next province that didn't have this problem, you see, well, they lived to be old and they never had any health problems. So yes, it has a health impact. All these things have a health impact on us. It's stress, it's mental, it's mental harassment. It's harassing our health. (Waldron 2016)

As this resident points out, illness can be produced from environmentally hazardous activities that transmit pollutants in several ways, such as through water and air.

The cancer risks associated with landfill-based disposal methods are approximately five times higher than the risks associated with waste-to-energy incineration (Moy et al. 2008). It is for this reason that community members in Lincolnville attribute high rates of prostate, stomach, lung, and skin cancers in their community to the landfill. According to a Lincolnville resident who participated in a study the ENRICH Project conducted, her community has experienced worsening health since the first-generation landfill was placed in the community, including increasing rates of cancer and diabetes:

> If you look at the health of the community prior to 1974 before the landfill site was located in our community, our community seemed to be healthier. From 1974 on until the present day, we noticed our people's health seems to be going downhill. Our people seem to be passing on at a younger age. They are contracting different types of cancer that we never heard of prior to 1974. Our stomach cancer seems to be on the rise. Diabetes is on the rise. Our people end up with tumours in their body. And, we're at a loss of, you know, of what's causing it. The municipality says that there's no way that the landfill site is affecting

us. But, if the landfill site located in other areas is having an impact on people's health, then shouldn't the landfill site located next to our community be having an impact on our health too? (Waldron 2016)

This resident makes a case for the link between the landfill and increased rates of mortality among younger people, as well as increased rates of different types of cancer and other health issues, all of which were rare before the landfill was placed in the community.

Child and Maternal Health

High rates of congenital anomalies and developmental delays in communities near industries and other environmental hazards provide sound evidence for the gendered health effects of contamination and pollution. A study conducted by Caitlin E. Holtby, Judith R. Guernsey, Alexander C. Allen, John A. VanLeeuwen, Victoria M. Allen, and Robert J. Gordon (2014) used province-wide, population-based birth registry data to examine the association between nitrate concentrations in drinking water and incidence of major congenital anomalies in Kings County, Nova Scotia. They found an increased risk of congenital anomalies for nitrate exposure of 1.5–5.56 mg/L (2.44; 1.05–5.66) and a trend toward increased risk for >5.56 mg/L (2.25; 0.92–5.52). These results suggest that nitrate exposure through drinking water may contribute to increased risk of congenital anomalies at levels below the current Canadian maximum allowable concentration.

In their review of forty-one papers, Wahida Kihal-Talantikite, Denis Zmirou-Navier, Cindy Padilla, and Severine Deguen (2017) found that the following congenital malformations were associated with proximity to pollution sites: an excess risk of reproductive morbidity, including preterm births; low birth weights; small size for gestational age; and intrauterine growth restrictions. In addition, the authors found that women living close to industrial sites were at increased risk of giving birth to children with overall congenital malformations and specific congenital malformations, including neural tube defects and congenital heart defects. Abbey E. Poirier, Linda A. Dodds, Trevor J.B. Dummer, Daniel G.C. Rainham, Bryan Maguire, and Markey Johnson (2015) used a superior geostatistical method to show that adverse birth outcomes associated with increased neonatal morbidity and mortality, such as preterm births, small size for gestational age, and full-term low birth weights, are linked to even relatively low concentrations of certain pollutants in Halifax, Nova Scotia.

In a study conducted in Chemical Valley, Constanze A. MacKenzie, Ada Lockridge, and Margaret Keith (2005) found that the birth rate in the area had reached nearly 2:143, which is outside the range of normal. This statistical anomaly had only been seen previously in animal populations living in extremely polluted areas. In the period between 1993 and 2003, there was a significant decline in the proportion of live births of males, following relatively stable sex ratios from 1984 to 1992. The authors suggest that there may be a link between sex ratio, the proximity of petrochemical industries to Aamjiwnaang First Nation, and potential exposures to compounds — all of which warrant further assessment. The Reproductive Justice movement, which emerged in the late 1980s, was led by Indigenous women who felt they had no control over their reproductive choices (Hoover, Cook, Plain, Sanchez, Waghiyi, Miller, Dufault, Sislin, and Carpenter 2012). Reproductive justice refers to the right to have children or not, and to parent them in a healthy and safe environment. Since that time, the movement has been examining the ways in which environmental racism compromises women's reproductive rights, given that a woman's reproductive destiny is tied to the conditions of her community (Hoover et al. 2012; Scott et al. 2015).

In addition to studies indicating a link between environmental hazards and a number of congenital issues in babies, Vrijheid (2000) found that there is strong evidence to suggest a link between environmental hazards and learning problems. This issue was discussed by a resident of Eskasoni who shared his concerns about the relationship between environmental pollutants and high rates of autism in Mi'kmaw communities in Nova Scotia during a meeting the ENRICH Project held in 2013:

> There's a higher percentage of kids that are born in Nova Scotia that have autism. And then you can go around, you can go down the list and it is safe to say that a lot of these issues are directly linked with the way in which the environment is being compromised. (Waldron 2014a)

As this statement indicates, a woman's exposure to toxic chemicals while pregnant will pose risks to childhood development during pregnancy and postnatally.

As we move from the Reproductive Justice movement to environmental justice movements led by Indigenous and African Nova Scotian peoples in the following chapter, I would like to point out that it is primarily women who are taking the lead in struggles to combat environmental racism in their communities. Therefore, we need to consider both the impacts of chemical exposures *and* grassroots organizing and resistance activities on women's bodies, spirits, and souls.

Chapter 6

NARRATIVES OF RESISTANCE, MOBILIZING, AND ACTIVISM

The Fight against Environmental Racism in Nova Scotia

> Understanding marginality as position and place of resistance is crucial for oppressed, exploited, colonized people. If we only view the margin as a site marking despair, a deep nihilism penetrates in a destructive way the very ground of our being. It is there in that space of collective despair that one's creativity, one's imagination is at risk, there that one's mind is fully colonized, there that the freedom one longs for is lost. (hooks 1990: 150–51)

Real solutions to environmental racism in Nova Scotia and Canada lie in a transformative agenda premised on anticolonial and anticapitalist environmental organizing where the goal is to build collective power. For Indigenous peoples, resistance has centred mainly on land dispossession or being denied access to land, resource exploitation of Indigenous lands, the legacy of residential schools, and the extinguishment of their rights. The cumulative impacts of these injustices have resulted in Indigenous peoples' historical trauma, cultural dislocation, and psychological, physical, and financial dependency on the state. Anticolonial resistance in Indigenous communities has involved a demand for self-determination and sovereign independence, as well as a reconstituted partnership with the Crown (Veracini 2011).

Resistance is about grounding theories in liberatory struggles of Indigenous, Black, and other racialized peoples, as well as disrupting the colonial conditions that dehumanize them. It is also important to interrogate how deeply relations of power and privilege permeate and are embedded within white settler societies and institutions. Therefore, while borrowing from pioneering anticolonial scholars like Fanon (1963) and Albert Memmi (1965, 2003), I would like to call attention to the ways in which historical processes and relations of power shape present-day material realities of Indigenous and Black communities experiencing various forms of state-sanctioned racial and gendered violence. Memmi (2003: 50–51) makes explicit how these complex hierarchies of difference and their accompanying tensions underpin the relationship between the colonizer and the colonized:

> Having found profit either by choice or by chance, the colonizer has nevertheless not yet become aware of the historic role which will be his. He [sic] is lacking one step in understanding his new status; he must also understand the origin and significance of this profit. Actually, this is not long in coming. For how long could he fail to see the misery of the colonized and the relation of that misery to his own comfort? He realizes that this easy profit is so great only because it is wrested from others. In short, he finds two things in one: he discovers the existence of the colonizer as he discovers his own privilege.

Memmi (2003) describes the journey the colonizer must take to develop an understanding of how the privileges "he" enjoys are tied to the oppression experienced by the colonized. In other words, as I argued earlier in this book, colonizers demonstrate innocent forms of ignorance characterized by their lack of knowledge about how they benefit from white skin colour privilege (Mills 2007). It is only when they come into contact with the colonized are they able to comprehend their privilege in the context of the material disadvantages experienced by the colonized and, consequently, their complicity in oppressing the colonized. At the same time, colonized peoples will only engage in acts of resistance when they come to the realization that the material benefits enjoyed by the colonizer have been accrued at their expense.

At its core, anticolonial theory is one of liberation, which starts from a critical premise that solidarity can be realized through counter-hegemonic consciousness, acts of resistance, and, consequently, the transformative human agency of colonized peoples (Dei 2012). It is grounded in an oppositional politics that pushes toward a rereading, reimagining, and recentring of the counter-knowledges of colonized voices and that seek to amplify individual and collective experiences of resistance, opposition, and agency (Waldron 2002, 2010a, 2012). Central to anticolonial theorizing is a reassertion of Indigenous and traditional counter-knowledges, or ways of knowing, of Indigenous and African peoples, and the de-centring, subverting, and disrupting of "normative" Euro-Western narratives embedded in virtually every social institution. Freire, in *Pedagogy of the Oppressed* (2000: 39), describes transformation in this way:

The more radical the person is, the more fully he or she enters into reality so that, knowing it better, he or she can transform it. This individual is not afraid to confront, to listen, to see the world unveiled. This person is not afraid to meet the people or to enter into a dialogue with them. This person does not consider himself or herself the proprietor of history or of all people, or the liberator of the oppressed; but he or she does commit himself or herself, within history, to fight at their side.

Henry Giroux (1983) defines the concept of resistance in three main ways. First, he argues that intentionality and consciousness must be central to understandings of and responses to domination. His conceptualization of human agency as possessing a dialectal character suggests that resistance and domination cannot function independent of one another and need each other for their successful operation. Second, he argues that the dominant group does not have exclusive access to power and that colonized people, despite their subordinate position, have the capacity to engage in transformative actions that destabilize and rupture hegemonic systems. Finally, Giroux points out that resistance must involve support for other liberatory struggles focused on transforming oppressive social structures. However, change can only be realized when community members are incited to action, as one Mi'kmaw community member from Eskasoni asserted during a meeting the ENRICH Project held in 2013:

I'm sure that the actions that the people take for their communities, with the governments that are in place, the changes will not matter if the government doesn't care. Somehow, they have to make them care ... So, through the education process, and radical changes in community development and how the community looks and, you know, in terms of the effects of electricity, radiation, and other stuff, clean water, and if people don't want it, then it's not going to happen. If people don't do something about it, it's not going to happen. So, some sort of action, something has to be done in individuals, it has to start somewhere. So, I think that through education programs and with the knowledge of research and professional people, they understand the effects of what we do. (Waldron 2014a)

His assertion that "something has to be done in individuals" speaks to the central role decolonization plays in a transformative agenda.

For example, Freire (2000) observes that decolonization is premised on colonized people's resistance to colonial structures, as well as liberation from internalized negative stereotypes they hold about their own history, culture, and traditions. Several other scholars (Dei and Asgharzadeh 2001; Fanon 1963; Waziyatawin and Yellow Bird 2012) argue that resistance calls for a deep engagement with how colonization has impacted the minds of colonized people. Michael Yellow Bird's Conceptual Model of Decolonization (Waziyatawin and Yellow Bird 2012) describes decolonization as both an event and a process. Decolonization as an event refers to colonized people's level of critical consciousness and acknowledgement about the ways in which colonization leads colonized people to engage in limited, destructive, and externally controlled responses to life circumstances. Decolonization as a process describes colonized people's participation in activities where creating, restoring, and birthing are central. Creating involves the conscious use of strategies to liberate oneself from, adapt to, and survive oppressive circumstances. Restoring focuses on reclamation of cultural practices, beliefs, and values that were taken away or abandoned, but which are necessary for the survival of Indigenous, Black, and other racialized peoples. Finally, birthing describes the creation of new ideas, thinking, technologies, and lifestyles for the purpose of empowering and advancing colonized people. Decolonization must also lead to progress that involves some kind of societal transformation that is driven by colonized people's efforts to destabilize inequities in power, income, and status. Indigenous, Black, and other racialized peoples are more likely to participate in social movements when their social and economic conditions begin to worsen and their desire for gaining access to valued goods and resources are not met. Participation in social movements is often perceived as an alternative course of action for individuals looking to maximize their utility (Chowning Davies 1971; Gurr 1970). However, moving from ideology to action must be accompanied by a willingness to support the ongoing work of communities, as one Mi'kmaw community member in Eskasoni pointed out during a meeting the ENRICH Project held in 2013:

> By supporting the actions of some of our people that are doing it, whether you're a trapper, whether you're an environmentalist, whether you're an educator, is to be able to be given the opportunity of integrating into their work plans of who they are as Mi'kmaq, because if that integration does not happen, then we're only capable of this philosophical level and not moving to the practical application. (Waldron 2014a)

While there will always be a role for protest and agitation in addressing social injustices, they mean very little if they do not accompany the building of something constructive and sustainable. I have witnessed many social justice initiatives in Nova Scotia eventually flicker out because those in leadership did not want to or know how to do the hard work that is required to sustain the project over the long haul, or because they were not backed up by any strategic action or plan once the initial protest was over. In the end, social justice work is a marathon, not a sprint.

MI'KMAW AND AFRICAN NOVA SCOTIAN COMMUNITIES ON THE FRONTLINES

The most significant challenge Indigenous and Black communities face in addressing environmental racism is the absence of legal tools that acknowledge, respond to, and address the entrenched colonialism, capitalism, and patriarchy embedded within environmental racism and other forms of environmental violence. For many Indigenous and Black peoples, environmental racism can only be effectively addressed by laws that acknowledge and act on the intersecting crisis in their communities: environmental violence on the land and environmental violence on the body. Within Indigenous worldviews, this holistic understanding of violence highlights the inherent contradictions between the law imposed by settler-colonial nations and Indigenous beliefs about the need to respond not simply to violence upon the land, but also the full web of inequalities that inflict violence on the bodies and communities of Indigenous peoples (Konsmo and Kahealani Pacheco 2015).

Transformative resurgence that aims to create more options for justice can only be realized when the laws created within settler-colonial nations begin to acknowledge, enable, and support Indigenous sovereignty and self-determination, value community-based organizing focused on healing in Indigenous and Black communities, recognize Indigenous knowledge as a transformative site for responding to various forms of state-sanctioned violence, and honour female and youth-led, solutions-oriented, grassroots resistance (Konsmo and Kahealani Pacheco 2015).

Idle No More

Idle No More is a grassroots political movement initiated by four women activists in Saskatchewan that is committed to resistance and mobilization of all people against all forms of neocolonialism in Canada, including Indigenous collective rights, sovereignty, social safety nets, and environmental protections. Idle No More's main objectives are to affirm Indigenous rights to sovereignty and to reintroduce traditional laws and nation-to-nation relations. The movement began on Facebook and evolved to peaceful street protests, teach-ins, and rallies.

Idle No More is specifically demanding that Canada, the provinces, and the territories repeal provisions of Bill C-45 (*Jobs and Growth Act*), as well as a number of other bills. Bill C-45 has lowered the protective threshold of reserve land "surrenders" and dropped the number of protected waterways from 2.8 million to less than one hundred. Idle No More is also demanding that Canada, the provinces, and the territories commit to the following: deepen democracy in Canada by ensuring that there is proportional representation of and consultation with Indigenous peoples on legislation related to collective rights and environmental protections; recognize Indigenous peoples' right to oppose development on their territory; recognize Indigenous title and rights, including the inherent Indigenous right to land or a territory, as well as the collective rights of Indigenous peoples that flow from their continued use and occupation of certain areas; officially revoke the racist Doctrine of Discovery and the doctrine of terra nullius, both of which have been used to justify the exploitation of Indigenous lands for profit; and help combat violence against women, including holding a national inquiry into missing and murdered Indigenous women in collaboration with Indigenous women (Idle No More n.d.).

In eastern Canada, the movement has been focused on empowering youth through treaty education. Demonstrations on the East Coast have included the 2013 hunger strike to halt treaty negotiations until communities were educated on what exactly is at stake when their leadership and the government make agreements, the march to Citadel Hill in Halifax, and the anti-fracking protest in New Brunswick, among others (McMillan, Young, and Peters 2013). The East Coast movement has received support from and partnered with groups such as Solidarity Halifax, the Council of Canadians, Clean Nova Scotia, NSPIRG, Federation of Labour Unions, and Dalhousie Student Union.

Idle No More also seeks to ensure that free, prior, and informed consent is no longer denied to Indigenous peoples. It does so by educating Indigenous peoples about their right to participate in decision-making processes and engendering in Indigenous youth an ongoing commitment to defend and protect Indigenous rights and govern future sustainable resource management (McMillan, Young, and Peters 2013).

Pictou Landing First Nation: Boat Harbour

Idle No More has been at the forefront of mobilizing efforts with community members in Pictou Landing First Nation to have an effluent spill at the Northern Pulp mill near Indian Cross Point cleaned up. Pictou Landing First

Nation, which has been actively opposing the treatment facility from which effluent has been flowing into Boat Harbour for decades, began action against the federal government for breach of fiduciary duty in 1986. The federal government negotiated a settlement with the community in 1991, promising to minimize the negative effects of the waste water when the Scott Maritimes Limited Agreement expired in 1995. Although an agreement with the federal government was reached out of court in 1993, the government failed to identify an alternative site when that agreement expired. When the government failed to keep its promise to close Boat Harbour by December 2005 and transferred mill ownership to Neenah Paper in 2004, the Band Council Chief informed the province in 2008 that they would not agree to further extensions. When meetings and other requests by the Band did not result in a commitment by government, the Band filed a lawsuit against the province and Northern Pulp in 2010 (Brannen 2014; Idle No More 2014; Thomas-Muller 2014).

After inquiries made by Chief Andrea Paul about how the province and Northern Pulp planned to clean up the spill were ignored, she and her First Nation government ordered a blockade of the road leading to the site of the effluent leak from Northern Pulp mill on June 11, 2014. This peaceful protest sought a commitment from the province to provide firm deadlines for identifying a more appropriate location for Northern Pulp's effluent, and for the remediation of Boat Harbour by June 2015. The Band dismantled its peaceful protest after an agreement was eventually signed by Chief Andrea Paul and Minister of Environment Randy Delorey to shut down the Boat Harbour treatment facility by 2020 (Brannen 2014; Idle No More 2014; Thomas-Muller 2014).

Sipekne'katik First Nation and Millbrook First Nation: Alton Natural Gas Storage Project

Over the last few years since the Alton Natural Gas Storage project was announced, First Nation Bands Sipekne'katik and Millbrook, along with non-Indigenous allies and organizations, have engaged in a number of activities to halt the Alton Natural Gas Storage project, including highway blockades, development site encampment, and educational events. During that time, the Treaty Truck House Against Alton Gas has become a gathering point for grassroots resistance activities against Alton Gas. Led by Elder Dorene Bernard, the Truck House (and its associated Facebook page) has become the site where planning activities have been initiated to fight against the Alton Gas project, where funds are raised to support the Truck House, and where educational activities are implemented to educate and inform the public on ecological, anticolonial, and anticapitalist issues.

In January 2016, the province approved the application submitted by Alton Gas to store natural gas in three underground salt caverns near Stewiacke, Nova Scotia. Later that month, the local First Nation Bands sent a letter to Premier Stephen McNeil, Energy Minister Michel Samson, and new Environment Minister Margaret Miller requesting that they suspend further approvals and provide up-to-date evaluations, research, and cumulative risk assessments. A number of groups and organizations supported these demands, including the Council of Canadians, EAC, the Atlantic chapter of the Sierra Club Foundation, the Nova Scotia Fracking Research and Action Coalition, the Canadian Youth Climate Coalition, and Divest Dalhousie (Corfu 2016; Hubley 2016).

The Shubenacadie River Commercial Fishermen's Association and EAC are among several groups and organizations working in solidarity with Sipekne'katik and Millbrook, who submitted appeals to the provincial government in February 2016 to halt the development of the brine release site. These groups and organizations contend that Alton Gas failed to provide adequate research or consider the impacts of the project on local fish populations and groundwater sources, and that the province has not engaged in meaningful consultation with the community (Corfu 2016; Hubley 2016). On April 14, 2016, members of the Sipekne'katik First Nation held a protest against the project in front of the Nova Scotia Legislature (Corfu 2016; Hubley 2016). A number of other protests followed, including a demonstration on May 28, 2016 that caused traffic delays on Highway 102 near Stewiacke.

In early 2017, the Sipekne'katik First Nation won a court decision against the province and the operators of Alton Natural Gas after Justice Suzanne Hood of the Nova Scotia Supreme Court ruled that the province's decision to reject complaints about the storage proposal was unfair (Rhodes 2017). This was followed by a decision in September 2017 that ordered the Nova Scotia Government to pay most of a $75,000 judgment to the Sipekne'katik First Nation over plans to implement the project. In a supplementary decision, Hood ruled that Sipekne'katik should be reimbursed for the court fight, arguing that the $75,000 represents about half of what Sipekne'katik First Nation spent to mount its court challenge and that the province is liable for 65 percent of that amount. She also ordered that the remaining 35 percent be paid by Alton Natural Gas Storage (Rhodes 2017). Alton Gas plans to move forward on the project, however, and hopes to start the brining process in 2021. The company has also been in touch with local authorities and provincial officials to discuss the ongoing protest, which they will continue to assess. They are also open to a discussion with protesters and have been talking to members of Sipekne'katik First Nation about a possible benefits agreement (Corfu 2017).

Indigenous Communities across Canada: Energy East Pipeline

Before the $15.7 billion proposed Energy East Pipeline was cancelled in October 2017, Indigenous peoples in Nova Scotia and across Canada had been partnering with various groups and organizations to resist TransCanada's plans to move 1.1 million barrels of crude per day, including crude from tar sands. The pipeline, which was first proposed by TransCanada in 2013, was expected to lead to massive tanker exports of western crude to eastern coastal waters and the profitable markets of Europe, India, China, and the United States. The proposed pipeline was to run through the lands of more than fifty First Nation communities without their consent. Using grassroots organizing strategies, campaigns, education, activism, and non-violent direct action, Indigenous communities, organizations like EAC and the Council of Canadians, and other allies across Canada pressured the Canadian government to develop strong policies that focus on renewable and sustainable energy solutions and that protect land, air, and water.

There was considerable surprise and relief by many when it was announced in the media in early October 2017 that the project had been cancelled. While oil prices neared $100 a barrel when the project was first proposed, it faced challenges as economics changed and regulatory and environmental hurdles began to pile up (Evans 2017; Healing 2017; MacKay 2017). The decision came a month after TransCanada asked the National Energy Board to put regulatory hearings on hold (Healing 2017). Feeling vindicated, Grand Chief Serge Simon of the Mohawk Council of Kanesatake stated, "Both the Northern Gateway fight and this Energy East one show that when First Nations stand together, supported by non-Indigenous allies, we win" (Evans 2017).

Africville Genealogy Society: Africville

Following the forced relocation of Africville residents to Uniacke Square and other parts of the province, the daily stresses of everyday life made it very difficult for residents to focus on compensatory efforts. The Halifax Human Rights Advisory Committee was established to improve access to employment and high-quality housing by advancing human rights legislation. Unfortunately, plans were already underway to remove residents, and arrangements for compensation had commenced without community consultation (Fryzuk

1996; Halifax Regional Municipality n.d.; Tavlin 2013). Residents formed the Africville Action Committee in 1969 to seek redress and to keep the community alive. In 1983, the Africville Genealogy Society was formed for the same purpose (Historica Canada n.d.c). Throughout the 1990s, the Africville Genealogy Society put pressure on City Hall to renegotiate with residents for compensation and other requests, including the employment of former Africville residents in Seaview Park and compensation to individuals who were not adequately paid for their homes. In 1996, after failed negotiation attempts, the Africville Genealogy Society launched a lawsuit against the City of Halifax, requesting compensation for the current value of their lands.

Fourteen years later, in 2010, former Halifax Mayor Peter Kelly apologized to the former residents of Africville. This apology was supported by the allocation of land and $3 million for the construction of the Seaview African United Baptist Church in 2011, a replica of the church that had been located in Africville. There was a split in the community over the final settlement, however, with the Africville Genealogy Society in favour of it and other individuals and groups representing residents or descendants of Africville not in favour. Those not in favour believed that the political decision-making process that led to the settlement deal was discriminatory because its early stages failed to promote public participation of those directly affected by the final decision (Halifax Regional Municipality n.d.; Nelson 2001; Tavlin 2013).

Twenty years after the statement of claim was filed against the City of Halifax (which is now part of an amalgamated municipality), the suit was revived in 2016. In November 2016, over forty former residents showed up at Nova Scotia Supreme Court in Halifax to hear lawyers argue the case to see if it would be certified as a class-action lawsuit. The lawyer representing the plaintiffs was seeking compensation for their community, since they had never received compensation for the loss of their community (Borden Colley 2016).

In late January 2018, I sent an email to CBC *Nova Scotia* journalist Sherri Borden Colley to find out if a decision has been made on the case, as she had written about it. In her email response to me, she indicated that she receives Nova Scotia court decisions daily and also checks in periodically with the lawyers for both the City and the former residents, as well as with the judge's office. According to Borden Colley, neither an oral nor a written decision has been rendered on the case.

Lincolnville Reserve Land Voice Council: The Second-generation Landfill

Lincolnville community members have long voiced their concerns about the "unhealthy" or environmentally hazardous methods used to handle waste at the first-generation landfill. According to community members, dangerous items and substances were thrown into the landfill at that time, including dead horses and other animals, transformers that leaked PCBs into the ground, and over fifteen thousand bags of industrial waste associated with beach cleanups. There was little concern at the time about wildlife, since the landfill was small and collected waste only from the Guysborough region. That would change when the first-generation landfill was replaced by the second-generation landfill.

In 2006, the Concerned Citizens of Lincolnville (now renamed the Lincolnville Reserve Land Voice Council) was formed to oppose the opening of the second-generation landfill. The community alleges that the Municipality of Guysborough improperly consulted them about this development. When the Concerned Citizens finally met with the municipality, they discussed their desire to be compensated for the economic fallout from the landfill site, as well as the impact of the landfill on the community's health. They insisted that they receive a portion of the revenue if the landfill remained in their community. After persistent lobbying and a letter to the Minister of Environment, community members received a survey from the municipality asking the community if they were willing to pay for a water well treatment and storage facility in Lincolnville. Not surprisingly, community members responded that they should not have to front the capital costs for cleanup efforts associated with someone else's garbage from a landfill they never wanted (Benjamin 2008). As one Lincolnville community member explained in the study the ENRICH Project held on environmental health issues in African Nova Scotian communities, her community has been organizing protests and demonstrations to force the government to remove the landfill since the early 1970s, despite intimidation from the police:

> We've had marches. We had the standoff at the dump and a march in Halifax in 2006. We had all kinds of protests about this. And we protested in 1974 when they started just dumping the stuff in a hole. We had a big protest. The police were called on us and all that. I don't know how many times the police were called and how many demonstrations I've been to where the cops have been called on us just because we

were walking, saying, you know, "take your garbage somewhere else
and take the rats somewhere else." You know? (Waldron 2016)

The standoffs, marches, and other kinds of protests that have taken place
in Lincolnville over the years have been supported by organizations from
multiple sectors in the province. For example, the Save Lincolnville Coalition
— an alliance of community partners composed of social justice and environmental groups throughout Nova Scotia — assisted residents in mounting
the Save Lincolnville Campaign. These partners included former residents of
Lincolnville, as well as organizations such as Bound To Be Free, African Nova
Scotian Brotherhood, NSPIRG, African United Baptist Association, Halifax
Coalition Against Poverty, and Halifax-Central Education Committee. The
objective of this province-wide campaign was to expose and challenge institutionalized oppression in the province. The campaign also wanted to send
a message to municipal and provincial levels of government (including the
Guysborough Municipality and Natural Resources Canada) that they opposed
the landfill, and that it was a clear example of environmental racism (Save
Lincolnville Campaign n.d.).

The Save Lincolnville Coalition demanded the following: that the
Guysborough Municipality review alternative locations and commence the
closure and relocation of the landfill site; that the land be redeveloped and
recovered; that all municipal resource management programs and planned
waste management infrastructure in Nova Scotia be preceded by an inclusive
and transparent consultative process with all sectors of the community; that
full reparations and compensation be given for land displacement, health
costs, and environmental contamination; that public policy be grounded in
mutual respect and justice for all people; and that all people be guaranteed
universal protection against nuclear testing, extraction, production and
disposal of toxic/hazardous wastes and poisons, regardless of race or class
(Save Lincolnville Campaign n.d.). Despite the considerable mobilizing the
community has done over the last forty years, their requests continue to be
ignored, as one Lincolnville resident explains:

> Opposition and fight has been going on for some years. A lot of
> people come to the conclusion, you know, they're fed up with what
> they're being dished out by the councillor and the Municipality of
> Guysborough. And, it seems like they've reached their wit's end com-
> ing to the table and trying to hammer out some resolve to these here
> concerns that's coming out of the community regarding these toxic

waste facilities. And they say, "hey, you know, we're sick and tired of beating our heads against the wall with no results." And sooner or later, sometimes people feel defeated if they are not making any progress on an issue. Should they feel defeated? Yeah, they should feel defeated. Should they accept defeat? No, they shouldn't accept defeat. Should they take action and try to make change? Yes, they should take action and try to make change. What should they do? Well, we should organize and put somebody in the position to take the position as councillor that's going to give us a voice at the table. And yeah, we should start a letter writing campaign to our MLA and to our government that's in power to say "hey, you know, we have some concerns here and we need those concerns addressed." (Waldron 2016)

In 2016, some members of the community organized to support Mary Desmond (a member of the Lincolnville Reserve Land Voice Council) in her bid for a councillor seat in District Two, which includes the communities of Lincolnville, Sunnyville, and Upper Big Tracadie. Unfortunately, Desmond failed to top Sheila Pelly, who was first elected in 2004.

The Prestons and East Lake: The East Lake Landfill

There were similarities between the Africville and East Lake cases. Preston and East Lake residents filed a complaint with the Nova Scotia Human Rights Commission against the Metropolitan Authority, Nova Scotia Environment, and the Provincial Government after the announcement by the Metropolitan Authority that East Lake was selected as the site for a landfill. The community alleged that the decision to site a landfill in East Lake was a clear example of environmental racism. A second human rights complaint was launched by the Shelburne County Cultural Awareness Society to oppose the location of a landfill in Birchtown. After EAC, the African United Baptist Association, the Lawrencetown Citizens Committee, Porters Lake and Myra Road Residents Against Site H Association, and the Lake Echo-Mineville Group Opposed to Site H joined the African Nova Scotian community's protest and growing community mobilization, the Metropolitan Authority voted to reverse their decision and removed East Lake from the list of potential sites for the landfill (Fryzuk 1996).

In addition to preventing the siting of the landfill near the community, the East Lake campaign united the entire community through strong political leadership. Despite these efforts, a toxic waste disposal site was eventually located near the community centre. According to an East Preston resident who participated in a study the ENRICH Project conducted, environmental racism and other community issues can only be addressed if residents develop the same sense of community they had in the past:

> We need to sit down and do a focus group. And you know, years ago, that was one thing we talked about — our community, we did a lot of work at the church. People would sit around at the table. After they'd go to church on Sunday night, they would sit around the table with a coffee and sit down and discuss things to get things moving.... But we have to start doing that stuff within our community. And we need to bring people together that care. Like you said, not self-motivated but we need to bring back that piece in the community about community. What is community? That's what we're lacking. (Waldron 2016)

This resident's assertion about the importance of bringing the community together and cultivating a stronger community voice was echoed by North Preston residents in that same study.

For example, a resident in North Preston discussed how important it is for her community to become more assertive and proactive in getting the government's attention and addressing various environmental concerns:

> The politicians will only respond to the community if there's some sort of mutiny. Because the community marches or they cause a riot or if they block off the road. But then you'll get public attention. The politicians really do not have the interest of the community at heart. The politician might not have money in their funds *per se,* but they have access to whatever funds that the government has, if they are willing to make the community's issues their priorities. But they're not. (Waldron 2016)

Another North Preston resident in the study shared a similar sentiment, arguing that it is time for community members to take back their community:

> So, if there's three people in the community who do read the paper and who are online, one person who's online, we need to make sure that everybody is aware of what's happening. And stop just sitting around our roundtables and discussing this stuff as opposed to inviting everybody into what's going on. Have more community meetings. Like get back to our Ratepayers Association [refers to the North Preston Ratepayers Association, which is an organization that advocates on

behalf of the community on matters relevant to the community, such as housing and land] and have our monthly meetings so that we can know what's happening and what's going on. Get people more actively involved and take back our own community. Like be more proactive in what's happening and what's going on instead of reactive to everything that is just forced down our throats. (Waldron 2016)

The importance of being proactive, rather than reactive was not lost on a group of concerned citizens residing in East Preston, Porters Lake, Lake Echo, and Mineville who came together in 2015 to initiate the Dump the Dump Campaign.

This campaign was opposing the application submitted to the City by Kiann Management Limited to rezone the 14.7-acre portion of the property on the north side of Highway 7, west of Parker Lane in Porters Lake. Residents had learned that there was a plan in place to relocate this construction and demolition materials processing facility, or dump, to a parcel of Crown land near the African Nova Scotian community of East Preston (Waldron 2016). There was a general sentiment in the African Nova Scotian community in East Preston that the decision to relocate the dump in their community was made to squelch the uproar from the largely white communities of Porters Lake, Lake Echo, and Mineville. A community member in East Preston discussed efforts in her community to halt the relocation of the dump:

I know there's a movement out here, they're trying to put that construction debris site out here in Porters Lake, which is in our proximity. And that's what's happening now. And, there's communities combined to try to stop that. (Waldron 2016)

Kiann Management Limited's plan to relocate the dump near East Preston eventually failed, however, when area residents and the East Preston Ratepayers Community Development Association contacted local, provincial, and municipal representatives about their concerns.

Lucasville Community Association: Memento Farm

Over the last fourteen years, the African Nova Scotian community of Lucasville has been dealing with the smell of manure, manure runoff, dust, increased traffic, noise, and rats from Memento Farm, a large commercial equestrian farm in the community. The Lucasville Community Association has been leading the fight to get the farm to leave the community and to preserve the 200-year-old

African Nova Scotian community. Several years ago, residents discovered that the farm was offering riding lessons and equestrian events illegally and was, therefore, not compliant with zoning for the area. Although the farm eventually stopped offering these lessons and events, it continues to board horses. Residents remain concerned that the development department has yet to address the smell, dust, and manure runoff. A petition was circulated in the community and a number of community meetings held after City Hall failed to address these issues.

Community members are also concerned about the failure of the owners of Memento Farm to consult them when the farm was built, as well as with the fact that government officials have continued to ignore their concerns. They see similarities between their situation and the experiences of African Nova Scotians in the North End of Halifax, fearing that their community will also be squeezed out by big business development (Devet 2015a, 2015b, 2016). Similar to other African Nova Scotian communities, actions taken by Lucasville residents to address the farm have been to no avail, as one community member discussed in a study the ENRICH Project conducted on environmental health issues in African Nova Scotian communities:

> Well, in the beginning when they [Memento Farm] first went there, my first call was to the municipality, telling them that they should have never let these people go in behind me without contacting me first to see how I felt about it. And I told them then "if I see any rats running on my property, you guys are going to have a big problem because I am scared to death of them." And I also called the Department of Environment. I called the Department of Agriculture. I contacted Clean Nova Scotia. I talked to so many people, to no avail. No answer, nothing. And I was even told at one time that if I didn't like the smell there that I should move. I don't see why I should move. I was born here. I was raised here. This is my homestead. (Waldron 2016)

Lucasville residents have also tried to address the issue as a collective, with few results, according to another community member who participated in the study:

> We did a petition in our community. We had over 150 signatures, if not more. And our councillor and I guess the MLAs, they didn't hear us at a community meeting at all. They just went and did what they felt as though they had to. But, they didn't listen to the people

of the community. They didn't come out and talk with the people of the community. But yet, we went to a meeting they had down in Sackville about this issue with Memento Farm. And they listened to a number of people not only in the community, outside the community — advocates for Black communities. And they just went straight ahead and did what they wanted to do. And when we found out, it was months later. Months later, we found out that they had granted them some grandfather status, or they gave them what they were looking for. And that's part of the problem we have in our Black community. (Waldron 2016)

As these two statements from African Nova Scotian residents in Lucasville indicate, actions taken by marginalized communities to have the government address their concerns often get ignored, because Black and Indigenous communities often lack the kind of political power required to resist the siting of industrial polluters in their communities.

Truro: Flooding and the Dump

The Marsh, one of three communities in Truro where African Nova Scotian people reside, has experienced issues with flooding. This led to community members moving into rental housing because they were unable to afford to repair their homes, and because they were ineligible for flood insurance. Community members residing on the Island also have concerns about flooding, as well as the health risks associated with a nearby dump, as do those who live on the Hill. Despite these ongoing concerns, community members have had little success getting the government to address these issues, according to one community member who participated in an ENRICH Project study:

Every year I try to address the flood with government. And even to the town representatives. And it gets back with trying — "We're trying." That's been going on for over sixty years. And the big problem with that is we have no political clout. We have no political organizations in our community. But if we had an organization speaking on behalf of the communities, that would have a lot more clout. (Waldron 2016)

This sentiment not only reflects an ongoing pattern by Nova Scotia Environment in addressing environmental concerns in African Nova Scotian and Indigenous communities; it also highlights how important it is for community members to cultivate a stronger community voice, become more involved in boards and commissions that make decisions about where industries are placed, and become more engaged in the political process.

In August 2015, African Nova Scotian community members in Truro organized a conference to address their community's ongoing failure to work together in addressing the many issues affecting their community. They have long been concerned that the lack of African Nova Scotian representation on various boards and commissions in Truro, as well as their community's lack of involvement in the political process, make it difficult for their voices to be heard or to impact policy decisions. As one community member pointed out in an ENRICH Project study, encouraging more community involvement by African Nova Scotians in Truro is important if the community wants to have more of a voice in the issues facing them:

> I'd just like to see the people in our community get more involved with each other. Like, there's three Black communities, and we don't have any communication. And if we all got together then it would be a bigger voice. And, you know, I visit all communities. I can recall coming down there and helping the people in the floods. To help them and the older people. It was appreciated. People from the Hill, I always got along with people from the Hill. But, it just seems like something's got to happen in the community, like a death or something, before we can get together and be all on one accord. (Waldron 2016)

This resident highlights how difficult it is to address long-standing environmental concerns when community cohesiveness has eroded over the years. It is only when community members come together as an empowered entity with shared goals and objectives that it will be possible for them to advocate on their own behalf through community mobilizing and consistent government pressure.

South End Environmental Injustice Society: The Morvan Road Landfill

Shelburne provides an excellent case study of how "grassroots" activism can effectively address environmental racism. Shelburne is a town located in southwestern Nova Scotia, settled by Loyalists in the late 1700s. This town became one of the largest Black settlements in North America at the time and remains a prominent African Nova Scotian community today (Nova Scotia Museum n.d.; Waldron 2016). Shelburne's south end, which is home to the majority of African Nova Scotian residents in the area, is currently the only area in Shelburne without access to the town's drinking water supply (Waldron, 2016).

For the past several decades, the Morvan Road landfill (commonly referred to as the Shelburne Town Dump by residents) has been located within the boundaries of the Town of Shelburne on Morvan Road on the southeastern outskirts of the town, where the largest concentration of African Nova Scotian residents has lived for decades (Waldron 2016). At the end of 2015, I hired community leader Louise Delisle to facilitate two focus groups with members of her community to discuss their perspectives on the landfill's impact on the community's health and well-being over the years. Following these focus groups and a meeting the ENRICH Project held with the community in late April 2016, several members of the community banded together to form the South End Environmental Injustice Society (SEED), a non-profit organization.

Although factual and accurate information is not currently available about the type and quantity of waste deposits made at the landfill over the years or about the background to its establishment, anecdotal evidence provided by community members suggests that it accepted municipal and medical waste from the adjacent hospital, the community college, the former naval base, and the municipality's industrial park, with little record keeping or documentation (Waldron 2016). In recent decades the landfill had "officially" been more restricted, but with little supervision of day-to-day administration and control by the Town of Shelburne, which is responsible for the location and operation of the landfill. In recent years, the town had "reopened" the landfill, although it had failed to consult in any meaningful way with community members about this. Visual investigation conducted by community members, as well as photos taken by one community member in 2016 showed evidence of continued use of the landfill — for at least the past twenty years — as an uncontrolled, or poorly controlled, repository for assorted materials not intended for the facility.

Since forming, SEED has collaborated with concerned citizens in the community; the ENRICH Project; social, environmental, and health organizations; and federal, provincial, and municipal governments to ensure proper cleanup and closure of the landfill. In June 2016, Nova Scotia Environment conducted an inspection of the landfill and found a number of environmental concerns, including a recent oil spill. This prompted them to issue an inspector's directive that the Shelburne Town Council was required to address. Nova Scotia Environment also hired engineers from the private sector to follow up and independently investigate the site. The landfill was finally closed in late 2016 (Waldron 2016). Since 2016, SEED has also been pursuing a collaboration with the town to initiate the following activities: establish a reliable database on the relationship between the landfill and its socioeconomic, health, and environmental effects; implement a plan for environmental, health, and community infrastructure and associated remedial issues; and identify potential federal and provincial funding sources for the necessary remedial work required. SEED also plans to carry out the following activities in collaboration with the ENRICH Project and various other partners: document the chronological development of the landfill, its use, and its administration, as well as results from any previous testing undertaken; conduct soil and water testing to identify which pollutants from the landfill community members have been exposed to; conduct a study on the ongoing health impacts of the landfill in the African Nova Scotian community, including cancer rates; seek compensation for residents who have contracted cancer over the last several decades; address mould in homes; and investigate the economic impacts of the landfill on local property values in the past, present, and future (Waldron 2016).

The grassroots mobilizing efforts that Mi'kmaw and African Nova Scotian communities have initiated to transform their communities have been inspiring to me over the years. They reflect Freire's (2000: 36) characterization of transformation in *Pedagogy of the Oppressed*:

> One of the gravest obstacles to the achievement of liberation is that oppressive reality absorbs those within it and thereby acts to submerge men's consciousness. Functionally, oppression is domesticating. To no longer be prey to its force, one must emerge from it and turn upon it. This can be done only by means of the praxis: reflection and action upon the world in order to transform it.

The long history of social and environmental justice struggles in Mi'kmaw and African Nova Scotian communities across the province have been premised on building collective power; communicating demands for self-determination and sovereign independence; and engaging in anticolonial, anticapitalist, and counter-hegemonic acts of resistance — including non-violent civil disobedience (blockades, marches, sit-ins) — to challenge historical and contemporary forms of possession, dispossession and other forms of state-sanctioned violence.

Struggles for social and environmental justice will only succeed, however, if they are accompanied by critical analysis that unpacks the larger socio-spatial processes of inequality that lead to possession and dispossession; they must also be grounded in theories that understand how environmental racism manifests within the context of colonialism, racial capitalism, patriarchy, neoliberalism, racialized and gendered forms of state-sanctioned violence, and other substantive and structural issues.

Conclusion

THE ROAD UP AHEAD

> Now, comrades. Now is the time to decide to change sides. We must
> shake off the great mantle of the night which has enveloped us, and
> reach for the light. The new day, which is dawning must find us deter-
> mined, enlightened and resolute. (Fanon 1963: 235)

As I left Province House on April 29, 2015 after witnessing Lenore Zann's
introduction of the *Environmental Racism Prevention Act* (Bill 111) (Nova
Scotia Legislature n.d.a), I was naively hopeful that the bill would become
legislation, and that the province would finally recognize and legitimize long-
standing concerns in Mi'kmaw and African Nova Scotian communities.

Unfortunately, a few weeks after the bill was introduced, my spirits were
dampened when Zann contacted me to let me know that she had heard through
the grapevine that the Liberal Party had no intention of putting the bill forward
to second reading during the spring 2015 sitting of the House. Disappointed,
but undaunted, I "gathered up the troops" and launched a coordinated and
strategic email-writing campaign in May 2015 to put pressure on members
of the House. Within the span of a few weeks, several hundred emails were
sent by members of the public to Premier Stephen McNeil, MLAs, and other
government officials across the province. It was to no avail, however, since the
bill failed to be put forward to second reading when the House finished sitting
a few weeks later. We would now have to wait until the fall to find out if acting
NDP Leader Maureen MacDonald would allow the bill to be put forward to
second reading and debated on the floor.

In the fall of 2015, I was again disappointed to learn from Zann that Bill 111
was not one of the bills MacDonald was planning to put forward for debate.
Recognizing that we needed to up the ante by taking a more aggressive approach
to ensuring that the bill would be debated, I scheduled a phone conversation
with MacDonald. During that phone conversation, I discussed not only the
importance of Bill 111 for addressing the long-standing concerns of community
members, but also emphasized that it would show the rest of Canada that Nova
Scotia was a leader in addressing environmental racism. While MacDonald

was gracious, listening attentively to my request, she explained that she had yet to decide which bills she would put forward and that other bills would, most likely, take precedence.

Concerned that I had not made any headway, the ENRICH Project team launched a second Bill 111 campaign on October 22, 2015. This was a more aggressive, multi-pronged, and multi-platform campaign whose purpose was to garner wider public and political support for the introduction of Bill 111 at second reading at the House of Assembly. The campaign involved the creation of a Bill 111 campaign page on the ENRICH Project website, where the Bill 111 campaign letter template, a video on the implications of white privilege for environmental racism, a filmed spoken-word piece on environmental racism, and an online petition were posted. Two student volunteers kept up the pressure by sending daily tweets to MacDonald, former environment minister Randy Delorey, Premier McNeil, and other government officials. Several volunteer students also initiated on-campus activities that included coordinated petition signings and class talks to mobilize students on campus. A few weeks later, we were all thrilled to learn that the team's efforts seemingly paid off when I received word from Zann on November 22 that MacDonald had selected Bill 111 to be put forward to second reading on November 25. Although I will never really know what precipitated MacDonald's change of heart, I would like to think that our campaign had something to do with it.

On November 25, all three parties debated the bill on the floor of the House, a historic event since no such bill had ever been debated — or even introduced — at the House of Assembly in Canada. Unfortunately, the bill failed to be put forward to the Law Amendments Committee, which gives clause-by-clause consideration and hears representations from any interested persons or organizations about the contents of referred public bills after they have received second reading in the House. This was a crushing blow to me, as well as to the team members and volunteers who had put so much effort into letter-writing campaigns, social media campaigns, student mobilizing on campus, and other activities. Although numerous people cautioned me about not expecting too much, since private members' bills rarely, if ever, pass into law, I had held out hope that our bill would be different. However, I am pleased to say that since November 25, 2015, the bill has been resurrected twice by the NDP, which reintroduced it on October 14, 2016 and on October 6, 2017. Although there's no telling what will come of Bill 111, I remain encouraged by the ongoing efforts made by the NDP to see the bill pass into law, as well as the attention it has given to environmental racism in the province and country.

On April 21, 2017, the ENRICH Project collaborated with the Nova Scotia Environmental Rights Working Group to launch another groundbreaking bill, the first provincial *Environmental Bill of Rights* (Nova Scotia Environmental Rights Working Group 2017), at a press conference in downtown Halifax. A few years earlier, in 2015, I had been invited to become a member of the working group to share the activities the ENRICH Project was involved in and to collaborate on a new, non-partisan *Nova Scotia Environmental Bill of Rights* with several environmental organizations, including the East Coast Environmental Law Association, the Blue Dot Movement, and EAC. The bill (Nova Scotia Environmental Rights Working Group 2017: 4) lays out the general purposes of the Act in the following way:

> (1) The General Purposes of this Act are:
> (a) To safeguard the rights of all present and future generations of Nova Scotians to a healthy and ecologically balanced environment by supporting and promoting the protection, enhancement and prudent use of the environment;
> (b) To protect the people of Nova Scotia from environmental hazards and guarantee that everyone living in Nova Scotia has a right to live and thrive in a healthy and ecologically balanced environment;
> (c) To address environmental racism that has disproportionately and negatively affected and continues to so affect historically marginalized, vulnerable or economically disadvantaged individuals, groups and communities, particularly Indigenous people and African Nova Scotians;
> (d) To confirm the Government's public trust duty to protect the environment; and
> (e) To protect, preserve and, where reasonable, restore the integrity of the environment by the means provided in this Act.

The failure to highlight the specific concerns of Mi'kmaw and African Nova Scotian communities disproportionately located near polluting industries is the main reason I was disappointed in the provincial *Environmental Bill of Rights* introduced by the NDP caucus a year earlier on May 5, 2016 (which had no relationship to Bill 111 or the *Nova Scotia Environmental Bill of Rights* developed by the Nova Scotia Environmental Rights Working Group). While the *Environmental Bill of Rights* "spells out the need to protect our environment, address climate change, and provide opportunities for meaningful consultation and public participation around environmental questions" (NDP 2016, n.p.), nowhere in the bill does it mention those communities most impacted by environmental hazards. While I recognize that the decision to omit any mention of race and Mi'kmaw and African Nova Scotian communities may have been based on the NDP's failure to get Bill 111 officially recognized as legislation throughout 2015, an approach that omits any mention of race or the concerns of those communities will do little to address the concerns of those most affected by environmental hazards. Regardless, the bill failed to move past its first reading. It was reintroduced in October 2017, this time with a stronger emphasis on the environmental issues affecting Mi'kmaw and African Nova Scotian communities.

Any environmental legislation concerned with the needs, priorities, and rights of Mi'kmaw and African Nova Scotian communities, whether it be Bill 111 or an *Environmental Bill of Rights*, should determine whether there is potential to enshrine into law clauses that hold Nova Scotia Environment accountable, and whether preventative steps can be taken to address environmental concerns in the communities most impacted by industry and other environmental hazards. It is also important to assess whether or not the proposed legislation will put in place built-in mechanisms to ensure that there are community-defined best practices around the siting of facilities.

Environmental legislation that speaks to the priorities of Indigenous and racialized communities in Nova Scotia and Canada must also bring increased awareness about and attention to environmental racism in Canada; recognize Indigenous treaty rights; review the ongoing environmental assessment process in collaboration with affected communities; and identify gaps in existing policies related to citizen engagement, community consultations, and other decision-making processes related to the location, monitoring, regulation, evaluation, and remediation of facilities and other environmental hazards.

A MULTI-PRONGED STRATEGY
FOR ADDRESSING ENVIRONMENTAL RACISM

Addressing environmental racism in Nova Scotia and Canada must involve a comprehensive, multi-pronged strategy designed to dismantle the underlying structural elements that drive and sustain it. This strategy must include the following: an environmental justice lens that unapologetically centres race and understands how it intersects with class, gender, and other social identities to shape the experiences of communities disproportionately impacted by a web of inequalities and environmentally hazardous industries; environmental policy that acknowledges and addresses structural and environmental determinants of health and culturally relevant participatory democracy approaches; partnerships between white-led environmental justice organizations and Indigenous and Black communities; and alliances and solidarities between Indigenous and Black communities.

Centring Race in an Environmental Justice Framework

It is important that policymakers, environmental organizations, activists, and others involved in environmental and social justice struggles acknowledge the central role that racism plays through the enduring impacts of colonialism and capitalism on the cultures, lands, and bodies of Indigenous and Black communities. A race analysis must be explicit in analyses of environmental concerns affecting these communities, as well as in decisions, policies, and strategies developed to promote more equitable distribution of industry. Reducing inequitable siting of polluting industries can't be achieved unless deliberate attention is paid to educating environmentalists and others about the systemic ways in which racist ideologies get written into environmental decision making and policy. In other words, antiracism initiatives must be connected to anti-capitalist struggles in the pursuit of a social system premised on equality and cooperation, rather than competition and hierarchical relationships based on race, colour, gender, and other social identities (Leong 2013).

Several factors can be attributed to a general reticence in the environmental movement to acknowledge and address the ways in which the movement has been complicit in environmental harms in Indigenous and Black communities. For example, many environmental organizations and activists lack education about or a critical understanding of how systemic racism shapes environmental decision making and policy in ways that harm already-vulnerable communities. They have a tendency to embrace a colourblind approach that fails to acknowledge the histories of struggle in Indigenous, Black, and other racialized communities and, consequently, may dismiss any notion of racism as an underlying factor in environmental decision making and policymaking. There is a perception by many in the movement that class inequalities, rather than race inequalities, are at the root of many of the barriers Indigenous and Black communities face. There is also a general unease or discomfort about discussing racism within the environmental movement, despite the fact that many of these individuals take an environmental justice approach to their work. Finally, many environmental organizations and activists lack the skills required to dismantle structural racism and other inequalities at the institutional and structural levels.

While many environmental organizations will argue that it is primarily the lack of financial and human resources that prevents them from taking on the "added" work of addressing racism and other inequalities, it is possible to take action on these issues without a lot of resources. This may include providing opportunities for ongoing conversations among staff or volunteers, as well as training about the implications of white privilege, white supremacy, and racism for organizational relationships, community building, workforce diversification, leadership development, and environmental policy. It may also involve the development of organizational policies, programs, and initiatives using available data on environmental racism and other types of state-sanctioned racial violence. Environmental organizations must also identify and develop relationships with broad and diverse networks of partners to leverage the necessary expertise and resources that can support them in addressing racism and other structural factors that drive and sustain environmental racism.

Environmental Policy: Addressing Structural and Environmental Determinants of Health

Environmental policy must begin to address, in a more forthright way, the cumulative health and mental health impacts of environmental racism. In doing so, it must acknowledge the complex web of inequalities that create greater biological susceptibility and social vulnerability and that, consequently, drive and sustain health disparities between white, Indigenous, and Black communities. As Morello-Frosch et al. (2011) observe, environmental policy has traditionally had a singular focus on pollutants, ignoring the social and economic inequalities that may render Indigenous and Black communities more vulnerable to the synergistic effects of social and environmental stressors on their health. Since Indigenous and Black communities often reside in racially segregated, low-income neighbourhoods with high rates of unemployment and underemployment, income insecurity, food insecurity, transportation barriers, and other social stressors, environmental policy must begin to pay more attention to the role that residential context plays in health disparities.

It is also important that health scholars contribute in more significant ways to a multi-level analysis of environmental health inequities that can inform research, environmental governance and policy, and advocacy in health promotion. For example, Jeffrey Masuda, Blake Poland, and Jamie Baxter (2010) explore ways in which health promotion and environmental justice can be combined into an integrated movement for environmental health justice in health promotion. Similarly, government health promotion policies and programs have not acknowledged some of the more salient environmental issues of our times and their impacts on our most vulnerable populations. They have not paid attention to the kinds of community knowledge and expertise that could improve the political legitimacy of conventional environmental knowledge. As Masuda, Poland, and Baxter observe, a commitment to healthy public policy and environmental racism within the environmental and health arenas, respectively, requires that those working in health and environment within academia, government, and community transcend sectoral and disciplinary boundaries.

Environmental assessments:
Incorporating a health equity impact assessment

As Roy E. Kwiatkowski, Constantine Tikhonov, Diane McClymont Peace, and Carrie Bourassa (2012) argue, impact assessments are not designed to consider the social, economic, environmental, and health issues facing Indigenous communities (or, for that matter, Black communities) because they are premised on western and scientific constructs and conceptualizations of the environment. Therefore, Indigenous methods of data collection and knowledge, as well as Indigenous conceptualizations of the environment that are premised on holism, are not acknowledged or validated in the environmental impact assessment process. One of the most important steps Nova Scotia Environment can take in addressing environmental racism in Mi'kmaw and African Nova Scotian communities — communities that are already experiencing greater vulnerability due to unemployment, poverty, poor-quality housing, and other structural determinants of health — is to incorporate a health equity impact assessment (HEIA) (Ontario Ministry of Health and Long Term Care 2012) into Nova Scotia's environmental assessment and approval process. HEIA is used to support improved health equity through the reduction of avoidable health disparities between communities. It is a tool to support decisions, which walks users through the steps for identifying how a program or policy will impact communities in different ways. The end goal is to maximize the positive impacts and reduce the negative impacts that could potentially widen health disparities between communities — in short, it supports more equitable delivery of programs, services, or policies (Harris-Roxas, P. Harris, E. Harris, and Kemp 2011).

Culturally relevant participatory democracy

Culturally relevant participatory democracy is also an important approach for addressing ways of knowing in Indigenous and Black communities and engaging these communities in environmental issues. Participatory democracy provides people with the education and competence to understand and communicate in the technical jargon often used by environmental professionals. If done in a culturally relevant way, it can provide Indigenous and Black communities with more opportunities and avenues for meaningful public participation and public consultation in decision-making processes related to environmental assessments and other environmental issues affecting their communities. In other words, it can ensure that the people most affected by these decisions are involved early on and throughout the process.

Participatory democracy may look different in Indigenous and Black communities, since there are constitutional differences between these and other communities in Canada as they relate to consultation and participation. While section 35 of the *Constitution Act* (Government of Canada 1982) sets out a legal requirement to consult with and accommodate Indigenous peoples where treaty rights or title interests are engaged, there is no such legal requirement for Black or other peoples in Canada. Despite this, African Nova Scotians have long demanded that they be consulted and involved in environmental decision making and policies that impact their community, as one North Preston resident points out in a study the ENRICH Project conducted on environmental health issues in African Nova Scotian communities:

> I'd like two things when it comes to government. I'd like for government to involve or invite every community to be a part of the major infrastructure. Let me give an example. If there's a committee that speaks directly to the premier and is the representation from around the province, well, then they need to send an invite to North Preston. So, they have a committee structure in terms of how to get people to sit on committees and so on. And they send them to people who have already been involved, people that they have a rapport with, and these people may not necessarily represent us. Okay? Send information to people that have been politically involved. Someone who has been highly involved with the NDP, well, when something comes down the pipe, they will let you know. The other thing is that I'd like for government to provide information upon which the community can have input. Like focus groups are good. But it's not the government that is doing the focus groups. It's more community-based organizations. But the government needs to have focus groups in the community in regards to whatever policies they're making. They need to have input from the community in terms of what they intend to do that affects them. And that would only come by recruiting people to sit

on committees and boards. Now, the way they do that is in the paper. There will be an invite. But then those people that are suggested, their names will be for a committee. If the committee doesn't like you, for example, you won't get approved. (Waldron 2016)

This statement reflects sentiments expressed to me over the years by Indigenous and African Nova Scotian communities that they have felt excluded from processes that would allow them to have a voice in decisions and policies that directly impact their community. They attribute this to the government's failure to reach out to their communities, as well as their communities' lack of involvement in the political process.

Following Roy E. Kwiatkowski et al. (2012) who assert that a pan-Indigenous approach to consultation is inadequate, I would also like to suggest that a "one size fits all" approach to the consultation process in Indigenous and Black communities is insufficient because it does not consider the distinct identities, beliefs, customs, and ways of knowing within each Indigenous Nation or Black community. Therefore, communication or engagement tools developed for consultation in these communities must be culturally specific and inclusive.

Building Coalitions and Solidarities for Environmental Justice Organizing

Collaborative partnerships

More reciprocal relationships and alliances must be forged between white-led environmental organizations and Indigenous and Black communities to address, in more serious ways, the lack of diverse and representative voices within their organizations. These organizations must learn to listen in a new way, unpack their biases, and engage in more strategic outreach initiatives that support environmental initiatives already underway in communities on the frontline of community-based struggles for environmental justice. They must also validate the unique histories, values, traditions, and epistemologies in these communities, as one Mi'kmaw Elder who participated in a meeting the ENRICH Project held in 2013 explained:

My greatest challenge of course is to convince the white people that we, the Mi'kmaw people, not only have something to say, but kind of raise a question in which people probably, in a humble way, ask themselves, you know, "what am I doing?" Because everything that I do onto her, our Mother Earth, I do unto myself. That, when are we going to be able to convey this message that if governments are anti-environmentalist, are anti-this, anti-that, because they're using the socioeconomic impact as a tool to justify the way things are going to be done? And let's look at what's happening in this part of the country, fracking, pipelines, etcetera ... that's just the tip of the iceberg. And what the government does is okay, they say "we're going to create x number of jobs." Now, how can anyone in any shape or form, justify that by saying okay, here's my uncle, my brother, my cousin who's going to work for this, but what am I doing, not only to the future generations, but what am I doing to lessen the chances of me surviving for whatever time I may have left because I don't have clean air, clean drinking water. That's the challenge I'm seeing. What must we say to get the majority of those white people on board? And I say a majority because I know a lot of nice and wonderful white people, but the majority, unfortunately, is on the same wavelength as the government and the industry. And that's a challenge. I think my challenge is, you know, how do we convey that message to the general population, that it is about time that we come together as one and say enough is enough? We're not going to allow you to desecrate Mother Earth, because by desecrating her, you're compromising my chances of survival. So, these are the challenges that I see and I applaud this project. (Waldron 2014a)

White-led environmental organizations must also become more proactive in collaborating with communities that are often perceived as "out of the way" or "off the map," according to a North Preston resident, who participated in the ENRICH Project's study on environmental health issues in African Nova Scotian communities:

I would like to see some of the groups that do work on this stuff like all the time, like the Ecology Action Centre, for example, or there's probably so many other environmental groups ... Like I'd like if they're government or funded by government, that they actually stretch to here. Because I don't think that they ... It's almost as if when it gets to Dartmouth or whatever, they stop. Like that's their geographic area. They don't always include Preston. But they may get money from the government to serve all of Halifax or HRM. But North Preston is often left out of that demographic. So, thinking about how they can actually expand who they're serving. (Waldron 2016)

The reality is that unless environmental organizations and groups make it a strategic priority to involve affected communities in decision-making activities, either as staff, board members, or in other ways, their efforts to represent these communities when they meet with government and other decision makers will remain disconnected from the real-life struggles and priorities facing those communities most impacted by environmentally hazardous activities.

Building bridges between Indigenous and Black communities

Even more important than forging alliances between affected communities and environmental organizations and groups are initiatives that seek to build bridges between Indigenous and Black communities in their struggles for social and environmental justice. We need to consider how these solidarities can centre on the shared and distinct experiences Indigenous and Black communities have around settler colonialism, white supremacy, patriarchy, racial capitalism, neoliberalism, and other injustices. At the same time, we must recognize that the unique ways in which each community experiences these issues can pose challenges to building solidarities for social, economic, political, and environmental justice. For example, one of the more significant factors that may deter Indigenous and Black communities from building alliances with each other, in my view, is the level of importance each community places on land versus racial inequalities. For Indigenous peoples, land has long been the more pressing issue, while racism the more important issue for Black peoples.

In Nova Scotia, efforts to become good allies of Mi'kmaq are led mainly by white people and white-led environmental organizations. Unfortunately, these same white allies often fail to consider the specific and unique ways in which African Nova Scotians are implicated in their work, judging by the dearth of collaborative projects and other initiatives between African Nova Scotian communities and white allies in the province. Therefore, to converge social justice struggles that are often isolated in Indigenous, Black, and other communities — to build solidarities — there must be greater efforts to create discursive spaces within which to think through how white supremacy, settler colonialism, racial capitalism, and other injustices structurally implicate Indigenous, Black, other racialized peoples, and white allies in each other's lives.

Such efforts call for a deeper engagement with how, for example, Indigenous concerns about land, underfunding of housing, education and the enduring impacts of residential schools, economic development, the epidemic of missing and murdered women, environmental racism, and health are not separate from the issues Black peoples and other racialized or marginalized communities

(LGBTQ+ communities, immigrants, Muslim communities, persons with disabilities) are also grappling with. However, when we endeavour to shed light on our commonalities, we must be prepared to consider our own complicity in each other's oppression, and how that complicity often serves to maintain the status quo.

FINAL WORDS

As the ENRICH Project moves forward to engage affected communities, the public, and environmental and other organizations in conversations this book has brought up, I would like to reflect on the many challenges, milestones, and successes the project has experienced over the past several years. While the project has been successful in engaging a diverse team composed of Mi'kmaw and African Nova Scotian community leaders, volunteers, environmental professionals, faculty, students and other individuals, considerably more work needs to be done building and sustaining collaborative relationships and partnerships with other Indigenous and Black communities that are on the frontlines of grassroots mobilizing efforts to address environmental struggles in Nova Scotia but often don't get attention.

One of the most important lessons I have learned over the past few years is that engaging marginalized communities requires a shift in thinking about how power, privilege, and equity are implicated in relationship building, partnerships, and research. For example, considerations about how researchers can work *with* rather than *for* or *on behalf of* communities must be premised on organic, trusting, collaborative, reciprocal, and equitable relationships with community members. This involves recognizing and respecting community members as experts in their own lives, ensuring that frontline communities are leading research, policy initiatives, and mobilizing efforts, and ensuring that these communities are involved at every stage of the research process — that they are full participants in the co-creation and dissemination of knowledge.

The ENRICH Project exemplifies the creative, innovative, timely, and culturally relevant ways in which research can be conducted, bringing together critical academic inquiry, the core principles and values of community-based research, and a creative mix of new technologies, media, and art. Most importantly, however, it seeks to support marginalized struggles for social and environmental justice in the province and, more broadly, in Canada. In closing, I would like to thank the community members who have shared their experiences with me and with whom I have been privileged to develop relationships over the past several years. These relationships have impressed upon me how crucial it is to conduct research that is grounded in and evolves out of the priorities, concerns, and needs of community members first and foremost. Moreover, I have come to a greater appreciation for how important it is to create spaces and opportunities for divergent voices to resonate throughout the project.

In moving forward, I hope to remain open, flexible, and accommodating to new ways of thinking about how the ENRICH Project can stay true to the core principles of community-based research, while continuing to interrogate and challenge research, policy actions, and activism that are rooted in colonial and white supremacist ideologies that perpetuate genocide.

Appendix A

SOCIAL MEDIA, MAPS, AND CASE STUDIES

The ENRICH Project website: <www.enrichproject.org>.

The ENRICH Project brochure: <http://www.enrichproject.org/wp-content/uploads/2017/03/ENRICH-Brochure-2017.pdf>.

The ENRICH Project Facebook page: <https://www.facebook.com/TheENRICH-Project/>.

The ENRICH Project Twitter page: <https://twitter.com/inwhosebackyard>.

The ENRICH Project map: <http://www.enrichproject.org/map/>.

Africville story map (created by Dalhousie Master of Planning Student Caitlin Hinton for use by the ENRICH Project): <https://dalspatial.maps.arcgis.com/apps/MapSeries/index.html?appid=8821561a4f2c44689bc02b172241883c>.

The ENRICH Project case study outline, published by National Collaborating Centre for the Determinants of Health <http://nccdh.ca/resources/entry/learning-from-practice-advocacy-for-health-equity-environmental-racism>.

Case study on the ENRICH Project, published by National Collaborating Centre for the Determinants of Health <http://nccdh.ca/images/uploads/comments/Learning_from_Practice_Advocacy_for_health_equity_Environmental_racism_EN_FV.pdf>.

Interactive Guide for the Lincolnville Water Monitoring Project: <http://www.enrichproject.org/wp-content/uploads/2013/12/Lincolnville-Interactive-PDF-for-Water-Monitoring-Project.pdf>.

Appendix B

AWARDS AND PRIZES

Advocate of the Year Award for 2015 for the ENRICH Project, Better Politics Award. Awarded by Springtide Collective, 2016.

Green Campaign of the Year Award, 6th Annual Greenie Awards, for *Time to Clear the Air: Art on Environmental Racism by Mi'kmaw and African Nova Scotian Youth*. Awarded by Dalhousie Student Union Sustainability Office, Dalhousie University, 2015.

Annual Sunshine Award Second Place Prize for the ENRICH Project. Awarded by the Ecology Action Centre, 2015.

Appendix C

THE ENRICH PROJECT DOCUMENTARY FILM AND VIDEOS

In Whose Backyard? released March 22, 2014: <http://www.enrichproject.org/
resources/>.

Outreach video for *Time to Clear the Air: Art on Environmental Racism by
Mi'kmaw and African Nova Scotian Youth,* released January 11, 2015:
<http://www.enrichproject.org/programs/time-to-clear-the-air/>.

Video for the symposium Over the Line: A Conversation on Race, Place & The
Environment, released November 14, 2017: <http://www.enrichproject.
org/programs/workshops/>.

Appendix D

SEVENTEEN PRINCIPLES OF ENVIRONMENTAL JUSTICE

Developed by delegates at the First National People of Color Environmental
Leadership Summit

- Environmental Justice affirms the sacredness of Mother Earth, ecological
  unity and the interdependence of all species, and the right to be free from
  ecological destruction.
- Environmental Justice demands that public policy be based on mutual
  respect and justice for all peoples, free from any form of discrimination or
  bias.
- Environmental Justice mandates the right to ethical, balanced, and responsible uses of land and renewable resources in the interest of a sustainable
  planet for humans and other living things.
- Environmental Justice calls for universal protection from nuclear testing,
  extraction, production and disposal of toxic/hazardous wastes and poisons
  and nuclear testing that threaten the fundamental right to clean air, land,
  water, and food.
- Environmental Justice affirms the fundamental right to political, economic,
  cultural and environmental self-determination of all peoples.
- Environmental Justice demands the cessation of the production of all
  toxins, hazardous wastes, and radioactive materials, and that all past and
  current producers be held strictly accountable to the people for detoxifica-
  tion and the containment at the point of production.

- Environmental Justice demands the right to participate as equal partners at every level of decision making, including needs assessment, planning, implementation, enforcement and evaluation.
- Environmental Justice affirms the right of all workers to a safe and healthy work environment without being forced to choose between an unsafe livelihood and unemployment. It also affirms the right of those who work at home to be free from environmental hazards.
- Environmental Justice protects the right of victims of environmental injustice to receive full compensation and reparations for damages as well as quality health care.
- Environmental Justice considers governmental acts of environmental injustice a violation of international law, the Universal Declaration On Human Rights, and the United Nations Convention on Genocide.
- Environmental Justice must recognize a special legal and natural relationship of Native Peoples to the US government through treaties, agreements, compacts, and covenants affirming sovereignty and self-determination.
- Environmental Justice affirms the need for urban and rural ecological policies to clean up and rebuild our cities and rural areas in balance with nature, honoring the cultural integrity of all our communities, and provided fair access for all to the full range of resources.
- Environmental Justice calls for the strict enforcement of principles of informed consent, and a halt to the testing of experimental reproductive and medical procedures and vaccinations on people of color.
- Environmental Justice opposes the destructive operations of multi-national corporations.
- Environmental Justice opposes military occupation, repression and exploitation of lands, peoples and cultures, and other life forms.
- Environmental Justice calls for the education of present and future generations which emphasizes social and environmental issues, based on our experience and an appreciation of our diverse cultural perspectives.
- Environmental Justice requires that we, as individuals, make personal and consumer choices to consume as little of Mother Earth's resources and to produce as little waste as possible; and make the conscious decision to challenge and reprioritize our lifestyles to ensure the health of the natural world for present and future generations.

REFERENCES

Access Alliance Multicultural Community Health Centre. 2007. *Racialization and Health Inequalities: Focus on Children*. Toronto: Access Alliance Multicultural Community Health Centre.

African Canadian Legal Clinic. n.d. *Policy Paper on Poverty*. pp. 17–18.<aclc.net/wp-content/uploads/Policy-Papers-1-11-English-FINAL.pdf>.

African Nova Scotian Affairs. n.d. "African Nova Scotian Community." <ansa.novascotia.ca/community>.

Alimahomed-Wilson, Jake and Dana Williams. 2016. "State Violence, Social Control, and Resistance." *Journal of Social Justice*, 6: 1–15.

Allen, Denise. n.d. "Remember Africville." <web.net/sworker/En/SW2002/383-09-Africville1.html>.

Arsenault, Dan. 2015. "Supporters Hold Silent Auction for Activist Annie Clair." *Chronicle Herald*, April 12. < thechronicleherald.ca/metro/1280191-supporters-hold-silent-auction-for-activist-annie-clair>.

Atari, Dominic Odwa, Isaac Lugina and Jamie Baxter. 2011. "This is the Mess that We Are Living In: Residents Everyday Life Experiences of Living in a Stigmatized Community." *GeoJournal*, 76, 5: 483–500.

Atari, Dominic Odwa, Isaac Luginaah, Kevin Gorey, Xiaohong Xu, and Karne Fung. 2012. "Associations Between Self-Reported Odour Annoyance and Volatile Organic Compounds in 'Chemical Valley', Sarnia, Ontario." *Environmental Monitoring and Assessment*, 185, 6: 4537–49.

Atiles-Osoria, Jose M. 2014. "Environmental Colonialism, Criminalization and Resistance: Puerto Rican Mobilizations for Environmental Justice in the 21st Century." *RCCS Annual Review*, 6: 3–21.

Auld, Alison. 2017. "Police Numbers Show Black Men Three Times More Likely to Be Street Checked in Halifax." *Toronto Star*, January 12. <thestar.com/news/canada/2017/01/12/police-numbers-show-black-men-3-times-more-likely-to-be-street-checked-in-halifax.html>.

Barlow, Maude and Elizabeth May. 2000. *Frederick Street: Life and Death on Canada's Love Canal*. Toronto: HarperCollins.

Basdeo, Maya and Lalita Bharadwaj. 2013. "Beyond Physical: Social Dimensions of the Water Crisis on Canada's First Nations and Considerations for Governance." *Indigenous Policy Journal*, 23, 4: 1–14.

Beaumont, Hilary. 2017. "United Nations Report Blasts Canada for Destruction of Historic Black Community." *Vice News Canada*, September 25. <https://<news.vice.com/story/united-nations-report-blasts-canada-for-destruction-of-historic-black-community>.

Benjamin, Chris. 2008. "Lincolnville Dumped on Again." *The Coast*, August 7. <thecoast.ca/halifax/lincolnville-dumped-on-again/Content?oid=993619>.

Benton, Winnie and Sandra Loppie. 2001. *Navigating the Cancer Care System: African Nova Scotians' Experience*. Halifax: Cancer Care Nova Scotia.

Bharadwaj, Lalita, Suzie Nilson, Ian Judd-Henrey, Gene Ouellette, Laura Parenteau, Cela

Tournier, Daryl Watson, Darcy Bear, Gilbert Ledoux, and Austin Bear. 2006. "Waste Disposal in First-Nations Communities: The Issues and Steps Toward the Future." *Journal of Environmental Health,* 68, 7: 35–39.

Black Community Action Network of Peel. 2015. *Pathways and Prevention of African Canadian Disproportionalities and Disparities in the Child Welfare System: A Position Paper.* Brampton: Black Community Action Network of Peel.

Black Cultural Centre for Nova Scotia. n.d. "Black Migration in Nova Scotia." <bccnsweb.com/web/our-history/>.

Black Lives Matter — Montreal. n.d. "Posts." <facebook.com/blmmontreal/>.

Black Lives Matter — Toronto. n.d. "Demands." < blacklivesmatter.ca/demands/>.

Blackstock, Cindy. 2010. "The Canadian Human Rights Tribunal on First Nations Child Welfare: Why if Canada Wins, Equality and Justice Lose." *Children and Youth Services Review* 33, 1, 187–94.

Blades, Lincoln Anthony. 2016. "What You Should Know About Environmental Racism." *Teen Vogue,* December 21. <teenvogue.com/story/what-you-should-know-about-environmental-racism>.

Bonner, Fred, Wilber Menendez Sanchez, Courtney Bonner, Angele Clarke, and Robyn Beckett. 2016. *Lincolnville Water Monitoring Report.* Halifax: Dalhousie University.

Boon, Jacob. 2016. "A Q&A With Nova Scotia's New Environment Minister." *The Coast,* January 21. <https://www.thecoast.ca/halifax/a-qanda-with-nova-scotias-new-environment-minister/Content?oid=5166748>.

_____. 2015. "Nova Scotia's Sad State of Environmental Racism." *The Coast,* July 28. <thecoast.ca/halifax/nova-scotias-sad-state-of environmentalracism/Content?oid=4823237>.

Booth, Annie L. 2017. "Northern Environmental Justice: A Case Study of Place, Indigenous Peoples, and Industrial Development in Northeastern British Columbia, Canada." *Case Studies in the Environment:* 1–19. <http://cse.ucpress.edu/content/ecs/early/2017/07/31/cse.2017.sc.454154.full.pdf>.

Borden Colley, Sherri. 2016. "Hundreds of Former Africville Residents Could Join Class-Action Lawsuit." cbc *News Nova Scotia,* November 30. <cbc.ca/news/canada/nova-scotia/africville-proposed-class-action-lawsuit-in-court-1.3874538>.

Brannen, John. 2014. "Updated: Pictou Landing Votes to Accept Government Offer, Dismantle Blockade." *The News,* June 16. <ngnews.ca/News/Local/2014-06-16/article-3765124/UPDATED%3A-Pictou-Landing-votes-to-accept-government-offer,-dismantle-blockade/1>.

Bullard, Robert D. 2002. "Confronting Environmental Racism in the 21st Century." *Global Dialogue: The Dialogue of Civilization,* 4: 34–48.

_____. 1993. *Confronting Environmental Racism: Voices from the Grassroots.* Boston: South End Press.

_____. 1990. *Dumping in Dixie: Race, Class, and Environmental Quality.* Boulder, CO: Westview Press.

_____. 1983. "Solid Waste Sites and the Black Houston Community." *Sociological Inquiry,* 53, 3–3 (April): 273–88.

Bullock, Brian K. 2015. "Reviving the Fight Against Environmental Racism."

Internationalist 360, March 11. <https://libya360.wordpress.com/2015/03/11/reviving-the-fight-against-environmental-racism/>.

Bundale, Brett. 2015. "Weekend Focus: The Toxic Sites of Nova Scotia Racism." *Chronicle Herald*, April 25. <thechronicleherald.ca/novascotia/1282706-weekend-focus-the-toxic-sites-of-nova-scotia-racism>.

Campbell, Francis. 2014. "Pictou Landing Chief Hails Boat Harbour Clean-Up 'Victory'." *Chronicle Herald News*, June 16. <thechronicleherald.ca/novascotia/1215271-pictou-landing-chief-hails-boat-harbour-cleanup-victory>.

Campbell, Robert A. 2002. "A Narrative Analysis of Success and Failure in Environmental Remediation: The Case of Incineration at the Sydney Tar Ponds." *Organization and Environment*, 15, 3: 259–77.

Campbell, Anita, Sivasankaran Balaratnasingam, Catherine McHugh, Aleksandar Janca, and Murray Chapman. 2016. "Alarming Increase of Suicide in a Remote Indigenous Australian Population: An Audit of Data from 2005 to 2014." *World Psychiatry*, 15, 3: 296–97.

Canadian Press. 2017. "UN Report on Canada to Address Anti-Black Racism." *Toronto Star*, September 24. <thestar.com/news/canada/2017/09/24/un-report-on-canada-to-address-anti-black-racism.html>.

Cancer Care Nova Scotia. 2013. *Navigating the Cancer Care System: Has the Experience of African Nova Scotians Improved?* Halifax: Cancer Care Nova Scotia.

Carothers, John Colin D. 1953. *The African Mind in Health and Disease: A Study in Ethno-Psychiatry.* WHO Monograph Series (Number 17). Geneva: World Health Organization.

_____. 1951. "Frontal Lobe Function and the African." *The British Journal of Psychiatry*, 97 (406): 12–48.

_____. 1940. "Some Speculations on Insanity in Africans and in General." *East African Medical Journal*, 17: 90–105.

Carrington, C. H. 1980. "Depression in Black Women: A Theoretical Appraisal." In L. F. Rodgers-Rose (ed.), *The Black Woman* (pp. 265–271). London: Sage.

CBC News. 2010. "Oilsands Poisoning Fish, Say Scientists, Fishermen." September 16. <cbc.ca/news/canada/edmonton/oilsands-poisoning-fish-say-scientists-fishermen-1.939507>.

_____. 2016. "Ontario Commits $300K to Grassy Narrows Water, Fish Sampling." June 28. <cbc.ca/news/canada/thunder-bay/grassy-narrows-ontario-committement-1.3655451>.

Chalifour, Nathalie J. 2013. "Environmental Discrimination and the Charter's Equality Guarantee: The Case of Drinking Water for First Nations Living on Reserves." *Revue Générale de Droit*, 43: 183–222.

Chen, Yiqun. 2009. "Cancer Incidence in Fort Chipewyan, Alberta 1995–2006." <albertahealthservices.ca/rls/ne-rls-2009-02-06-fort-chipewyan-study.pdf>.

Chiefs of Ontario. 2008. *Water Declaration of Anishinaabek, Mushkegowuk and Onkwehonwe in Ontario.* Toronto, ON: Author.

Choi, Jennifer. 2015. "Annie Clair, Anti-Shale Gas Protester Free, Charges Dropped." *CBC News New Brunswick*, September 21. <cbc.ca/news/canada/new-brunswick/protests-shale-gas-annie-clair-elsipogtog-1.3237337>.

Chowning Davies, James. 1971. *When Men Revolt and Why — A Reader in Political Violence and Revolution.* New York: Free Press.

Clement, Dave. 2003. "As Long as the River Flows." DVD. Ontario: Thunder Bay Indymedia.

Coates, Ken. 1999. "The 'Gentle' Occupation: The Settlement of Canada and the

Dispossession of the First Nations." In Paul Havemann (ed.), *Indigenous Peoples' Rights in Australia, Canada and New* Zealand (pp. 141–61). Auckland: Oxford University Press.

Commission for Racial Justice. 1987. *Toxic Wastes and Race in the United States: A National Report on the Racial and Socio-Economic Characteristics of Communities with Hazardous Waste Sites.* United Church of Christ. <reimaginerpe.org/files/toxics-racerace87.pdf>.

Community Tool Box. 2014. "How to Conduct Research: An Overview" <ctb.ku.edu/en/table-of-contents/advocacy/advocacy-research/overview/main>.

Corfu, Nina. 2017. "Protesters Build Permanent Structure, Plan to Overwinter at Alton Gas Site." CBC *News Nova Scotia*, December 19. <cbc.ca/news/canada/nova-scotia/protesters-alton-natural-gas-storage-project-altagas-mi-kmaq-stewiacke-treaty-rights-straw-bale-house-1.4451648>.

Corfu, Nina. 2016. "Sipekne'katik First Nation Protestors Rally Against Alton Natural Gas Project." CBC *News*, July 22. <cbc.ca/news/canada/nova-scotia/sipekne-katik-first-nation-protestors-alton-natural-gas-altagas-appeal-stewiacke-1.3535709>.

Cornwall, Andrea, Jasmine Gideon and Kalpana Wilson. 2008. "Introduction: Reclaiming Feminism: Gender and Neoliberalism." *IDS Bulletin*, 39, 6: 1–9.

Correctional Investigator Canada. 2013. *Annual Report of the Office of the Correctional Investigator 2012–2013*. Ottawa: Correctional Investigator Canada.<oci-bec.gc.ca/cnt/rpt/pdf/annrpt/annrpt20122013-eng.pdf>.

Coulthard, Glen Sean. 2014. *Red Skin, White Masks: Rejecting the Colonial Politics of Recognition*. University of Minnesota Press.

Courville, Cindy. 1993. "Re-Examining Patriarchy as a Mode of Production: The Case of Zimbabwe." In Abena P.A. Busia and Stanlie M. James (eds.), *Theorizing Black Feminisms: The Visionary Pragmatism of Black Women* 1st Edition (pp. 31–43). New York: Routledge.

Crouse, Dan L., Paul A. Peters, Paul J. Villeneuve, Mark Olivier Proux, Hwashin H. Shin, Mark S. Goldberg, Markey Johnson, Amanda J. Wheeler, Ryan W. Allen, Dominic Adwa Atari, Michael Jerrett, Michael Brauer, Jeffrey R. Brook, Sabit Cakmak, and Richard T. Burnett. 2015. "Within- and Between-City Contrasts in Nitrogen Dioxide and Mortality in 10 Canadian Cities: A Subset of the Canadian Census Health and Environment Cohort (CanCHEC)." *Journal of Exposure Science and Environmental Epidemiology*, 5: 482–89.

Cryderman, Diana, Lisa Letourneau, Fiona Miller, and Niladri Basu. 2016. "An Ecological and Human Biomonitoring Investigation of Mercury Contamination at the Aamjiwnaang First Nation." *EcoHealth*, 13, 4: 784–95.

Cutter, Susan L. 1995. "Race, Class, and Environmental Justice." *Progress in Human Geography*, 19, 1: 111–22.

Dawson, Susan E. and Gary E. Madsen. 2011. "Psychosocial and Health Impacts of Uranium Mining and Milling on Navajo Lands." *Health Physics*, 101, 5: 618–25.

Deacon, Leith and Jamie Baxter. 2013. "No Opportunity to Say No: A Case Study of Procedural Environmental Injustice in Canada." *Journal of Environmental Planning and Management*, 56, 5: 607–23.

Dei, George Sefa. 2012. "Indigenous Anti-Colonial Knowledge as 'Heritage Knowledge' for Promoting Black/African Education in Diasporic Contexts." *Decolonization: Indigeneity, Education and Society*, 1, 1: 102–19.

Dei, George Sefa and Alirezah Asgharzadeh. 2001. "The Power of Social Theory: The

Anti-Colonial Discursive Framework." *The Journal of Educational Thought,* 35, 3: 297–323.

De Leeuw, Sarah. 2015. "Activating Place: Geography as a Determinant of Indigenous People's Health and Well-Being." In Margo Greenwood, Sarah de Leeuw, Nicole Marie Lindsay and Charlotte Reading (eds), *Determinants of Indigenous Peoples' Health in Canada: Beyond the Social* (pp.90–103). Toronto: Canadian Scholars Press.

De Leeuw, Sarah, Nicole Marie Lindsay, and Margo Greenwood. 2015. "Rethinking Determinants of Indigenous Peoples' Health in Canada." In Margo Greenwood, Sarah de Leeuw, Nicole Marie Lindsay and Charlotte Reading (eds.), *Determinants of Indigenous Peoples' Health in Canada: Beyond the Social* (pp.xi-xxix). Toronto: Canadian Scholars Press.

Democracy Now. 2005. "Professor Preacher Michael Eric Dyson on the State of the Country: Some of Us Are in First Class, But the Plane Is in Trouble." October 14. <democracynow. org/2005/10/14/professor_preacher_michael_eric_dyson_on>.

Devet, Robert 2018. "You Have Mail, and It Isn't Very Nice – When White Residents Don't Want to Live in a Black Community." *The Nova Scotia Advocate,* February 1. <https://nsadvocate.org/2018/02/01/you-have-mail-and-it-isnt-very-nice-when-white-residents-dont-want-to-live-in-a-black-community/>

_____. 2017a. "Historic Black Community of Lucasville Continues to Fight Horse Farm, Feels Abandoned by HRM." *The Nova Scotia Advocate,* July 11. <https://nsadvocate. org/2017/07/11/historic-black-community-of-lucasville-continues-to-fight-horse-farm-feels-abandoned-by-hrm/>.

_____. 2017b. "Putting Lucasville on the Map: African Nova Scotian Community Wants its Boundaries Finally Resolved." *The Nova Scotia Advocate,* February 23. <nsadvocate. org/2017/02/23/putting-lucasville-on-the-map-african-nova-scotian-community-wants-its-boundaries-finally-resolved/>.

_____. 2016. "Lucasville: A 200-Year Old African Nova Scotian Community Fighting for Survival." *The Nova Scotia Advocate,* February 8. <nsadvocate.org/2016/02/08/lucasville-a-200-year-old-african-nova-scotian-community-fighting-for-survival/>.

_____. 2015a. "Lucasville Residents Have Their Say at Rowdy Community Council Meeting." *Halifax Media Co-op,* September 28. <halifax.mediacoop.ca/story/lucasville-residents-have-their-say-rowdy-communit/33948>.

_____. 2015b. "Lucasville: Fighting City Hall, Racism and the Smell of Horse Manure." *Halifax Media Co-op,* September 20. <halifax.mediacoop.ca/story/lucasville-fighting-city-hall-racism-and-smell-hor/33904>.

Dhillon, Christina, and Michael G. Young. 2010. "Environmental Racism and First Nations: A Call for Socially Just Public Policy Development." *Canadian Journal of Humanities and Social Sciences,* 1, 1: 25–39.

Donovan, Moira. 2015. "Will Nova Scotia Take Environmental Racism Seriously?" *Halifax Examiner,* July 29. < halifaxexaminer.ca/province-house/will-nova-scotia-take-environmental-racism-seriously/>.

Downey, Liam and Marieke Van Willigen. 2005. "Environmental Stressors: The Mental Health Impacts of Living Near Industrial Activity." *Journal of Health and Social Behaviour,* 46, 3: 289–305.

Dyer, Richard. 1988. "White." *Screen,* 29, 4: 44–65.

Dyson, Michael Eric. 2016. *The Black Presidency: Barack Obama, and the Politics of Race in America.* Boston: Houghton Mifflin Harcourt.

Elson, Diane. 1992. "Male Bias in Structural Adjustment." In Haleh Afshar and Carolyne Dennis (eds.), *Women and Adjustment Policies in the Third World* (pp. 46–68.) London: Macmillan.

Evans, Pete. 2017. "TransCanada Pulls Plug on Energy East Pipeline." CBC *News*, October 5. < cbc.ca/news/business/transcanada-energy-east-1.4338227>.

Evans-Campbell, Teresa. 2008. "Historical Trauma in American Indian/Native Alaska Communities: A Multilevel Framework for Exploring Impacts on Individuals, Families, and Communities." *Journal of Interpersonal Violence,* 23: 316–38.

Fanon, Frantz. 1963. *The Wretched of the Earth.* New York: Grove Press.

Feagin, Joe R.and Hernan Vera. 1995. *White Racism: The Basics.* New York: Routledge.

Fellows, Mary Louise and Sherene Razack. 1998. "The Race to Innocence: Confronting Hierarchical Relations Among Women." *Journal of Gender, Race and Justice,* 1: 335–52.

Fernando, Suman. 1991. *Mental Health, Race and Culture.* London: Macmillan Education.

First Nations Information Governance Centre. 2012. *First Nations Regional Health Survey (RHS) Phase 2: National Report on Adults, Youth and Children Living in First Nations Communities.* Ottawa: The First Nations Information Governance Centre.

Free Grassy Narrows. n.d. "Province Ignored Minister's 1984 Recommendation to Clean Up Mercury in River Near Grassy Narrows: Star Investigation." *Free Grassy Narrows.* <freegrassy.net/2016/07/04/province-ignored-ministers-1984-recommendation-to-clean-up-mercury-in-river-near-grassy-narrows-star-investigation/>.

Freire, Paulo. 2000. *Pedagogy of the Oppressed* (30th Anniversary Edition). London: Bloomsbury Academic.

Fryzuk, Lori Anne. 1996. "Environmental Justice in Canada: An Empirical Study and Analysis of the Demographics of Dumping in Nova Scotia." Masters Thesis, Environmental Studies, School for Resource and Environmental Studies, Dalhousie University, Halifax.

Gazso, Amber, Susan MacDaniel, and Ingrid Waldron. 2016. "Networks of Social Support to Manage Poverty: More Changeable Than Durable." *Journal of Poverty,* 20, 4: 1–24.

Gazso, Amber and Ingrid Waldron. 2009. "Fleshing out the Racial Undertones of Poverty for Canadian Women and Their Families: Re-Envisioning a Critical Integrative Framework." *Atlantis: A Women's Studies Journal,* 34, 1: 132–41.

Gilbert, Ruth, John Fluke, Melissa O'Donnell, Arturo Gonzalez-Izquierdo, Marni Brownell, Pauline Gulliver, Staffan Janson, and Peter Sidebotham. 2012. "Child Maltreatment: Variation in Trends and Policies in Six Developed Countries." *The Lancet,* 379, 9817: 758–72.

Giroux, Henry. 1983. *Theory and Resistance in Education: A Pedagogy for the Opposition.* South Hadley, MA: Bergin and Garvey.

Goldberg, Mark S., Jack Siemiatyck, Ron DeWar, Marie Desy, and Helen Riberdy. 1999. "Risks of Developing Cancer Relative to Living Near a Municipal Solid Waste Landfill Site in Montreal, Quebec, Canada." *Archives of Environmental Health,* 54: 4.

Goldman Environmental Foundation. n.d. "The Goldman Environmental Prize." <goldmanprize.org/recipient/ken-saro-wiwa/>.

Goldstein, Alyosha. 2017. "On the Reproduction of Race, Capitalism, and Settler

Colonialism." *Race and Capitalism: Global Territories, Transnational Histories Conference*, October 20. <challengeinequality.luskin.ucla.edu/race-and-capitalism/#about>.

Gosine, Andil and Cheryl Teelucksingh. 2008. *Environmental Justice and Racism in Canada: An Introduction.* Toronto: Emond Montgomery Publications.

Government of Canada. 1982. *Constitution Act.* <laws-lois.justice.gc.ca/eng/const/page-15.html#h-38>.

_____. 2013. *Safe Drinking Water for First Nations Act.* June 19. <laws-lois.justice.gc.ca/eng/acts/S-1.04/FullText.html>.

Gurr, Ted. 1970. *Why Men Rebel.* Princeton: Princeton University Press.

Halifax Regional Municipality. n.d. "Remembering Africville Source Guide." *Halifax Online.* <www.halifax.ca/archives/AfricvilleSources.php>.

Haluza-Delay, Randolph. 2007. "Environmental Justice in Canada." *Local Environment,* 12, 6: 557–63.

Harris-Roxas, Ben F., Patrick J. Harris, Elizabeth Harris, and Lynn A. Kemp. 2011. "A Rapid Equity Focused Health Impact Assessment of a Policy Implementation Plan: An Australian Case Study and Impact Evaluation." *International Journal for Equity in Health* (January): 2–12.

Harvey, David. 2003. *The New Imperialism.* Oxford: Oxford University Press.

Hawkesworth, Mary. 2006. *Globalization and Feminist Activism.* New York: Rowman and Littlefield.

Healing, Dan. 2017. "TransCanada Blames 'Substantial Uncertainty' for Killing Energy East Pipeline." *Canadian Press,* October 6. <atlantic.ctvnews.ca/transcanada-blames-substantial-uncertainty-for-killing-energy-east-pipeline-1.3620152>.

Henry, Frances and Carol Tator. 2006. *The Colour of Democracy: Racism in Canadian Society.* Toronto: Thomson Nelson.

Hernandez, Sergio. 2016. "What You Need to Know to Understand the Flint Water Crisis." *Mashable,* January 19. <mashable.com/2016/01/19/flint-water-crisis-explainer/#TaEBYox2Cpqa>.

Hetzler, Olivia, Veronica E. Medina, and David Overfelt. 2006. "Gentrification, Displacement and New Urbanism: The Next Racial Project." *Sociation Today,* 4, 2. <www.ncsociology.org/sociationtoday/gent.htm>.

Hewitt, Mark L., Joanne L. Parrott, and Mark E. McMaster. 2006. "A Decade of Research on the Environmental Impacts of Pulp and Paper Mill Effluents in Canada: Sources and Characteristics of Bioactive Substances." *Journal of Toxicology and Environmental Health Part B: Critical Reviews,* 9: 341–56.

Hier, Sean P. and B. Singh Bolaria. 2007. *Race and Racism in 21st Century Canada: Continuity, Complexity and Change.* Peterborough: Broadview Press.

Hill Collins, Patricia. 1990. *Black Feminist Thought: Knowledge, Consciousness and the Politics of Empowerment.* London: Unwin Hyman.

Historica Canada. n.d.(a). "Black History Canada Timeline." <blackhistorycanada.ca/timeline.php?id=1600>.

_____. n.d.(b). "Grassy Narrows." <thecanadianencyclopedia.ca/en/article/grassy-narrows/>.

_____. n.d.(c). "Africville." <thecanadianencyclopedia.ca/en/article/africville/>.

Hoffman, Emma, Meagan Bernier, Brenden Blotnicky, Peter G. Golden, Jeffrey Janes,

Allison Kader, Rachel Kovacs-Da Costa, Shauna Pittipas, Sarah Vermeulen, and Tony R. Walker. 2015. "Assessment of Public Perception and Environmental Compliance at a Pulp and Paper Facility: A Canadian Case Study." *Environmental Monitoring and Assessment*, 187, 12: 766.

Hoffman, Kelly M., Sophie Trawalter, Jordan R. Axt, and M. Norman Oliver. 2016. "Racial Bias in Pain Assessment and Treatment Recommendations, and False Beliefs about Biological Differences Between Blacks and Whites." *Proceedings of the National Academy of Sciences*, 113, 16: 4296–301.

Holtby, Caitlin E., Judith R. Guernsey, Alexander C. Allen, John. A. VanLeeuwen, Victoria M. Allen, and Robert J. Gordon. 2014. "A Population-Based Case-Control Study of Drinking-Water." *International Journal of Environmental Research and Public Health*, 11: 1803–23.

hooks, bell. 1993. *Sisters of the Yam: Black Women and Self-Recovery*: South End Press.

_____. 1990. *Yearning: Race, Gender and Cultural Politics*. Boston: South End Press.

_____.1981. *Ain't I a Woman: Black Women and Feminism*. Boston: South End Press.

Hoover, Elizabeth, Katsi Cook, Ron Plain, Kathy Sanchez, Vi Waghiyi, Pamela Miller, Renee Dufault, Caitlin Sislin, and David O. Carpenter. 2012. "Indigenous Peoples of North America: Environmental Exposures and Reproductive Justice." *Environmental Health Perspectives*, 120, 12: 1645–49.

Howe, Miles. 2016. "Going Against the Tide: The Fight Against Alton Gas." *The Coast*, February 18. <thecoast.ca/halifax/going-against-the-tide-the-fight-against-alton-gas/Content?oid=5221542>.

Hubley, Jake. 2016. "The Alton Gas Project: An Analysis." *Solidarity Halifax*, March 31. <solidarityhalifax.ca/analysis/the-alton-gas-project-an-analysis/>.

Hunt, Sarah. 2015. "Embodying Self-Determination: Beyond the Gender Binary." In Margo Greenwood, Sarah de Leeuw, Nicole Marie Lindsayand Charlotte Reading (eds.), *Determinants of Indigenous Peoples' Health in Canada: Beyond the Social* (pp.103–19). Toronto: Canadian Scholars Press.

Hunter, Justine and Ian Bailey. 2017. "B.C. to Proceed with Site C Hydroelectric Dam." *Globe and Mail*, December 12. <https://www.theglobeandmail.com/news/british-columbia/bc-to-proceed-with-site-c-hydroelectric-dam/article37290570/>.

Hunter, Lori. M. 1998. "The Association Between Environmental Risk and Internal Migration Flows." *Population and Environment*, 19, 3: 247.

Hunter, Lori M., Michael J. White, Jani S. Little, and Jeannette Sutton. 2003. "Environmental Hazards, Migration, and Race." *Population and Environment*, 25, 1: 23–39.

Huseman, Jennifer and Damian Short. 2012. "A Slow Industrial Genocide: Tar Sands and the Indigenous Peoples of Northern Alberta." *The International Journal of Human Rights*, 16, 1: 216–37.

Idle No More. 2014. "Pictou Landing Erects Blockade Against Northern Pulp." June 13. <idlenomore.ca/pictou_landing_erects_blockade>.

_____. n.d. "Calls for Change." <idlenomore.ca/story>.

Indigenous and Northern Affairs Canada. 2014. "Registered Indian Population By Sex and Residence 2014 – Statistics and Measurement Directorate (2014)." December 31. <aadnc-aandc.gc.ca/eng/1429798605785/1429798785836>.

Israel, Barbara A., Amy J. Schultz, Edith A. Parker, and Adam B. Becker. 1998. "Review of

Community-Based Research: Assessing Partnership Approaches to Improve Public Health." *Annual Review of Public Health*, 19: 173–202.

Jackson, Jennifer; Elizabeth McGibbon, and Ingrid Waldron. 2013. "Racism and Cardiovascular Health: Implications for Nursing." *Canadian Journal of Cardiovascular Nursing*, 23, 4: 12–17.

Jacobs, Beverley. 2010. "Environmental Racism on Indigenous Lands and Territories." <cpsa-acsp.ca/papers-2010/Jacobs.pdf>.

Jiwa, Fazeela. 2017. "New Organization to Test Rural Water Quality When Government Doesn't." *The Nova Scotia Advocate*, October 6. <nsadvocate.org/2017/10/06/new-organization-to-test-rural-water-quality-when-government-doesnt/>.

Johnson, Shelly. 2014. "Knucwénte-kuc re Stsmémelt.s-kuc Trauma-Informed Education for Indigenous Children in Foster Care." *Canadian Social Work Review/ Revue canadienne de service social*, 31, 2: 155–74.

Johnston, Dawn, Tania Angelucci, Melissa Howey, Ingrid Waldron, Elizabeth Townsend, and Sharon Lawlor. 2009. "Social Influences on Primary Health Care in Occupational Therapy." *World Federation of Occupational Therapists Bulletin*, 60: 49–55.

Kelley, Robin D. G. 2017. "What Is Racial Capitalism and Why Does It Matter?" *Katz Distinguished Lecture in the Humanities and the John E. Sawyer Seminar on Capitalism and Comparative Racialization*, Simpson Center for the Humanities, University of Washington, November 7. <youtube.com/watch?v=REo_gHIpvJc>.

Kihal-Talantikite, Wahida, Denis Zmirou-Navier, Cindy Padilla, and Severine Deguen. 2017. "Systematic Literature Review of Reproductive Outcome Associated with Residential Proximity to Polluted Sites." *International Journal of Health Geographics*, 16: 20.

King, Deborah K. 1988. "Multiple Jeopardy, Multiple Consciousness: The Context of a Black Feminist Ideology." In Micheline R. Malson, Elisabeth Mudimbe-Boyi, Jean F. O'Barr, and Mary Wyer (eds.), *Black Women in America: Social Science Perspectives* (pp. 265–95). Chicago: University of Chicago Press.

King, Tiffany. 2013. "In the Clearing: Black Female Bodies, Space and Settler Colonial Landscapes." PhD dissertation, Maryland: University of Maryland.

Kirmayer, Laurence, Gregory M. Brass, Tara Holton, Ken Paul, Cori Simpson, and Caroline Tate. 2007. *Suicide Among Aboriginal People in Canada*. Ottawa: Aboriginal Healing Foundation.

Kisely, Steve, Mikiko Terashima, and Don Langille. 2008. "A Population-Based Analysis of the Health Experience of African Nova Scotians." *Canadian Medical Association Journal*, 179, 7: 653–58.

Knowles, Caroline and Sharmila Mercer. 1992. "Feminism and Anti-Racism: An Exploration of The Political Possibilities." In James Donald and Ali Rattansi (eds.), *"Race," Culture and Difference* (pp. 104–25). London: Sage, in association with The Open University.

Kobayashi, Audrey. 2000. "Racism Out of Place: Thoughts on Whiteness and an Antiracist Geography in the New Millennium." *Annals of the Association of American Geographers*, 90, 2: 392–403.

Kondo, Michelle C., Carol Ann Gross-Davis, Katlyn May, Lauren O. Davis, Tyiesha Johnson, Mable Mallard, Alice Gabbadon, Claudia Sherrod, and Charles C. Branas. 2014. "Place-Based Stressors Associated with Industry and Air Pollution." *Health & Place*, 28: 31–37.

Konsmo, Erin Marie and A.M. Kahealani Pacheco. 2015. "Violence on the Land, Violence

on Our Bodies: Building an Indigenous Response to Environmental Violence."
<landbodydefense.org/uploads/files/VLVBReportToolkit2016.pdf?>.

Kuokkanen, Rauna. 2008. "Globalization as Racialized, Sexualized Violence: The Case of Indigenous Women." *International Feminist Journal of Politics*, 10, 2: 216–33.

Kurtz, Hilda E. 2009. "Acknowledging the Racial State: An Agenda for Environmental Justice Research." *Antipode*, 41, 4: 684–704.

Kwiatkowski, Roy E., Constatine Tikhonov, Diane McClymont Peace, and Carrie Bourassa. 2012. "Canadian Indigenous Engagement and Capacity Building in Health Impact Assessment." *Impact Assessment and Project Appraisal*, 27, 1: 57–67.

Lambert, Timothy W., Lindsay Guyn, and Stephanie E. Lane. 2006. "Development of Local Knowledge of Environmental Contamination in Sydney, Nova Scotia: Environmental Health Practice from an Environmental Justice Perspective." *Science of the Total Environment*, 368, 2–3: 471–84

Lefebvre, Henri. 1991. *The Production of Space*. Cambridge, MA: Blackwell.

_____. 1976. "Reflections on the Politics of Space" (translated by M.J. Enders). *Antipode*, 8, 2: 30–37.

Leong, Nancy. 2013. "Racial Capitalism." *Harvard Law Review*, 126, 8: 2152–226.

Lightman, Ernie, Andrew Mitchell, and Dean Herd. 2005. "One Year On: Tracking the Experiences of Current and Former Welfare Recipients in Toronto." *Journal of Poverty*, 9, 4: 5–25.

Lindholm-Lehto, Petra C., Juha S. Knuutinen, Heidi S. Ahkola, and Sirpa H. Herve. 2015. "Refractory Organic Pollutants and Toxicity in Pulp and Paper Mill Wastewaters." *Environmental Science and Pollution Research*, 22: 6473–99.

Lindsay, Hillary Bain. 2011. "Lincolnville Protest Against Environmental Racism." *Halifax Media Co-op*, May 10. <halifax.mediacoop.ca/newsrelease/7215>.

Lipsitz, George. 2007. "The Racialization of Space and the Spatialization of Race: Theorizing the Hidden Architecture of Landscape." *Landscape Journal*, 26, 1: 10–23.

_____. 1998. *The Possessive Investment in Whiteness*. Philadelphia: Temple University Press.

Luck, Shaina. 2016. "Black, Indigenous Prisoners Over-Represented in Nova Scotia Jails." CBC *News Nova Scotia*, May 20. <cbc.ca/news/canada/nova-scotia/black-indigenous-prisoners-nova-scotia-jails-1.3591535>.

Lypny, Natascia. 2013. "Toxic Legacies." *Halifax Media Co-op*, November 13. <halifax.mediacoop.ca/fr/story/toxic-legacies/19765>.

Maantay, Juliana. 2002. "Mapping Environmental Injustice: Pitfalls and Potential of Geographic Information Systems in Assessing Environmental Health Equity." *Environmental Health Perspectives*, 110 (supp 2): 161–71.

Macias, Kelly. 2015. "Sisters in the Collective Struggle: Sounds of Silence and Reflections on the Unspoken Assault on Black Females in Modern America." *Cultural Studies Critical Methodologies*, 15, 4: 1–5.

MacIntosh, Constance. 2008. "Testing the Waters: Jurisdictional and Policy Aspects of the Continuing Failure to Remedy Drinking Water Quality on First Nations Reserves." *Ottawa Law Review*, 39, 1.

MacKay, Cody. 2017. "Turn the Page: Energy East Cancellation a Relief for Environmental Protection Group." CBC *News New Brunswick*, October 7. <cbc.ca/news/canada/new-brunswick/nb-energy-east-pipeline-cancellation-1.4345375>.

MacKenzie, Constanze A., Ada Lockridge, and Margaret Keith. 2005. "Declining Sex Ratio in a First Nation Community." University of Ottawa: Ontario, Canada. <ncbi.nlm.nih.gov/pmc/articles/PMC1281269/>.

Macklem, Patrick. 2001. *Indigenous Difference and the Constitution of Canada*. Toronto: University of Toronto Press.

Maddalena, Victor, Wanda Thomas Bernard, Josephine B.Etowa, Sharon Davis-Murdoch, Donna Smith, and Phyllis Marsh-Jarvis. 2010. "Cancer Care Experiences and the Use of Complementary and Alternative Medicine at End of Life in Nova Scotia's Black Communities." *Journal of Transcultural Nursing*, 21: 114–22.

Márquez, John. 2014. *Black–Brown Solidarity: Racial Politics in the New Gulf South*. Austin, TX: University of Texas Press.

Maiter, Sarah and Carol Stalker. 2011. "South Asian Immigrants' Experience of Child Protection Services: Are We Recognizing Strengths and Resilience?" *Child and Family Social Work*, 16, 2: 138–48.

Martinez, Elizabethand Arnoldo Garcia. n.d. "What Is Neoliberalism? A Brief Definition for Activists." *Corpwatch*. <corpwatch.org/article.php?id=376>.

Mascarenhas, Michael. 2007. "Where the Waters Divide: First Nations, Tainted Water and Environmental Justice in Canada." *Local Environment*, 12, 6: 565–77.

Massey, Doreen. 1992. "Politics and Space/Time." *New Left Review*, 196: 65–84.

Masuda, Jeffrey R., Blake Poland, and Jamie Baxter. 2010. "Reaching for Environmental Health Justice: Canadian Experiences for a Comprehensive Research, Policy and Advocacy Agenda in Health Promotion." *Health Promotion International*, 25, 4: 452–63.

Masuda, Jeffrey R., Tara Zupancic, Blake Poland, and Donald C. Cole. 2008. "Environmental Health and Vulnerable Populations in Canada: Mapping an Integrated Equity-Focused Research Agenda." *The Canadian Geographer*, 52, 4: 427–50.

Mattei, Ugo and Laura Nader. 2008. *Plunder: When the Rule of Law Is Illegal*. Hoboken, NJ: John Wiley & Sons.

Maudsley, Henry. 1879. *The Pathology of Mind*. London: MacMillan & Company.

Mays, Vickie M., Cleopatra Howard Caldwell, and James Sidney Jackson. 1996. "Mental Health Symptoms and Service Utilization Patterns of Help-Seeking Among African American Women." In Harold W. Neighbors and James Sidney Jackson (eds.), *Mental Health in Black America* (pp. 161–76). London: Sage.

McClintock, Anne. 1995. *Imperial Leather: Race, Gender, and Sexuality in the Colonial Contest*. London: Routledge.

McGibbon, Elizabeth, Ingrid Waldron, and Jennifer Jackson. 2013. "The Social Determinants of Cardiovascular Health: Time for a Focus on Racism." *Diversity and Equality in Health and Care*, 10, 3: 139–42.

McGregor, Deborah. 2012. "Traditional Knowledge: Considerations for Protecting Water in Ontario." *International Indigenous Policy Journal*, 3, 3: 1–21.

McKittrick, Katherine. 2011. "On Plantations, Prisons, and a Black Sense of Place." *Social and Cultural Geography*, 12, 8: 947–63.

_____. 2002. " 'Their Blood is There, and They Can't Throw it Out': Honouring Black Canadian Geographies." *Topia: Canadian Journal of Cultural Studies*, 7: 27–37.

McKittrick, Katharine, and Linda Peake. 2005. "What Difference Does Difference Make to Geography?" In Noel Castree, Alisdair Rogers and Douglas Sherman (eds.), *Questioning*

Geography: Fundamental Debates (pp. 39–54). Malden, MA: Blackwell Publishing.

McMillan, I. Jane, Janelle Young, and Molly Peters. 2013. "Commentary: The 'Idle No More' Movement in Eastern Canada." *Canadian Journal of Law and Society*, 28, 3: 429–31.

Memmi, Albert. 2003. *The Colonizer and the Colonized*. London: Earthscan Publications.

_____. 1965. *The Colonizer and the Colonized*. Boston: Beacon Press.

Menjívar, Cecilia. 2016. "A Framework for Examining Violence." In Maxine Baca Zinn, Pierette Hondagneu-Sotelo, Michael A. Messner and Amy M. Denissen (eds.), *Gender Through the Prism of Difference* (pp. 130–145). New York: Oxford University Press.

Mill, Charles. 2007. "White Ignorance." In Nancy Tuana and Shannon Sullivan (eds.), *Race and Epistemologies of Ignorance* (pp. 13–38). Albany: SUNY Press.

_____. 2001. "Black Trash." In Laura Westra and Bill E. Lawson (eds.), *Faces of Environmental Racism* (pp. 73–93). Lanham, MD: Rowman & Littlefield.

Minkler, Meredith, Victoria B. Vasquez, Mansoureh Tajik, and Dana Peterson. 2008. "Promoting Environmental Justice Through Community-Based Participatory Research: The Role of Community and Partnership Capacity." *Health Education and Behavior*, 35, 1: 119–37.

Minkler, Meredith and Nina Wallerstein. 2011. *Community-Based Participatory Research for Health from Process to Outcome*. San Francisco: Jossey-Bass.

Mirabelli, Maria C. and Steve Wing. 2006. "Proximity to Pulp and Paper Mills and Wheezing Symptoms Among Adolescents in North Carolina." *Environmental Research*, 102: 96–100.

Morello-Frosch, Rachel, Miriam Zuk, Michael Jerrett, Bhavna Shamasunder, and Amy D. Kyle. 2011. "Understanding the Cumulative Impacts of Inequalities in Environmental Health: Implications For Policy." *Health Affairs*, 30, 5: 879–87.

Morgan, Jennifer L. 2004. *Laboring Women: Reproduction and Gender in New World Slavery*. Philadelphia: University of Pennsylvania Press.

Morgan, Rachel. 2015. "We're Tired of Being the Dump: Exposing Environmental Racism in Canadian Communities." Honours thesis, Political Science Department, Dalhousie University, Halifax.

Movement for Black Lives. n.d. "Invest-Divest." <policy.m4bl.org/invest-divest/>.

Moy, Pearl, Nikhil Krishnan, Priscilla Ulloa, Steven Cohen, and Paul W. Brandt-Rauf. 2008. "Options for Management of Municipal Solid Waste in New York City: A Preliminary Comparison of Health Risks and Policy Implications." *Journal of Environmental Management*, 87, 1: 73–79.

Munkittrick, Kelly R., Mark E. McMaster, and Mark R. Servos. 2013. "Detection of Reproductive Impacts of Effluents from Pulp and Paper Mills: Shifts in Issues and Potential Causes." *Environmental Toxicology and Chemistry*, 32: 729–31.

Murakawa, Naomi. 2014. *The First Civil Right: How Liberals Built Prison America*. New York: Oxford University Press.

NDP. 2016. "NDP Introduces Historic Environmental Bill of Rights." *Nova Scotia NDP*, May 5. <classic.nsndp.ca/ns/ndp-introduces-historic-environmental-bill-of-rights>.

Nelson, Jennifer J. 2001. "The Operation of Whiteness and Forgetting in Africville: A Geography of Racism." Doctoral thesis, Toronto, Ontario Institute for Studies in Education, University of Toronto.

Newcombe, Charles P. and Digby. D. MacDonald. 2011. "Effects of Suspended Sediments on Aquatic Ecosystems." *North American Journal of Fisheries Management*, 11: 72–82.

Nickerson, Colin. 1999. "Hoping Blight Makes Might: Cape Breton Town Seeks Role as Toxic Waste Learning Site." *Boston Globe*, May 12. <highbeam.com/doc/1P2-8544389. html>.

Nixon, Rob. 2011. *Slow Violence and the Environmentalism of the Poor.* Cambridge, MA: Harvard University Press.

Nova Scotia Canada. 2016. "Alton Natural Gas Storage Facility Project." <energy.novascotia. ca/oil-and-gas/consumer-natural-gas/underground-storage>.

Nova Scotia Environment. 2010. "Water for Life: Nova Scotia's Water Resource Management Strategy." Halifax. <novascotia.ca/nse/water.strategy/docs/WaterStrategy_Water. Resources.Management.Strategy.pdf>.

_____. 2007. *Environmental Goals and Sustainable Prosperity Act.* Halifax. <nslegislature. ca/legc/bills/60th_1st/3rd_read/b146.htm>.

Nova Scotia Environmental Rights Working Group. 2017. *Nova Scotia Environmental Bill of Rights.* Halifax: ECELAW. <ecelaw.ca/images/PDFs/ER_event/EBR-Public-Release-June-2017.pdf>.

Nova Scotia Legislature. 2015. *Community of Sackville Landfill Compensation Act*, November 24. <http://nslegislature.ca/legc/bills/62nd_2nd/3rd_read/b130.htm>.

_____. n.d.(a). *Environmental Racism Prevention Act.* <nslegislature.ca/legc/ bills/62nd_2nd/1st_read/b111.htm>.

_____. n.d.(b). *Wilderness Areas Protection Act.* <nslegislature.ca/sites/default/files/legc/ statutes/wildarea.htm>.

Nova Scotia Museum. n.d. "Remembering Black Loyalists, Black Communities in Nova Scotia." <novascotia.ca/museum/blackloyalists/communities.htm>.

NSPIRG. n.d. "Save Lincolnville Campaign." <nspirg.ca/projects/past-projects/save-lincolnville-campaign/#sthash.9YV4BKxl.dpuf>.

O'Brien, Nicole L. and Keith W. Hipel. 2016. "A Strategic Analysis of the New Brunswick, Canada Fracking Controversy." *Energy Economics*, 55: 69–78.

Office of Aboriginal Affairs. n.d. "Facts Sheets and Additional Information." <novascotia. ca/abor/aboriginal-people/demographics/>.

Office of the Auditor General of Canada. 2005. *Report of the Commissioner of the Environment and Sustainable Development.* Ottawa: Minister of Public Works and Government Services Canada.Olsen, Frances. 1995. *Feminist Legal Theory, Volume 1.* New York: NYU Press.

Omi, Michael and Howard Winant. 1994. *Racial Formation in the United States* (2nd ed.), New York: Routledge.

Ontario Ministry of Health and Long Term Care. 2012. *Health Equity Impact Assessment Workbook.* Toronto: Ontario Ministry of Health and Long Term Care.

One Vision One Voice Steering Committee. 2016. *One Vision, One Voice: Changing the Ontario Child Welfare System to Better Serve African Canadians.* Toronto: Ontario Association of Children's Aid Societies.

Optis, Michael, Karena Shaw, Peter Stephenson, and Peter Wild. 2012. "Mold Growth in On-Reserve Homes in Canada: The Need for Research, Education, Policy, and Funding." *Journal of Environmental Health*, 74, 6: 14–22.

Orellana, Jesem. D., Antonio A. Balieiro, Fernanda R. Fonseca, Paulo C. Basta, and

Maximiliano Ponte de Souza. 2016. "Spatial-Temporal Trends and Risk of Suicide in Central Brazil: An Ecological Study Contrasting Indigenous and Non-Indigenous Populations." *Revista Brasileira Psiquiatria* 38, 3: 222–30.

Pellow, David N. 2016. "Toward a Critical Environmental Justice Studies: Black Lives Matter as an Environmental Justice Challenge." *Du Bois Review*, 13, 2: 1–16.

Pellow, David N. and Robert J. Brulle. 2005. *Power, Justice, and the Environment*. Cambridge, MA: MIT Press.

Pink Dog Productions. 2014. *In Whose Backyard?* Halifax: Dalhousie University. <enrichproject.org/resources/#IWB-Video>.

Poirier, Abbey E., Linda A. Dodds, Trevor J.B. Dummer, Daniel G. C. Rainham, Bryan Maguire, and Markey Johnson. 2015. "Maternal Exposure to Air Pollution and Adverse Birth Outcomes in Halifax, Nova Scotia." *Journal of Occupational and Environmental Medicine*, 57, 12: 1291–98.

Pokhrel, D. and T. Viraraghavan. 2004. "Treatment of Pulp and Paper Mill Wastewater — A Review." *The Science of the Total Environment*, 333: 37–58

Pritchard, Henderson W. 2009. "Race, Class and Environmental Equity: Study of Disparate Exposure to Toxic Chemicals in the Commonwealth of Massachusetts." Doctoral thesis, Boston, Northeastern University.

Province of Nova Scotia. 2016. *Meetings with African Nova Scotian Communities Regarding Amendments to the Children and Family Services Act*. Halifax: Province of Nova Scotia.

Pulido, Laura. 2017. "Geographies of Race and Ethnicity II: Environmental Racism, Racial Capitalism and State-Sanctioned Violence." *Progress in Human Geography*, 41, 4: 524–33.

_____. 2016. "Flint, Environmental Racism, and Racial Capitalism." *Capitalism Nature Socialism*, 27, 3: 1–16.

_____. 2000. "Rethinking Environmental Racism: White Privilege and Urban Development in Southern California." *Annals of the Association of American Geographers*, 90, 1: 12–40.

_____. 1996. "A Critical Review of the Methodology of Environmental Racism Research." *Antipode*, 28, 2: 142–59.

Raphael, Dennis. 2007. "Poverty and the Modern Welfare State." In Dennis Raphael (ed.), *Poverty and Policy in Canada: Implications for Health and Quality of Life* (pp. 5–26). Toronto: Canadian Scholars Press.

Razack, Sherene H. 2002. "Gendered Racial Violence and Spatialized Justice: The Murder of Pamela George." In Sherene H. Razack (ed.), *Race, Space, and the Law: Unmapping a White Settler Society* (pp. 123–278). Toronto: Between the Lines.

_____. 2000. "Introduction: Law, Race and Space." *Canadian Journal of Law and Society*, 15, 2: 1–8.

_____. 1998. *Looking White People in the Eye: Gender, Race, and Culture in Courtrooms and Classrooms*. Toronto: University of Toronto Press.

Reading, Charlotte. 2015. "Structural Determinants of Aboriginal Peoples' Health." In Margo Greenwood, Sarah de Leeuw, Nicole Marie Lindsay and Charlotte Reading (eds.). *Determinants of Indigenous Peoples' Health in Canada: Beyond the Social* (pp. xi-xxix). Toronto: Canadian Scholars Press.

Recoquillon, Charlotte. 2014. "Neoliberalization and Spatial (In) Justice: The Gentrification of Harlem." *Spatial Justice*, 6. <jssj.org/article/neoliberalisation-et-injustice-spatiale-le-cas-de-la-gentrification-de-harlem/>.

Reid, Daniel S. 1989. "Pictonians, Pulp Mill and Pulmonary Diseases." *Nova Scotia Medical Journal*, 68: 146–48.

Rhodes, Blair. 2017. "Province to Pay Sipekne'katik First Nation $48K in Court Costs." CBC *News Nova Scotia*, September 29. <cbc.ca/news/canada/nova-scotia/province-to-pay-sipekne-katik-first-nation-48k-in-court-costs-1.4313498>.

Riahi, Aru and Tim McSorley. 2013. "Another Layer of Colonialism': Resource Extraction, Toxic Pollution and First Nations." *Canadian Dimension*, 47, 6: 34–35,4.

Richmond, Chantelle. 2015. "The Relatedness of People, Land, and Health: Stories from Anishinabe Elders." In Margo Greenwood, Sarah de Leeuw, Nicole Marie Lindsay and Charlotte Reading (eds.). *Determinants of Indigenous Peoples' Health in Canada: Beyond the Social* (pp. 47–63). Toronto: Canadian Scholars Press.

Robinson, Deborah M. 2000. "Environmental Racism: Old Wine in a New Bottle." *World Council of Churches*. <wcc-coe.org/wcc/what/jpc/echoes/echoes-17-02.html>.

Robinson, William I. 2015. "Global Capitalism and the Global Police State: Crisis of Humanity and the Specter of 21st Century Fascism." Global Research, April 21. <globalresearch.ca/global-capitalism-and-the-global-police-state-crisis-of-humanity-and-the-specter-of-21st-century-fascism/5444340>.

Rodney, Patricia and Esker Copeland. 2009. "The Health Status of Black Canadians: Do Aggregated Racial and Ethnic Variables Hide Health Disparities?" *Journal of Health Care for the Poor and Underserved*, 20, 3: 817–23.

Rowat, Steven C. 1999. "Incinerator Toxic Emissions: A Brief Summary of Human Health Effects with a Note on Regulatory Control." *Medical Hypothesis*, 52, 5: 389–96.

Saulnier, Christine. 2009. *Poverty Reduction Policies and Programs: The Causes and Consequences of Poverty: Understanding Divisions and Disparities in Social and Economic Development in Nova Scotia*. Ottawa: Canadian Council on Social Development.

Save Lincolnville Campaign. n.d. "Our Demands." <savelincolnville.h-a-z.org/demands.php>.

Schmeichel, Mardi. 2011. "Feminism, Neoliberalism, and Social Studies." *Theory & Research in Social Education*, 39, 1: 6–31.

Schneir, Miriam. 1972. *Feminism: The Essential Historical Writings*. New York: Vintage Books.

Schreiber, Rita, Phyllis Noerager Stern, and Charmaine Wilson. 2000. "Being Strong: How Black West Indian Canadian Women Manage Depression and its Stigma." *Journal of Nursing Scholarship*, 32, 1: 39–46.

_____. 1998. "The Contexts for Managing Depression and its Stigma Among Black West Indian Canadian Women." *Journal of Advanced Nursing*, 27: 510–17.

Scott, Nadine, Lauren Rakowski, Laila Zahra Harris, and Troy Dixon. 2015. "The Production of Pollution and Consumption of Chemicals in Canada." In Dayna Nadine Scott (ed.), *Our Chemical Selves: Gender, Toxics and Environmental Health* (pp. 3–28). Vancouver: UBC Press.

Senate of Canada. 2007. *Safe Drinking Water for First Nations. Final Report of the Standing Senate Committee on Aboriginal Peoples*. <sencanada.ca/content/sen/committee/391/abor/rep/rep08jun07-e.htm>.

Sharp, Donald. 2009. "Environmental Toxins, A Potential Risk Factor for Diabetes Among Canadian Aboriginals." *International Journal of Circumpolar Health*, 68, 4: 316–26.

Shenk, Timothy. 2015. "Booked #3: What Exactly Is Neoliberalism?"

Dissent Magazine, April 2. <dissentmagazine.org/blog/booked-3-what-exactly-is-neoliberalism-wendy-brown-undoing-the-demos>.

Shoemaker, Nancy. 2015. "A Typology of Colonialism." *Perspectives on History*. October. <historians.org/publications-and-directories/perspectives-on-history/october-2015/a-typology-of-colonialism>.

Sibley, David. 1995. *Geographies of Exclusion: Society and Difference in the West*. London: Routledge.

Simon, Derek. 2016. "Vulnerable Waters, Anti-Fracking Solidarities, and Blue Theologies: Toward a New Brunswick Case Study between the Global and the Local." *Journal of New Brunswick Studies*, 7, 2: 92–111.

Sipekne'katik. n.d.(a) "History." <sipeknekatik.ca/history/>.

_____. n.d.(b) "Community Profile." <sipeknekatik.ca/community-profile/>.

Smith, Andrea. 2005. "Native Feminism, Sovereignty and Social Change." *Feminist Studies*, 31, 1: 116.

Smith, Anna Marie. 2008. "Neoliberalism, Welfare Policy, and Feminist Theories of Social Justice." Special issue, *Feminist Theory* 9, 2: 131–44.

Solidarity Halifax. 2017. *Guideposts for Environmental Organizing Against Capitalism*. September. <solidarityhalifax.ca/wp-content/uploads/2017/10/SH-EJC-AXIOMS.pdf>.

Soskolne, Colin L.and Lee E. Sieswerda. 2010. "Cancer Risk Associated with Pulp and Paper Mills: A Review of Occupational and Community Epidemiology." *Chronic Diseases in Canada*, 29 (Supplement 2): 86–100.

Sparr, Pamela. 1995. *Mortgaging Women's Lives: Feminist Critiques of Structural Adjustment*. London: Zed Books

Statistics Canada. 2017a. "Visible Minority (Black), Both Sexes, Age (Total), Canada, Nova Scotia and Census Metropolitan Areas and Census Agglomerations, 2016 Census – 25% Sample Data." October 25. <12.statcan.gc.ca/census-recensement/2016/dp-pd/hlt-fst/imm/Table.cfm?Lang=E&T=42&SP=1&geo=12&vismin=5&age=1&sex=1>.

_____. 2017b. "Visible Minority (15), Individual Low-Income Status (6), Low-Income Indicators (4), Generation Status (4), Age (6) and Sex (3) for the Population in Private Households of Canada, Provinces and Territories, Census Metropolitan Areas and Census Agglomerations, 2016 Census – 25% Sample Data." October 25. <http://www5.statcan.gc.ca/olc-cel/olc.action?objId=98-400-X2016211&objType=46&lang=en&limit=0)>.

_____. 2017c. "Visible Minority (15), Income Statistics (17), Generation Status (4), Age (10) and Sex (3) for the Population Aged 15 Years and Over in Private Households of Canada, Provinces and Territories, Census Metropolitan Areas and Census Agglomerations, 2016 Census – 25% Sample Data." October 25. <http://www5.statcan.gc.ca/olc-cel/olc.action?objId=98-400-X2016210&objType=46&lang=en&limit=0>.

_____. 2017d. "Visible Minority (15), Generation Status (4), Age (12) and Sex (3) for the Population in Private Households of Canada, Provinces and Territories, Census Metropolitan Areas and Census Agglomerations, 2016 Census – 25% Sample Data." October 25. <12.statcan.gc.ca/census-recensement/2016/dp-pd/dt-td/Ap-eng.cfm?LANG=E&APATH=3&DETAIL=0&DIM=0&FL=A&FREE=0&GC=0&GID=0&GK=0&GRP=1&PID=110531&PRID=10&PTYPE=109445&S=0&SHOWALL=

0&SUB=0&Temporal=2017&THEME=120&VID=0&VNAMEE=&VNAMEF=>.

_____. 2011a. "Nova Scotia Community Counts, Census of Population and National Household Survey." <12.statcan.gc.ca/nhs-enm/2011/dp-pd/prof/index. cfm?Lang=E>.

_____. 2011b. "Aboriginal Peoples in Canada: First Nations People, Metis and Inuit." <12. statcan.gc.ca/nhs-enm/2011/as-sa/99-011-x/99-011-x2011001-eng.cfm>.

Stoler, Ann Laura. 1991. "Carnal Knowledge and Imperial Power: Gender, Race, and Morality in Colonial Asia." In Micaela di Leonardo (ed.), *Gender at the Crossroads of Knowledge: Feminist Anthropology in the Postmodern Era* (pp. 51–101). Berkley, CA: University of California Press.

Sumarokov, Yury A., Tormod Brenn, Alexander V. Kudryavtsev, and Odd Nilssen. 2014. "Suicides in the Indigenous and Non-Indigenous Populations in the Nenets Autonomous Okrug, Northwestern Russia, and Associated Socio-Demographic Characteristics." *International Journal of Circumpolar Health,* 73, 10.

Tavlin, Noah. 2013. "Africville: Canada's Secret Racist History." *Vice,* February 4. <vice. com/en_ca/read/africville-canadas-secret-racist-history>.

Teelucksingh, Cheryl. 2007. "Environmental Racialization: Linking Racialization to the Environment in Canada." *Local Environment,* 12, 6: 645–61.

_____. 2002. "Spatiality and Environmental Justice in Parkdale (Toronto)." *Ethnologies,* 241: 119–41.

Teelucksingh, Cheryl, and Jeffery R. Masuda. 2014. "Urban Environmental Justice Through the Camera: Understanding the Politics of Space and the Right to the City." *Local Environment,* 19, 3: 300–17.

Thomas-Muller, Clayton. 2014. "Pictou Landing First Nation Government Erect Blockade Over Northern Pulp Mill Effluent Spill." *IC Magazine,* June 10. <intercontinentalcry. org/pictou-landing-first-nation-government-erect-blockade-northern-pulp-mill-effluent-spill-23337>.

Trocmé, Nico, Della Knoke, and Cindy Blackstock. 2004. "Pathways to the Overrepresentation of Aboriginal Children in Canada's Child Welfare System." *Social Service Review,* 78, 4: 577–600.

Truth and Reconciliation Commission of Canada. 2015. *Honouring the Truth, Reconciling for the Future. Summary of the Final Report of the Truth and Reconciliation Commission of Canada.* Winnipeg: Truth and Reconciliation Commission.

Udofia, Aniekan, Bram Noble, and Greg Poelzer. 2016. "Aboriginal Participation in Canadian Environmental Assessment: Gap Analysis and Directions for Scholarly Research." *Journal of Environmental Assessment Policy and Management,* 18, 3: 1–28.

Ujima Design Team. 2015. *The Nova Scotia Home for Colored Children Restorative Inquiry.* Halifax: Nova Scotia.

United Nations General Assembly. 2017. *Report of the Working Group of Experts on People of African Descent on Its Mission to Canada.* Geneva: UN Human Rights Council.

Veracini, Lorenzo. 2011. "Introducing Settler Colonial Studies." *Settler Colonial Studies,* 1, 1: 1–12.

Vives Miro, Sonia. 2011. "Producing a 'Successful City': Neoliberal Urbanism and Gentrification in the Tourist City – The Case of Palma (Majorca)." *Urban Studies Research:* 1–13.

Vrijheid, Martine. 2000. "Health Effects of Residence Near Hazardous Waste Landfill Sites: A Review of Epidemiological Literature." *Environmental Health Perspectives*, 108, 1: 101–12.

Waldron, Ingrid R.G. 2016. *Experiences of Environmental Health Inequities in African Nova Scotian Communities.* Halifax: Dalhousie University.

_____. 2015a. "Findings from a Series of Workshops Entitled 'In Whose Backyard? — Exploring Toxic Legacies in Mi'kmaw and African Nova Scotian Communities.'" *Environmental Justice*, 8, 2: 1–5.

_____. 2015b. *Final Report for North End Matters: Using the People Assessing Their Health Process to Explore the Social Determinants of Health in the Black Community in the North End of Halifax.* Halifax: Dalhousie University.

_____. 2014a. *Report on the Regional Meetings and Convergence Workshop for "In Whose Backyard? Exploring Toxic Legacies in Mi'kmaw and African Nova Scotian Communities."* Halifax: Dalhousie University.

_____. 2014b. *Report on Government Consultations for the Environmental Noxiousness, Racial Inequities and Community Health Project.* Halifax: Dalhousie University.

_____. 2012. "Out From the Margins: Centering African-Centered Knowledge in Psychological Discourse." *The Australian Community Psychologist* (Special Issue: Ignored No Longer: Emerging Indigenous Researchers on Indigenous Psychologies), 24, 1: 34–47.

_____. 2010a. "The Marginalization of African Indigenous Healing Traditions Within Western Medicine: Reconciling Ideological Tensions and Contradictions Along the Epistemological Terrain." *Women's Health and Urban Life: An International and Interdisciplinary Journal*, 9, 1: 50–71.

_____. 2010b. *Challenges and Opportunities: Identifying Meaningful Occupations in Low-Income, Racialized Communities in the North End.* Halifax: Dalhousie University.

_____. 2010c. "The Impact of Inequality on Health in Canada: A Multidimensional Framework." *Diversity in Health and Care*, 7, 4: 261–70.

_____. 2008. *Re-Conceptualizing "Trauma": Examining the Mental Health Impact of Discrimination, Torture and Migration for Racialized Groups in Toronto.* Toronto: Across Boundaries – An Ethno-Racial Mental Health Agency.

_____. 2005. "African Canadian Women Resisting Oppression: Embodying Emancipated Consciousness Through Holistic Self-Healing Approaches to Mental Health." In G. Sophie Harding (ed.), *Surviving in the Hour of Darkness: The Health and Wellness of Women of Colour and Indigenous Women* (pp. 13–31). Calgary: University of Calgary Press.

_____. 2003. "Examining Beliefs About Mental Illness Among African Canadian Women." *Women's Health and Urban Life: An International and Interdisciplinary Journal*, 2, 1: 42–58.

_____. 2002. *African Canadian Women Storming the Barricades! Challenging Psychiatric Imperialism through Indigenous Conceptualizations of 'Mental Illness' and Self-Healing.* Doctoral thesis, Toronto, Ontario Institute for Studis in Education, University of Toronto.

Waldron, Ingrid and Amber Gazso. 2018. "Managing Low Income in Families: The Importance of Institutions and Interactions." In Amber Gazso and Karen Kobayashi (eds.), *Continuity and Innovation: Canadian Families in the New Millennium* (pp. 80–96).

Toronto: Nelson Education.

Walker, Gordon. 2009. "Beyond Distribution and Proximity: Exploring the Multiple Spatialities of Environmental Justice." *Antipode*, 41, 4: 614–36.

Walker, Tony R. 2014. "Environmental Effects Monitoring in Sydney Harbor During Remediation of One of Canada's Most Polluted Sites: A Review and Lessons Learned." *Remediation: The Journal of Environmental Cleanup Costs, Technologies and Techniques*, 24, 3: 103–17.

Walkom, Thomas. 2013. "Stephen Harper's New Employment Insurance Rules Whack Hard." *Toronto Star*, November 1. <thestar.com/news/canada/2013/11/01/stephen_harpers_new_employment_insurance_rules_whack_ontario_hard_walkom.html>.

Walls, Melissa. L. and Les B. Whitbeck. 2012. "The Intergenerational Effects of Relocation Policies on Indigenous Families." *Journal of Family Issues*, 33, 1272–93.

Washington, Harriet A. 2007. *Medical Apartheid: The Dark History of Medical Experimentation on Black Americans from Colonial Times*. New York: Doubleday.

Waziyatawin and Michael Yellow Bird. 2012. "Introduction: Decolonizing Our Minds and Actions." In Waziyatawin and Michael Yellow Bird (eds.), *For Indigenous Minds Only: A Decolonization Handbook* (pp. 1–14). Santa Fe: SARS.

Wiebe, Sarah Marie. 2016. "Guardians of the Environment in Canada's Chemical Valley." *Citizenship Studies*, 20, 1: 18–33.

Wilkins, Russell, Jean-Marie Berthelot and Edward Ng. 2002. "Trends in Mortality by Neighbourhood Income in Urban Canada from 1971 to 1996." *Health Reports*, 13 (Supplement): 1–28.

Withers, Paul. 2015. "Boat Harbour Compensation Being Negotiated with Nova Scotia." *CBC News*, December 19. <cbc.ca/news/canada/nova-scotia/boat-harbour-compensation-pictou-landing-first-nation-1.3372761>.

Wolfe, Patrick. 2006. "Settler Colonialism and the Elimination of the Native." *Journal of Genocide Research*, 8, 4: 387–409.

_____. 1999. *Settler Colonialism and the Transformation of Anthropology: The Politics and Poetics of an Ethnographic Event*. London: Cassell.

INDEX